Information, Computers, and System Design

Information, Computers, and System Design

Ira G. Wilson / Marthann E. Wilson

John Wiley & Sons, Inc., New York · London · Sydney

INDIANA
UNIVERSITY
LIBRARY

NORTHWEST

Library of Congress Catalog Card Number: 65-21430
Printed in the United States of America

to our little i.g.

SYSTEMS ENGINEERING AND ANALYSIS SERIES

In a society which is producing more people, more materials, more things, and more information than ever before, systems engineering is indispensable in meeting the challenge of complexity. This series of books is an attempt to bring together in a complementary as well as unified fashion the many specialities of the subject, such as modeling and simulation, computing, control, probability and statistics, optimization, reliability, and economics, and to emphasize the interrelationship between them.

The aim is to make the series as comprehensive as possible without dwelling on the myriad details of each specialty and at the same time to provide a broad basic framework on which to build these details. The design of these books will be fundamental in nature to meet the needs of students and engineers and to insure they remain of lasting interest and importance.

Preface

In the past twenty years or so, two separate concepts have emerged: information theory and system theory. Each of these concepts is extremely important in its own right. Each has many different applications. The theme of this book is that they should be considered together. By a joint study, each concept can gain from the other; each concept can make large contributions to the other. For example, analysis of the information required for the various phases in the life of a "new" system reveals some tasks that computers might perform, some that human beings will always have to perform, and some that either may perform depending on the circumstances.

Since an understanding of the two concepts can be useful in many diverse disciplines, all the background needed to understand the exposition is included. Terms are carefully defined. To ensure clarity the development is purposely quite detailed. For some chapters selected references to pertinent books and papers are given. The mathematical aspects are confined to the last eight chapters. These eight chapters justify and amplify many statements made in the earlier chapters. However, a good understanding of the two sets of concepts can be gained, even if the mathematical details are skipped. A glossary is included for those not entirely familiar with the two vocabularies.

The head of the largest corporation in the world* has stated that "the successful union of business and science depends on systems thinking." Actually, information theory and system theory have far wider applications. Only a few of many possible examples illustrate the point. Thus, the mission of every educator is to teach his students to think (i.e., to process information). Behavioral scientists, psychologists, and psychiatrists also study the processing of informa-

---

*F. R. Kappel, Chairman of the Board of the American Telephone and Telegraph Co., in an address before the 13th Comité International de l'Organisation Scientifique (CIOS), September 16, 1963.

tion by the human mind and its effects on the emotions. Computers and automation are but two applications of the system concept. Actually, systems are everywhere. Telephone engineers design "switching systems," "transmission systems," and "data systems." Military men talk of their "weapons systems." Physicians and psychologists are concerned with the "muscular," "nervous," and other systems of the human body.

In this book, system concepts are examined in the light of information theory. A moment's reflection shows that all of the effort spent in planning and developing a new system is an information-processing operation up to the time that some hardware is built. Only when hardware is available can it be tested. And the purpose of the tests is to generate information for management's consideration. Further, management's activities are information-processing operations. No hardware is involved—except the documents and pieces of paper carrying written or printed information.

Existing information theory in America is based on mathematics. Definitions are precise. Theorems are proved rigorously. Today, system theory is in quite a different state. Mathematical computations are used in some cases. But today, system design and development are really more of an art than a science. Various authors sometimes disagree on definitions of words such as "system engineering," or even omit definitions entirely. System concepts are described—not proved.

In this book a system is defined as a set of components to perform some "wanted" operation on an object. The operation must be wanted by one or more human beings. Models (in this case, "pictures") can be used to represent systems. "Information" is always at least one input of any system. The information is necessary to show that the system operation is wanted. Careful analysis of the models makes it possible to classify the modest number of different kinds of building blocks that can be put together in designing a new system. All the possible kinds of changes that can be made in an information input are tabulated. Next, a "canonical" or prototype model for any complex system is described. How the model applies to numerous complex systems is explained. Thus, the first eight chapters present necessary background for the remainder of the book, enumerate and classify the building blocks of any system, and present a widely applicable model of complex systems.

To explain the importance of the information generation, transmission, and processing implicit in the system concept, the necessary steps in the life of a new system are described. The information-processing and other necessary functions performed during each step then can be put in chart form. There are only a modest number of different kinds of functions. These can be portrayed graphically, and their necessary inputs and outputs can be identified. This approach also makes it clear that the steps must follow a particular pattern. They are partially ordered in time because some steps must be completed—or almost completed—before the next step can be begun. It is also possible to see how the management, research, planning, engineering, production, operation, maintenance, and sales activities make necessary contributions at different times in the life of a "new" system. Analysis shows that a system design problem falls into one of sixteen classes. A design procedure is presented in the form of a particular kind of step-by-step flow chart. The flow chart shows that a system design involves four kinds of tasks: (1) finding a set of functional blocks which can jointly perform all wanted functions, (2) finding a set of devices to implement the functional blocks, (3) making various kinds of computations, and (4) choosing between possible alternatives. In this form the information that must be available so that each step can be performed is made quite clear. The design procedure has been tried out experimentally and proved to work. In theory most of the steps can be mechanized using suitable building blocks to form appropriate information-processing arrangements that form a "computer." The tasks can then be divided into three classes: (1) those that a computer can do, (2) those that a human or humans must do, and (3) those that either may do. For a particular design some tasks may be hard to classify. But even an imperfect classification points out where the uncertainties are. Chapters 9 through 16 present these ideas.

Mathematically, a system may be thought of as an operator that changes system inputs into outputs. To give meaning to this approach, appropriate variables to describe system inputs must be found. Information-carrying energy is always a system input. The variables necessary to describe such inputs are investigated. Any possible information-processing operator can only change one or more values of these variables. It follows that the number of kinds of system building blocks is also limited because such blocks can only mechanize the possible mathematical operations. In many system studies, cost and reliability estimates are necessary to help to decide between alternative proposals. Some simple formulas to help make such estimates are covered. These and other mathematical aspects of system design are covered in Chapters 17 through 24.

Mr. Estill Green encouraged the investigation of many of the ideas that resulted in this book. Mr. A. D. Hall worked with one of us (IGW) in early studies of the application of information theory to communication systems. We were privileged to have stimulating discussions with Herbert Holt, M.D. and psychiatrist. Mr. John Theiss carefully reviewed this manuscript and made many valuable suggestion. Their help is gratefully acknowledged.

April, 1965

IRA G. WILSON
MARTHANN E. WILSON

Contents

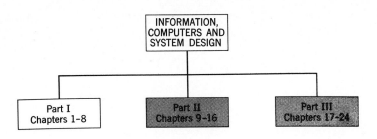

PART I

This part furnishes an adequate background for understanding the steps that occur from the conception of a "new" system until the last survivor is no more. No mathematics are used in the exposition.

The importance of the role played by an unpredictable energy flow is shown by models of simple systems. Such a flow can be called *information*. This simple concept has far-reaching implications. The many kinds of information used by humans and machines are explained.

The analysis shows that only a modest number of different kinds of building blocks are necessary in any system. The presentation of a *canonical* model of any complex system is followed by a number of examples.

1

Systems and System Design

"Systems"

In our modern world the word "system" is used to mean many different things used for many different purposes. For example, there are systems for breaking the bank at Monte Carlo or Las Vegas, for winning at bridge, and for beating the races. Such systems are not discussed here.

So some definitions are in order. In this book the word "system" is used to convey at least two different ideas:

1. A regular or orderly arrangement of components or parts in a connected and interrelated series or whole.

2. A series or group of components or parts necessary to some operation.

The word "operation" is defined as the bringing about of an effect.

More particularly, by definition, a system consists of a set of components arranged to perform some *wanted* operation. The word "wanted" is significant because it indicates that someone wants the operation performed.

The Environment of a System

Every system operates in an environment. By definition, the environment consists of everything outside a system that either affects the operation of the system or is affected by the system.

The dividing line between the system and the environment may be hard to draw. For many systems the air temperature, the relative humidity, and the barometric pressure are important enough effects to be considered part of the environmental conditions. Of course, these quantities vary with time, and usually a system must perform throughout the range of the variations. Some systems generate heat

3

which must be removed.   For example, the cooling system of an automobile keeps the engine temperature within safe working limits.

Included in the system and its environment is everything which
the designer feels is important.   For any real system, the conceivable
number of interactions between the system components and the environment is extremely large.   Therefore, in practice it is necessary
to select only a modest number from all the possibilities.   In other
words, the possibilities are divided by the designer into those considered to be important and those considered to be unimportant.
The choice between the important and unimportant may be difficult,
perhaps impossible.   For example, in complex social systems some
of the variables may not even be suspected, much less known precisely.

Organization of Complex Systems

In practice many systems must perform more than one wanted
operation.   It is assumed that any such complex system can be factored or resolved into subsystems.   The combination of the subsystems
performs all the wanted operations.   Experience leads to the belief
that the assumption is reasonable.

Each subsystem can be further factored or resolved and the fac-

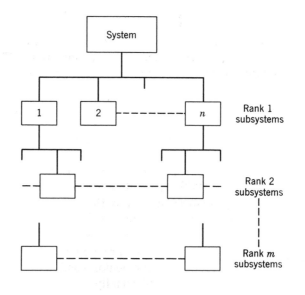

Figure 1-1

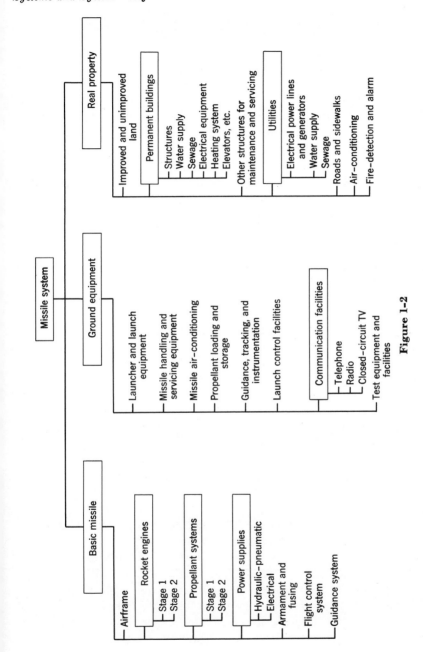

Figure 1-2

toring can be continued until further resolution would involve breaking down the molecules or atoms of the component parts.

Figure 1-1 shows such a hierarchical breakdown. The complex system is made up of n first-rank subsystems. In turn, each of these is made up of second-rank subsystems and so on until a lowest rank, m, is reached.

There is no restriction on the number of subsystems in a particular rank nor any significance in the order in which they are listed. The only requirement is that the subsystems operating together must perform all the functions of the next higher rank in the system.

As a familiar example of a complex system, take the automobile. Some of the subsystems in one possible factoring might be the engine, ignition system, cooling system, transmission, steering system, and instrumentation system. Frequently, a complex system may be factored into several, or even many, different sets of subsystems. Figure 1-2 represents a complex missile system in the form of a hierarchy. Only the first few top levels are shown.

Man-made and Material Systems

This book discusses the design of man-made systems. Many of the results seem to apply to a human being when he is thought of as a "system." Some results may not. And there may well be unknown "X factors." Time will furnish the answers. But even an imperfect theory may be helpful in studies of the brain mechanisms and how they might, or actually do, work.

Further, the discussion is intended to apply only to systems composed of material components or parts. For example, this restriction might exclude a "system" of mental telepathy.

As a practical matter, man-made systems composed of material parts are found everywhere. The family automobile is certainly such a complex system composed of material parts. So is a modern home—equipped with an automatic stereo high-fidelity, record-changing system, television, toasters and other appliances, in addition to twenty or more electric motors that run the clocks, mix the daiquiris, vacuum the floor, wash the laundry, and dry the clothes.

Also, telephone engineers speak of "switching systems," "transmission systems," and "data systems." Military men talk about "weapons systems," "early-warning radar systems," and "sonar systems"; chemical engineers, about "petro-chemical systems" which furnish us with many different petroleum products; industrial engineers, about "automation systems" for machine tools or even entire factories. These systems are also designed by men; they use sets of man-made parts (sometimes called "hardware"), and they are complex. Some contain millions of parts. And there is a trend toward even greater complexity.

Other professional people work with and study the human body. According to the definition, the human body is a system. Certain related components can also be called systems, for example, the "muscular" and "nervous" systems. These systems are not designed by men; and with only a few exceptions, such as some surgical repairs, they do not use man-made parts. But the human body is such a complex system that we are only beginning to understand some of its secrets.

Material-flow and Information Systems

Some authors have divided systems into two categories: material-flow systems and communication systems. Factories and oil refineries and automobile highways are examples of material-flow systems. Both the inputs and the outputs are material things or objects. Telephone, telegraph, radio, and television systems are cited as examples of communication, or information-flow, systems.

Earlier, the discussion was limited to systems composed of material objects. By definition, mechanics is the branch of physics that treats of phenomena caused by the action of forces on material bodies. A mechanism is a system that constitutes a working agency. Also, by definition, a machine is any combination of mechanisms for utilizing, modifying, applying, or transmitting energy whether simple or complex. Obviously, the definitions apply to material-flow systems.

Information systems can be subdivided into information-flow and information-handling systems.

According to the definition, the information-flow systems are also composed of machines. Take a television system as an example. One machine, the transmitter, transmits energy to be received by other machines called receivers which modify their input energy so it can be displayed by a cathode-ray tube and radiated by loudspeakers. Hopefully, there is no information loss in the many energy conversions involved.

Computers are examples of information-handling systems. So are many subsystems of telephone-switching systems that set up and take down wanted connections. Both the inputs and outputs of computers are information, in other words, data. The computer function is to change the input information in some way. Such information-handling systems are also composed of machines.

To repeat, some information systems take in input information and deliver it at the output without change; other systems take in input information, change it, and deliver the resultant information at the output. The distinction between the two kinds of operations is basic to understanding the system design problem.

Machine Capabilities

Machines can gather information, make measurements, send signals which control other machines, calculate, predict, and change physical objects. At least in principle, any specified behavior which does not contain physical impossibilities or logical contradictions can be built into a machine. The complexity of the behavior patterns that a machine can exhibit is limited only by the design of its control.

A machine can generate a program for its own future operations. In other words, it can change its operations as time goes on. If the results of the change are reactions more favorable to the inputs (including the environment), then the machine is said to show "adaptation."

The human body shows many examples of adaptation. For example, mechanisms tend to keep body temperature and pH of the blood within rather narrow limits. Some primitive adaptation systems have been built by men. For example, a giant computer has been programmed to play chess. It "remembers" its poor moves and thus gradually tries to improve its game. But it still cannot beat a good human opponent.

Machine-Man Systems

Today, we have many man-made systems in which a man or men perform some operations. In some the man acts as the error detector. Men play such a role in steering ships, in driving automobiles, in piloting airplanes, and in tracking objects with gun and missile directors.

But the complexity of future systems may well make greater demands on their human operators. In such sophisticated systems, more of man's present-day functions may be taken over by machines. In some instances, the men will perform only those functions that are not feasible to automate. Such "semi-automatic" systems will fall short of "full automation."

It will become apparent that the term "full automation" must be used with care. In fact, "full automation" can never be achieved, because human beings must always supply initiative, set criteria of satisfactory performance, and take action if an unforeseen crisis arises. For such reasons, the space ships of the future are likely to have astronauts aboard. Some of these information-generating and information-handling functions are best performed by human beings; some must be.

Systems Composed of Men

Some systems are composed entirely of men, such as the Congress or a business organization. Even in such systems, both information flow and information handling are essential in the functioning. Business and management literature is full of samples of organization charts showing the formal lines of communication. And besides the formal lines of communication, many informal lines of communication usually exist. The "decision-makers" process the information available to them to direct the business operation.

System Design

By definition, to *design* is to map out in the mind; to plan mentally; to conceive of as a whole, completely or in outline; to organize a scheme of (e.g., a system); to invent. Further, a design may arise in the mind for something to be done or produced; or for a mental project or scheme in which means to an end are laid down.

Design refers to the adaptation of means to an end; the coordination of parts or separate acts to produce a result.

Note particularly the presence of the words "mentally" and "mental" in the definition. Thus, the design of a system is the work of a human mind or minds.

Perhaps just because a design is the result of mental operations, there are some who almost lead you to believe that the practice of system design is akin to the practice of black magic. To such people the design process is elusive, undefinable, almost ethereal, and certainly incapable of successful analysis. To a system designer with years of experience, it can hardly be so mysterious. At least a start can be made on an analysis.

There are other people who have described system design as just quantified common sense. Now, common sense is defined as sound and ordinary sense; specifically good judgment or prudence in estimating affairs, especially as free from emotional bias or intellectual subtlety. Expressed differently, system design should utilize both sound logic and estimated or measured values of quantities to create new designs.

The use of logical reasoning is an information-processing operation. To get correct answers, the rules of correct reasoning must be followed. Otherwise, errors can occur. But, in creating a new design, to what kinds of quantities should estimated or measured values be attached? The identification of the quantities needed to describe systems composed of physical objects is a prerequisite to understanding system design. To make such an identification is a major objective of this book.

Unquestionably, system design involves mental effort. Hence, to analyze the system design process, it is necessary to study how the mind may handle the available information to create the design.

The steps in system design cannot be derived from a study of the organization of companies doing systems work. The departmental organizations of companies with large research, development, engineering, and design departments differ. And quite different titles are given to departments performing essentially the same functions. In this book the attention will be solely on the steps in the design of a system—not on corporate structure or departmental titles.

System Design by Computer

According to the definition of the word "machine," computers are machines. As stated earlier, in theory computers can perform any specified task that does not contain physical impossibilities or logical contradictions. Hence, computers should be able to perform some of the tasks of system design. But which tasks? The concept that system design is an information-processing operation makes it possible to show some tasks computers may perform or help to perform, and other tasks that they certainly cannot perform today—and never will be able to perform.

2
System Models

Models of Systems

Any theory (and a theory of system design is no exception) deals with models. By definition, a *model* is an approximate or simplified representation of the operation of the actual system being studied. Its purpose is to help us to understand the system operation, and to predict its behavior under particular chosen conditions.

Models are useful because they can be studied abstractly. They facilitate the synthesis and analysis of quite different kinds of systems by a uniform approach.

For ease in making studies, a model should be simple. But by the very nature of things, simplicity can be had only by neglecting some effects believed to be of minor importance to the operation. So a model always is a compromise between simplicity and reality.

If we can duplicate in the real world the conditions assumed in the model, then predictions can be checked by experiment. If predictions are verified, confidence that the model is "adequate" increases. On the other hand, if predictions are not verified, and the experimental analog of the model duplicates the conditions assumed in setting up the model, then that model is "inadequate" for understanding and prediction. It must be revised. If one or more important effects are neglected in setting up a model, then the study of that model can lead to incomplete or even completely wrong results. To avoid such unfortunate outcomes, models should be chosen with great care. Further, predictions should be checked by experiment.

Two Useful Kinds of Models

In system design two quite different kinds of models are widely used: block diagrams and mathematical models. Another kind of model called a "signal flow graph" has been applied to a rather restricted class of design problems.

Block diagrams and signal flow graphs are "iconographic" models. Such models are pictorial representations used to describe the system

11

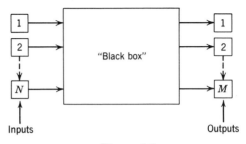

Figure 2-1

and its functional relationships. They are useful both in the synthesis and analysis of a system.

As an example, Fig. 2-1 shows a block diagram of a generalized system to perform some wanted operations. It consists of a set of inputs, a "black box," and a set of outputs. Many a systems engineer has hopefully (but vainly) wished some genie would present him with such a "black box" to solve the problem for which he needed the answer yesterday. And many patent claims try to come as near to claiming a "black box" as the examiner will allow.

As it stands, Fig. 2-1 can represent an automated factory, a telephone-switching system, a digital computer, or even a human being. Thus this single block diagram can apply to systems studied in many widely different disciplines.

Figure 2-2 shows how the representation of Fig. 2-1 can be applied to the "human system." The arrows within the "brain" represent signal flows that control the muscles. Of course, Fig. 2-2 is still a greatly simplified representation. But more details can obviously be added, details about the input sensors, about the brain, and about the output effectors.

"Understanding a model" means understanding how the outputs vary with the inputs. Mathematical models express the relations between the inputs and outputs of the actual system by an equation or set of equations. In situations where the equations can be set up and solved, such models can be a powerful tool for analyzing system performance. They will be used in the later chapters.

Unfortunately, mathematical models are not always as helpful as we would like. Such a model requires that all of the important variables and the relations between them be known. At the present time, this just is not so in many systems, particularly those involving man-machine relationships. Further, the number of variables must not be so large that the solution will require excessive time or cost

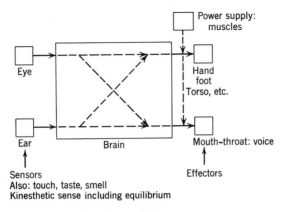

Figure 2-2

or both. For many complex systems this requirement is not met. Next, as you learn in college, some innocent-looking equations are easy to write but extraordinarily difficult to solve. Exact solutions may be beyond the reach of known mathematical methods. Finally, all material objects can show nonlinear effects. Approximations to exact solutions are possible for some nonlinear equations, but not for all. In some cases, computers can be helpful in getting approximate solutions—if the answer to the problem justifies the costs incident to getting it.

Electrical and communication system designers seem to prefer block diagrams to represent a system. Many hydrodynamic and aeronautical engineers, and also operation research specialists, prefer mathematical models and use block diagrams rather sparingly.

In this book, the system design problem is first explained using block diagrams and in later chapters in terms of mathematical models. Each representation contributes to understanding.

Model of the Simplest System

Figure 2-1 can represent a generalized system. But the complexity of large systems makes it difficult to tabulate similarities and differences except in a very elementary way.* In fact, it is difficult to make any meaningful general statements about very large systems.

---

* See, for example, W. A. Malthaner and H. E. Vaughan, "An Automatic Telephone System Employing Magnetic Memory," Proceedings IRE, Vol. **41**, October 1953.

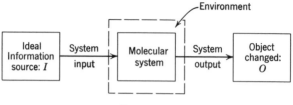

Figure 2-3

Since the model of Fig. 2-1 is too general to be of much practical use, it must be made more detailed. Now Fig. 2-3 shows a model consisting of one input, a system to perform one operation, and one output.

According to the earlier definitions, Fig. 2-3 is a "model" of a "system"—and further, it is a model of the simplest complete system.

The purpose of this system is to change a physical object in some wanted way. To do this the system components respond to the supplied input information. The system output changes the object. This system has only one behavior pattern, and this pattern can be initiated in only one way. The system is determinate. Event B (the output) occurs only if prior Event A (the input) occurs, and vice versa. Event A can be called "information," supplied by an information source as shown in Fig. 2-3.

In Fig. 2-3, all flows are assumed to be one way. Arrows indicate the direction of flow. The input is acted on by the system to produce the output. Interchange of the input and output is impossible.

Examples can be found of material objects in which flow can take place in either direction. When such objects are represented, the wanted direction of flow is indicated by an arrow.

The word "molecular" has been chosen for the model of Fig. 2-3 because it suggests that such a system can be used as a building block.

Complex systems are considered to be aggregates of many molecular systems of the kind shown in Fig. 2-3. Some large systems involve many human beings—for example, the United States postal system. Just as in putting molecules together to make useful chemical combinations, rules must be followed in putting molecular systems together. These rules are presented later.

In turn, the blocks in Fig. 2-3 can be broken down into simpler parts, the "atoms." Chemical molecules are composed of atoms.

By analogy, the term "molecular" is used in the model shown in Fig. 2-3. There are relatively few kinds of "atoms" that can be combined to form the "molecular" model.

The Model Input and Output

In Fig. 2-3, the input stimulus or "information" indicates that the system operation is wanted. The word "stimulus" is defined as an agent or form of excitation which influences the action of an organism (e.g., a system) as a whole or in any of its parts. Obviously it is an appropriate word for the molecular system input. The definition and discussion of the word "information" given in the next chapter will include *stimulus* as a special case.

The input stimulus or "information" from the source to the system must be in the form of an energy flow in space that varies with time and thus conveys the information. The information energy flow may be continuous over an interval of time (as in speech) or discontinuous (as in telegraph signals).

The system output is also time-varying energy. The output energy changes a material object that exists in space and time from one state to another. The change can be observed and measured by a human being. In fact, to satisfy the want for which the system is intended, the output *must* be observed or measured by a human being. To make the change, energy must be expended. The changed object may be thought of as an information or energy "sink" or absorber.

The energy flow and hence the information flow is one-way from the source to the object.

Thus the molecular model represents a set of components that performs the wanted energy conversion between the system input and output.

In some important practical cases, the conversion operation can be described mathematically by a transfer function which converts the time-varying input energy into the time-varying output energy.

Any deterministic system is an energy-conversion system. Now, certain energy conversion systems have been carefully studied—for example, the conversion of mechanical into electrical energy by a dynamo and the inverse conversion by an electric motor. The problem of causal systems is more complex because the conversion involves variations with time.

Components of the Model

The model of Fig. 2-3 is made up of several components (functional blocks). The word "component" often is used to mean a widely used unit of equipment with a definite name and a prescribed performance standard. The word "part" is used for a portion, piece, or fragment of a component. Thus the distinction between the meanings of component and part is somewhat hazy. But, in the present usage, a component can be thought of as a rather small collection of parts.

Environment of the System

In Fig. 2-3, the environment surrounds only the molecular system. Of course, both the information source and object also exist in environments. These three environments may or may not be the same.

Built-in Connections

The built-in, invariable-with-time connections of a system determine the operation. Even a few parts can be assembled in many ways. In many practical cases, all but one possibility is eliminated when the system is assembled. For example, a particular set of vacuum tubes, sockets, resistances, capacitors, and other parts may be used to build many different circuits, say an amplifier or an oscillator. But, after the parts are assembled and wired, the circuit either amplifies or oscillates. The same parts may be used for either circuit, but the wiring (built-in connections) determines what the circuit actually does.

The connections are sometimes called built-in "memory"—that is, they "remember" how the parts were put together.

Some Examples of Simple Systems

Examples of simple systems which the model can represent are found everywhere. Take a buzzer that operates when the switch is closed. The information supplied by a human being is discontinuous (on and off); the output is sound waves.

Sunlight may turn a street light off; darkness may turn it on. The system has two states (on and off). The information energy is the sunlight as it is varied in time by the earth's rotation, clouds, etc.

A water faucet is turned on by a movement of the hand, i.e., by mechanical energy directed in space. The handle can be moved smoothly and continuously over its range. It is not just open or closed. When the faucet is open, hydraulic energy causes the water to flow.

Idealized Model Invariant with Time

Figure 2-4 shows the model of Fig. 2-3 divided into two functional portions connected together by an energy transmission medium. This model is called "idealized" because the components are assumed to be perfect and to dissipate no power.

As in Fig. 2-3, the input is "information" from a human being or "information" obtained by observation or measurement of some natural phenomenon.

The information portion of Fig. 2-4 takes the input "message" energy and changes it into "signal" energy suitable for delivery to the effector portion. To make the change a power source may be necessary.

In some engineering practice, the word "message" is used to mean the original modulating wave in a communication system. The word "signal" means the physical embodiment of a message.

The effector portion (1) responds to the input signal, (2) changes the signal energy into a form suitable for the effector, and (3) furnishes the time-varying energy output to cause the wanted change

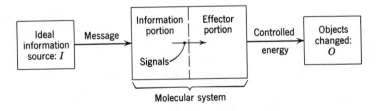

Figure 2-4

in the object. The effector itself carries out the final action with respect to the physical object. Thus, the message from the information source controls the effector, and thereby the changes in the object.

In performing the wanted operation, several controlled changes of energy with time are involved. For this reason, the information and effector portions of the model have several similar functions that differ only in the intended result—not in the operation. The functions of the two portions are interdependent and interrelated.

Two physical objects cannot occupy the same space at the same time. So, in a physical system the two portions in Fig. 2-4 must be separated in space. Therefore they must be connected together by a transmission "medium."

Reasons for Dividing the Model into Two Portions

The model of Fig. 2-4 is divided into two portions. To see why, suppose that the primary information source (I) is a human brain. For a human to affect an object in a wanted way, the information from (I) is converted into signals to control the muscles and thereby to produce speech or a muscular movement.

Now take the effector portion. Assume the object (O) is a human brain. After sensing (e.g., by the ear or tactile sensors), the signal is converted into a form (nerve impulses) that the brain can recognize. Exactly how the conversion is done and how the impulses are recognized are not completely understood, but to conform to the molecular system model it is only necessary to understand that the functions must be performed. Thus, in human speech and hearing the two portions of the model are both necessary and sufficient.

Also, if *either* (I) or (O) is a human being, the two portions of the model are necessary and sufficient. For example, the information source may be a television picture and the affected object the brain. Then the signal to the human being is in the form of light energy from the cathode-ray tube. As another example, consider turning on an electric light. Then the brain is the information source, and the lamp filament the object affected. In each example, the information and effector functions can be identified.

Finally, if neither the information source nor the object changed is a human being, the two portions are certainly sufficient. As yet, no example has been found in which either portion is unnecessary, but, conceivably, examples may exist. So the question is open. In

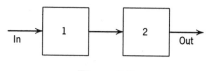

Figure 2-5

such an example, the functions of the information and effector portions would be combined.

Generality of the Model

The simple molecular model has one input (information energy) and one output (effector energy) which makes the wanted change in a material object. This model is strictly causal. Given this model, two questions that arise are: "How general is it?" and "To what sort of phenomena does it apply?"

It may never be possible to prove that the molecular model usefully describes all systems that change objects. But few models are completely general. A useful model need only apply satisfactorily to a sizable class of important phenomena. The molecular model certainly does apply in many cases.

Combinations of Models

Complex arrangements of molecular models can usually be separated into sets of models connected in a series or in parallel (see Figs. 2-5 and 2-6). For the parallel case, "combiner" and "divider" functions are necessary. These functions are discussed later. By their

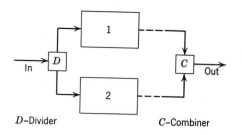

D–Divider   *C*–Combiner

Figure 2-6

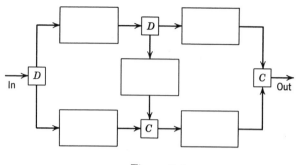

Figure 2-7

use more complicated arrangements are possible, such as the "bridge circuit" of Fig. **2-7**.

For any configuration, a set of molecular models can only: (1) receive information from one or more sources; (2) combine, divide or otherwise change information; (3) change or divide an object or combine two or more objects.

3

An Elementary Description
of Some Information Concepts

Introduction

As has been stated, the input to the molecular model is called "information," and the function of the first portion of the model is to handle "information." In fact, all systems designed to make wanted changes in physical objects require one or more information inputs. In some systems the emphasis is on the information handling. For example, a telephone system is furnished information about wanted connections. To be sure, to set up the wanted connections, material objects must move to close metallic contacts, or their equivalent. Present-day contacts are moved by electromechanical switches. In the future, connections may be set up by controlling the movements of carriers in solid-state materials. But even to many telephone system engineers, contact closures are much less important design problems than the devices that handle the information needed to set up and take down the connections.

On the other hand, in an automated factory, the wanted output may be particular automobile parts machined to certain tolerances. The production line function is to produce the wanted parts and then assemble them. But before any parts can be made, information (manufacturing drawings) must be prepared that describes exactly what is to be produced. Further, the line must be designed, set up and started, and eventually stopped. All these operations require the handling and preparation of information.

Information flow is essential in any system, whether it be a "communication" system, an automated factory, a man-machine system, or an all-human system. This is a fundamental fact.

It has been conjectured elsewhere* that if a system design were carried through on the basis of information flow, then provision for the flow of material objects might not require much change in the

---

* Goode and Machol, *System Engineering*, McGraw-Hill Book Company, Inc., New York, 1957, p. 315.

information flow. This concept distinguishes between information flow (e.g., the desired telephone number) and the flow of material objects (component parts in an automated factory).

The molecular model goes beyond this conjecture because it shows that material objects cannot be changed except by a system controlled or stimulated by information. Later chapters will show clearly that system design is almost entirely an information-handling process.

Because of the importance of these two quite different concepts involving the idea of "information," it is essential to make clear what we mean by the word.

Although very important contributions had been made by earlier workers, the beginning of modern information theory is usually ascribed to Shannon.* There have been hundreds of publications since his now classical paper.

Information Theory had made contributions to understanding important aspects of information handling in communication systems. As it exists today, Information Theory does not directly apply to many problems encountered in system design, but it can be used as a starting point.

Much of the existing theory has been developed by mathematicians. Some of their basic formulas and results are covered in a later chapter. Here, some important definitions, assumptions, and concepts are summarized so that they can be used in the course of the exposition. The intent is to be brief, so many details not important for the exposition are only mentioned or even omitted. Furthermore, no proofs of theorems are given.

Definitions

One value of modern information theory lies in the fact that it carefully defines the words it uses. So, as a beginning, the definitions of the words that we shall use are given.

Information-in-general can add to a representation of what is known, believed, or alleged to be so. In other words, information is the *capacity* for increasing knowledge. Actually, it may or may not do so.

An *information source* generates information.

Communication of information is the reproduction of generated in-

---

* C. E. Shannon, "A Mathematical Theory of Communication," Bell System Technical Journal, Vol. 27, July, October 1948.

formation at some other location or locations, either exactly or approximately.

Measures of Amount of Information

An *amount of information* may be measured in terms of at least three different concepts. In all three, the amount of information can be defined by what it does, just as force can be defined in terms of the acceleration it causes or could cause.

1. Unexpectedness. "I got little information because I knew what he'd say before he opened his mouth."

To measure an amount of information using this concept, a communications engineer puts himself in the position of the receiver of the information or possible information. He then considers a particular amount of information as *selected* from a set of possible alternative amounts of information by some standard procedure. The important word is "selected." His criterion of the amount of information is the *unexpectedness* or *improbability* of the particular information, without attention to the structure. In other words, he is not interested in the semantic content at all. In fact, no satisfactory definition of semantic content is yet available.

According to the unexpectedness concept, the word "information" excludes meaning in the semantic sense. Somewhere a story is told about a telegrapher handling a message arranging for his wife to run away with another man. In his official capacity, that particular message would be just one more for him to transmit in such a way that no additions, subtractions, or errors occurred. His job required that he pay no attention to meaning—only to the unexpectedness of the individual symbols. Despite such practical drawbacks, the unexpectedness concept has many useful applications.

One possible difficulty with such a measure is that the recipient of the supposed information may know or be able to guess part of it. Shannon's definition in terms of probabilities avoids such difficulties. Stated another way, if the received message is *predictable,* no information is gained by receiving it.

Shannon further showed that this measure of information has the form of entropy as defined in thermodynamics and statistical mechanics. The mathematical details are covered later. For the present, it suffices to say that entropy is a measure of disorder, or of the improbability of the next state. It always tends to increase, and is a maximum where the sequence of events is random, i.e., completely unpredictable.

Conversely, a completely predictable source of energy furnishes no information whatever. Such a source is called a "zero-entropy (0-entropy) energy source." The wave shape and the kind of energy are unimportant. Thus, the direct-current flow from a battery, the sine-wave output from an oscillator or alternating-current generator, the regular ticking of a clock, and the flow of heat from a radiator are all predictable and hence the energy sources are 0-entropy.

2. Complexity of Structure. "An instrument which can respond in 0.01 second can give more information per second (i.e., more possible readings per second) than one which can respond in 0.1 second."

The number of distinguishable groups in a pattern—its dimensionality or number of degrees of freedom—is a measure of its structural information content. Clearly, a color picture contains more information than a black and white picture of the same scene.

3. Metrical Information. "An experiment yielding a result accurate to 1% gives more information than one accurate to 10%."

For a numerical value, the amount of metrical information is a measure of the "precision" with which it is determined.

Messages

The word "message" is used with two different meanings in the literature: (1) an ordered selection from an agreed set of signs intended to convey information, and (2) the original modulating wave in a communication system. The first definition is the sense in which the word is used in information theory; the second, the sense in which it is often used in engineering practice.

By definition (1) a message is a selected amount of information. Thus one newspaper paragraph is a message, and so are the entire contents of the newspaper. In this example the individual paragraphs may be considered as separate messages, but their sum may still be called one message. It is not to be inferred that this curious conclusion follows from a general rule.

Some kinds of messages have prescribed (or at least similar) formats. For example, in telegraph messages the usual information order is date and time, address, text, and signature. Formal, social, and business letters even specify placement of the component parts of the message on the page.

For our purposes, messages are assumed to be generated by an information source. By a further assumption, all messages generated by information sources are error-free. In a human being quite obviously the message source is the brain. Even though a child speaks nonsense syllables, there is no way of knowing that they are not exactly the sounds specified by his brain. Hence the assumption seems reasonable.

Signals

By definition, signals are the manifestations of some physical phenomena (e.g., electrical or light waves) by which a message is transmitted. Signals have an information content because they are conveying a message.

Signals are the only physical manifestation of any information. Hence, any operations on information can only involve operations on the physical phenomena carrying the message. Far-reaching conclusions can be drawn from this fact.

Direction of Information Flow

Energy flows from a generator to a receiver or an energy sink. So does information. Few, if any, information generators can be used as receivers, or vice versa. We talk with our mouths and listen with our ears—never the other way around.

In some media, energy can be transmitted equally well in two or even more directions. Such media can be used for two-way signals. Sound waves in air are a familiar example. Wires carrying electric energy are another.

By suitable arrangements, one-way transmitters and receivers can sometimes use a medium capable of carrying signals in two directions for two-way information transmission.

The Concept of Noise

In many practical systems, for some reason two separate signals are present at the destination where only one is wanted. The unwanted signal is regarded as a nuisance. Such a situation is often called "a signal corrupted by noise."

In some cases, noise signals cannot be distinguished in any intrinsic way from the wanted signal waves. Only their relative importance to the receiver makes possible a distinction between wanted signal and noise. But the fundamental difference between a wanted signal and noise is the fact that the two cannot be completely separated. If the two (or more) signals can be completely and simultaneously recovered, then the concept of "noise" has little use.

With regard to information, there is no such thing as "pure noise." Radio static may give information about the ionosphere; cosmic noise, information about the stars (as in radio astronomy). Noise can always tell something about its source. In this way, noise can become information.

When noise is purposely added to a signal, it is called "camouflage."

Delay and Distortion

The information generator, object, and other components of a physical system are separated in space. Signals travel with finite velocity, so some finite transmission time is always required to traverse the distance in space. The time interval is sometimes called the "delay."

If a particular input signal always produces the same output signal, but the output signal differs in a definite way from the input signal, then the effect may be called "distortion."

If the distorting function has an inverse, then (at least in principle) the distortion can be corrected by an inverse functional operation on the received signal. For example, attenuation of a signal may be made up by amplification.

But if the input signal does not always undergo the same change, then it is not always possible to reconstruct the input signal with certainty. Some information is lost.

Some Information-handling Systems

The information-handling systems by which human beings communicate with each other are an important subclass of all information systems.

Much information is passed between humans by voice, i.e., by talking and listening. Spoken communication uses about forty phonemes (i.e., elementary sounds) which go to make up human speech. The information is carried by sound-pressure waves in air. Sound waves are also used for communication by the "talking-drums" used by some African tribes and the human whistlers in parts of the Canary Islands.

As a substitute for the spoken word, deaf and mute people learn to communicate by "signs" expressed by the hands. Some people can convey information—sometimes a great deal of information—by a lifted eyebrow or a wince, a smile or a frown. The signals are carried by light waves. For other reasons, light waves are also used by North American Indians to carry their smoke signals, and by the military for wig-wag or semaphore signals and blinkers or heliographs.

A vast amount of information is passed between humans in written form. The received signals are also carried by light waves. In this case, the "signs" are the letters of the alphabet or the ideographs of the language.

Today, humans also communicate with machines and machines with humans. Except to a limited extent, machines are not yet able to read human handwriting or to understand human speech. With time, machines will exhibit both of these skills. So far, humans design the machines, so the machine communicates with humans with "signs" that humans can understand, at least most of the time—because upon occasion even a normally well-behaved machine can act like a temperamental human.

Finally, some machines now communicate with other machines. For nation-wide dialing of telephone calls, thousands of central offices must be able to communicate with each other. These central offices are of many different kinds. Unless something is done, they cannot communicate. The situation is worse than an English-speaking American trying to talk to a non-English-speaking Chinese—worse, because humans can sometimes make understandable signs for simple wants. Today, machines are not yet that capable. But the study of how machines communicate with other machines is very enlightening, because some necessary but abstract requirements for "understanding" become clear.

Table 3-1 on the following page gives some examples of messages and signals.

Table 3-1   *Examples of Messages and Signals*

Systems	Messages	Signals
A. Telegraphy	Sequences of letters and spaces	Series of discrete pulses for each letter
B. Telephony	Groups of voiced syllables	A single continuous function of time in terms of current or voltage amplitude
C. Radio broadcasting (AM)	Groups of voiced syllables and arrangements of musical sounds	A carrier frequency, modulated by a single continuous function of time in terms of current or voltage amplitude
D. Black-and-white television	Three-dimensional images varying with time (4 variables)	A carrier frequency modulated by a single continuous function of the horizontal dimension in terms of current or voltage amplitude. The function varies discontinuously with respect to the vertical dimension and time
E. Television with an associated AM audio channel	A combination of C and D	A combination of C and D
F. Typed or printed matter	Sequences of letters and spaces	Reflected light from the paper and letters
G. Business machine cards	Pattern of punched holes	Mechanical, electrical, or light signals showing presence or absence of holes in the possible positions

4

Properties Involved in Message and Signal Transmission

Introduction

A description of all the properties of messages and signals is necessarily lengthy. It must include descriptions of:

1. A predictable (zero-entropy) energy flow
2. Generation of an information-carrying signal
3. The structure in space and time of the information carried by the signal.
4. Changes in amount of information
5. Properties of a particular message.
6. Signal path and receiver
7. Additional effects that must be considered with multiple sources, paths, receivers, and messages.

Furthermore, it is necessary to have units in which to express the amount of information contained in a message or signal.

Predictable Energy Flow

To describe the energy flow, we can assume a suitable power receiver or power meter is connected to a predictable (i.e., zero-entropy) source by a perfect medium which in no way changes the output from the source. Then, at any instant the energy flow can be described in terms of the form of energy and a structure in space. Variations with time can only be variations of the space structure.

1. Any *form of energy* can or may be used to convey information. Examples of various forms are familiar to all of us. Acoustic waves carry human speech as well as many other sounds, such as jungle drum messages. Electric energy guided by wire conductors is used for telegraph, telephone, and other signals. The energy in electromagnetic fields carries information for our radio and television pro-

grams, and for microwave radar signals, and about distant galaxies. Higher-frequency electromagnetic fields are used in infrared photography and systems to detect warm or hot objects. Light waves are also electromagnetic waves. Of course, light waves can carry many kinds of information. The Indian's smoke signals and the Navy's wig-wag, semaphore, and blinker signals are carried by light waves. Further up the electromagnetic spectrum lie the waves used in electron microscopes, x-rays, and cosmic rays.

In a loudspeaker, mechanical energy launches the acoustic waves that we hear. The chemical energy produced during a reaction can give information about the progress of the reaction. The thermal energy of a heat source can give information about the temperature.

2. In principle, zero-entropy energy flow comes from a *source* or *origin*. The source is at a *location in space*. The location in space may change with time. For example, a storage battery or 400-cycle generator in an airplane moves as the plane's location in space changes.

3. At such a source, the energy flow has an *extent in space*. In a particular case, the extent may be described in terms of zero, one, two or three dimensions. For example, the physicist may assume a "point source" of light energy—i.e., a zero-dimension source. A one-dimension source may launch an electric wave to be carried by a pair of wires. A planar or two-dimensional source may furnish heat energy to a conducting rod or pipe. Spherical or three-dimensional waves may be radiated by a suitable radio antenna. Analogous examples can be found for the receiver or destination.

4. The energy flow has a *structure in space*. For the present purpose the word "structure" is defined as: an arrangement of organic units or parts in a whole; the arrangement of constituent particles of a substance or body; the manner of organization. By the definition of a zero-entropy source, the structure must be completely predictable. A completely uniform, invariable structure in space obviously complies with the definition. But the definition does not mean that the structure can not vary—only that, if it does, the variations be predictable.

In general, the structure in space contains a number of distinguishable groups or clusters of elements. The elements in each group are indistinguishable. Thus there are two numerical features of a structure: (*a*) the number of distinguishable groups, (*b*) the number of elements in each group.

For the human eye, an incandescent lamp can be considered to be a zero-entropy source of light waves. It is continuous in space over the extent of the lamp, and invariable with time. With suitable instruments, an unpredictable fine structure is revealed. Because the unaided eye cannot see this structure, to it the lamp is a zero-entropy source.

These examples illustrate the point that the structure may be simple or complex. But any structure, however complex, can be described mathematically in terms of the amplitudes and phases of space frequencies. Such a description permits breaking the structure down into elementary areas.

5. At a source, in each elementary area, the energy flow has a *direction in space*. In some systems this property is very important. Thus, the designer traces individual light rays from a source as his proposed camera lens changes their direction so that they are focused on the photographic film (receiver). The astronomer points his telescope at the object he wants to observe or measure.

6. A single zero-entropy source exists at a *location in time*—for example, on June 17, 1965.

7. Also, the energy flow has an *extent in time* determined by the starting and ending instants. The extent may be only a few seconds or it may be many years.

8. In each elementary area of the structure in space the energy flow has a *structure in time*. The structure may be simple or complex, but it must be predictable. The structure is predictable or certain because there is reason to believe that the future structure will have a particular pattern. The belief is based on prior knowledge about the source. Because the structure is certain, it can be predicted ahead of time.

The structure in the time domain contains a number of distinguishable groups or clusters of elements. The elements in each group are indistinguishable. Thus, there are two numerical features of such a structure in time (*a*) the number of distinguishable groups (i.e., time intervals) and (*b*) the number of elements in each group (e.g., different kinds of phenomena in each interval).

An unvarying source of power over the time interval—such as a storage battery—is a zero-entropy source. In fact, storage batteries are used in telephony for exactly this purpose. Predictable structures in time such as a square wave or a sine wave are also frequently used as a source in communication systems. Energy sources such as a smoking fire or a random-noise generator can be considered to have zero entropy if the fine structure can be neglected. After all, American Indians used smoke signals to convey information.

No matter how complex the time structure in any elementary space area, in theory it can be described mathematically in terms of the amplitudes and phases of the frequencies present in the wave. Such a description permits breaking the wave structure down into elementary time intervals.

9. The *rate of energy supply* from a source may be measured in power units, for example in watts, milliwatts or kilowatts. In some communication systems, the *power level* relative to a reference level (such as one milliwatt) is a useful concept.

10. Because time's arrow has only one *direction,* this property is seldom thought about in practical system design.

Table 4-1 lists the properties of a zero-entropy energy source.

Table 4-1   *Properties of a Zero-entropy Energy Flow*

At any instant:
  Form of energy
  Properties in the space domain—
    Location
    Extent in 0, 1, 2, or 3 dimensions
    Structure—simple or complex wave shape in space
    Directions of flow of elementary areas of the structure

Any variations of the space structure with time are expected because of some prior knowledge and hence are predictable:
  Properties in the time domain—
    Location of the changes of the space structure in time
    Extent (duration) in time of the changes
    Structure of the changes—a simple or complex wave shape in time for each
      elementary area of the space structure
    Power and power level
    Direction—there is only one in the time domain

Generation of an Information-carrying Signal

Information is carried by unexpected variations of energy flow with time. The only way to create information-carrying energy is for a message source to control the flow from a zero-entropy source so that some property (or properties) is not predictable. A modulating wave carries the specification of the message and varies some property of the zero-entropy wave to generate a modulated wave, the signal. The message is recovered from the signal at the destination. An important question therefore is: What properties of a zero-entropy source can be used to create a signal?

1. Any *form of energy* may be used to convey information. Since zero-entropy energy flow is controlled to create the signal, the signal

energy has the same form as that of the zero-entropy source. On the other hand, the message and signal energies may or may not be of the same form. In many cases, the message energy is used to control an electrical source, because of the advanced technology available for transmitting and handling electrical signals.

2. By definition, the structure of the energy flow from a zero-entropy source must be predictable. To convey information, some property of the output of such a source must be controlled so that the resulting signal is unpredictable.

Some property or properties of a zero-entropy energy flow in the *space domain* may be changed with time to convey information. This process may be called *modulation in the space domain* to distinguish it from an analogous process in the time domain which is usually called simply *modulation*. By definition, the signal energy is always changed in time to carry various parts of the message serially in time.

In the space domain, the unexpected changes with time may involve the location and extent of the energy flow from the zero-entropy generator.

Alternatively, the structure of the energy flow in space may be changed in some way. The only possible changes are unexpected variations with time of the amplitudes, frequencies, and phases of the space frequencies in the output of the zero-entropy source.

These changes may be described in terms of a power spectrum in space that varies with time. For example, the amplitude of the energy flow in space may be controlled in some way. Black letters on white paper reflect less white light than the paper. Hence they can be observed and thus carry information. Also, different areas of a color slide transmit different parts of the electromagnetic spectrum.

In the time domain, the structure of the energy flow with time may be changed in some way to convey information. The possible changes are limited to variations of the amplitudes, frequencies, and phases of the frequencies in the output of the zero-entropy generator. The resulting waves may be described in terms of a power spectrum in the time domain.

The signal power output is measured in units of milliwatts, watts, kilowatts, or even megawatts.

In considering the various possibilities, assume that the zero-entropy source wave (carrier) is dc or a sinusoidal wave. Many information transmission systems use such simple carriers, but others do not. For example, information can be transmitted by modulating a complex wave shape. Examples are smoke signals and light waves keyed on and off by a heliograph.

For amplitude modulation, two or more different amplitude conditions may be used; for frequency modulation of a sinusoidal carrier, two or more frequencies; for phase modulation, two or more phases. Two-condition transmission is sometimes called binary. The possible number of different conditions that may be used depends on the permissible error rate considering the noise present while information is being sent. The noise tends to reduce the intended differences between conditions and thus to cause ambiguities or errors.

Communication systems may be classified as discrete, continuous, or mixed. In a discrete system, information is transmitted in the form of sequences of pulses as in telegraphy; in a continuous system, by a continuous function over an interval as in a musical recital. In a mixed system, both discrete and continuous information is transmitted. The vertical and horizontal synchronizing pulses of a television system furnish information in discrete form; the audio channel in continuous form. Both are essential parts of the program information.

The possible modulation methods can be tabulated as one result of the mathematical description of a zero-entropy generator. It is likely that all possible modulation methods have been used. Further, almost all of the methods using a single carrier over a single channel are in use in one or more modern information transmission systems. Those not in use have drawbacks.

3. The signals resulting from the modulation have properties in both the space and the time domain. Thus the signal energy flow has an *origin* and *one or more destinations in space*. Of course, for physical reasons the origins and destinations as well as the zero-entropy sources are at different locations.

In many practical systems, the origins and destinations are known or even specified, as in a telephone call. But some signals are generated by an unknown or unidentifiable source (e.g., cosmic rays). In radio broadcasting, the destinations are known only in a general way. Some signals are produced for delivery to an unknown destination (or person) at an unknown later time, for example, phonograph records and library file cards. On the other hand, in telephony selected channels are linked together upon request for the signal transmission between particular instruments. The calling subscriber originates the information about the wanted connection to a destination, the called party. A ringing signal informs the called party of the progress of his call. For example, if the wanted line is reached, ringing tone is returned to the calling subscriber; if not, a busy signal may be returned. When the called party answers, the two parties exchange messages by using the telephone instruments and the telephone channel to generate, transmit, and receive appropriate electrical signals. When they are through, another auxiliary signal indicates the connection is no longer wanted, and the channels are released.

The location in space of the origin or destination of a message—or both—may vary with time. Relative motion of the origin and destination can be described in terms of a time-varying velocity vector and a time-varying acceleration vector.

4. The signal energy flow resulting from the modulation has an *extent in space*. The number of dimensions of the input and output may not be the same—nor of the signal in all parts of the signal transmission path. The exact extent may be difficult to determine, as in a vignetted portrait. Appropriate devices may change the extent. For example, a document may be microfilmed and then the copy enlarged to the original size.

5. The signal energy flow has *direction* in space. This property may or may not be of importance in a particular case. A satellite relay of electromagnetic energy is an example where directed energy flow is extremely important. Both the transmitting and receiving antennas must point quite exactly at the satellite as it whirls around the earth. If either antenna (or both) cannot "see" the satellite, signals can not be sent from the source to the receiver.

The direction can be changed in some cases. Heated steam can be directed by a steam pipe; a prism can selectively change the direction of various wavelengths of a beam of light.

6. The signal energy flow has a *structure* in space. As defined earlier, information-in-general can add to a representation of what is known, believed, or alleged to be so. By this all-inclusive definition, information includes any phenomenon that can be perceived or measured as any means whatsoever.

The signal energy structure in space may be relatively simple or very complex.

The view of the sky, mountains, trees and houses from the window of our study has structure in space. Were an artist to paint this view, he might change this structure to convey some mood to those who see his painting.

A structure in space in two or three dimensions may be continuous (or substantially continuous), as in large areas of a picture or photograph; or discontinuous, as in printed or typed material.

A complex signal source may generate several kinds of signals. To illustrate the point, consider the signals from a person talking to you in a lighted room. He is a source of a group of light signals seen by your eyes, and also a group of sound waves heard by your ears. As another example, an airplane emits heat and acoustic energy from its engines and light energy from its own lights and reflects light energy reaching it from external sources.

To transmit structural information about a "describee" (i.e., "the real thing") over a distance or to store the information for a time, several methods are possible:

a. A small sample (such as a mineral sample) furnishing adequate information

b. A replica, or a miniature representation, which simulates the unique features (although possibly incompletely)

c. A code representation such as a graphic or written description

Direct observation of the describee permits immediate interpretation by the observer without further information transmission. Sending a sample avoids transmitting the real thing, permits direct interpretation, and avoids interference by any form of noise. Sending a replica also permits direct interpretation, but the information may be incomplete. A code representation may permit misinterpretation and the coding itself may contain errors.

The signal energy from a source may flow over one *path* or *simultaneously over plural paths*. Local telephone calls within a city are ordinarily carried over one path that uses two wires to carry both directions of transmission. The picture and sound information that together furnish the information to a television transmitting station may go over different kinds of facilities and over quite different geographical routes. For example, the video may go over a microwave radio relay system and the audio over a broad-band channel in a carrier system in underground cable.

7. The signals have a *location in time*. Most (if not all) signals involving humans or machines or both have an identifiable *start and end at instants in time*.

8. The *extent or duration in time* of the signal energy flow is the time interval between the start and the end. In some cases, information about the extent in time may be more useful than that about the exact starting and ending instants. For example, the duration of a long-distance telephone call is a factor in the cost of the call to the customer.

9. The *structure* of the signal energy *in the time domain* is the result of modulating the zero-entropy energy source. It contains a number of distinguishable groups or clusters of elements. The ele-

ments in each group are indistinguishable.   Thus there are two numerical features of such a structure

 a. The number of distinguishable groups
 b. The number of elements in each group

The signal that results from tapping a telegraph key can be observed by measuring the energy at an appropriate point in the path.   The information is conveyed by an unpredictable function of time.   Telephone and many other communication systems transmit information serially in time in this way over one path.

Other systems also transmit information serially in time but some information is sent over one path; other information over other paths. Business-machine card punches can punch all the holes in one column simultaneously and then all the holes in the next column.

As another example, take the structure formed by the leaves of a tree as it is blown by the wind.   It varies in space because the leaves move.   It also varies with time because at one instant the leaves may be motionless, at another, blown violently by a storm.

As quite a different example, take a page in a book.   The information is invariant in space (assuming the page is stationary during the time of observation) and it is also invariant in time from the time the page is turned until the page is turned again.

Table 4-2 summarizes the factors involved in signal generation.

Table 4-2   *Generation of Information-carrying Signal*

Signal generation changes any expected variations with time of the output of a zero-entropy generator into unexpected variations.

Signal energy form is that of the zero-entropy generator.

Unexpected changes may involve the properties of the zero-entropy generator in the:

 Space domain (see Table 4-1) with time, or
 Time domain only

The process of changing the zero-entropy energy flow with time is called modulation.   Changes in the amplitude, frequency, or phase properties of the modulated wave are three important examples of modulation.

The information-carrying signal has an origin and a destination in space. These may vary with time.

The modulated wave may be described in terms of the variations of average power with time or of the power spectrum in time.

The signal has a location in time and an extent in time.

Modulation of the space structure of the zero-entropy generator permits a maximum information density per unit area; modulation in the time domain, a maximum information rate per unit time.

Structure in Space and Time of Signal Information

So far, this chapter has described the properties of messages and signals without regard to the abstract structure of the information itself. To be sure, all information does not have an easily described structure. On the other hand, many different English words are used to describe the structures used in certain kinds of communication. Communication is an extremely important part of information-in-general, but it is by no means the whole story.

Signs and Symbols

Communication, human, animal or machine, cannot take place without a system of signs. There are many kinds of "signs." The signs used in communicating information and the rules operating upon them and upon their users are essential parts of a theory of communication and information-handling.

A *sign* is defined as a written mark conventionally used for a word or a phrase; a thing used as a representation of something; a natural or conventional motion or gesture used instead of words to convey information.

A *symbol* is defined as a thing regarded by general consent as naturally typifying or representing or recalling something by possession of analogous qualities or by association in fact or thought.

In accordance with the definitions, Cherry* suggests that the word "sign" should be used for a physical event used in communication; and that the word "symbol" be reserved for Uncle Sam, Father Time, and other cultural symbols interpretable only in a specified historical context. His suggestion seems quite reasonable for many communications. But—at least in American usage—the word "symbol" is applied to the letters used for the chemical elements, and to the conventional graphic marks used in mechanical drawings and electronic circuit drawings.

Codes and Coding

A *code* is defined as a set of rules on any subject; a system of military or navigational signals.

A *coding* is a transformation or mapping. The transformation may or may not be one-to-one. Coding or encoding is the application

---

* Colin Cherry, *On Human Communication*, The M.I.T. Press, Cambridge, Mass., 1957.

of a set of transformation rules to a message or signal. Decoding is the inverse operation. Writing and reading are examples of the coding and decoding of information. Thus, a written or typed letter travels to its destination and scatters light in a pattern which the reader (if he uses the same language) decodes in his brain. In television, telephony, and telegraphy, the signals travel through space as a sequence of coded waves or impulses in time. The coding is built into the transmitter and the decoding into the receiver. The ultimate observer senses the information without interpreting the code.

The users of a code must both understand the intended point-by-point correspondence between the elements of the code and the things denoted by them. This understanding is called "meaning." On this basis, all oral and written languages are codes. Telegraph codes and cryptographic signs are codes of codes.

Language; Alphabet; Words

Many communications are expressed in a language and the signs are characters in some sort of alphabet.

In many communications involving humans, the *language* is defined: a vocabulary and way of using it. Thus, language is a generic word denoting any mode of conveying ideas, for example:

1. Human speech
2. A particular set of articulate sounds used in the expression of thoughts; the aggregate of the words used in the expression of thoughts.
3. The expression of thought in any way, articulate or inarticulate, conventional or unconventional, as "the language of signs."

In the sense of human language, it is the set of signs and rules used in everyday speech and conversation to represent ideas. Language is a body of words and methods of combining these words. A language is developed over a long period of time. Formalized systems of signs and rules, such as those of mathematics and logic, may be called *language systems* or *sign systems*.

An *alphabet* is the letters or signs of a language. They are sometimes arranged in a customary order, as in the English alphabet. In some information-handling systems, a simple "binary," or two-condition, alphabet is used—a signal is either present or not present. Written language represents other signs: the sounds of spoken words that represent ideas.

In a communication, the message and signal signs may be coded in different languages and alphabets. Thus, information can be coded even though it is already expressed by signs (e.g., letters of the English alphabet may be transmitted by a telegraph code).   The information content of the two sets of signs may differ.

Words are groups of signs.   A word is defined as a single articulate sound or combination of articulate sounds or syllables uttered by the human voice and by custom expressing an idea or ideas; the smallest portion of human language forming a grammatical part of speech; the letter or letters or other characters, written or printed, which represent such a sound or combination of sounds.

Almost all modern written languages are punctuated into word blocks.   In most languages, spaces or punctuation marks are used to divide sequences of written signs into words.

Spoken English uses nearly forty different sounds (phonemes).   Words, or even sentences, may be run together.   But pauses occur in all speech.

Spelling; Grammar; Syntax

Spelling is the order of signs within words.

Grammar or *syntax* is the order of words in a communication or portion of communication such as a phrase, clause, or sentence.

Redundancy

Redundancy is a property of spoken and written languages, and of many codes and sign systems.   An excessive number of rules (e.g., those of spelling) facilitate communication despite factors such as noise or other interference that act against the transmission.

Simple repetition is an elementary way to introduce redundancy. English text is still readable if nearly half of the letters are omitted and must be guessed.   Another example is repetition of the same information in the form of a picture or sketch and in accompanying text.

Ordering in Space and Time

Ordering is a very important factor in the structure of signals. Letters are ordered to spell a word; words are ordered in sentences; in turn, sentences are ordered.   In some written languages, vowels may precede consonants after which they are sounded in the spoken language.

Rearrangement of the letters of a word or words is called anagramming.   Sometimes, anagramming can generate a new word or words. But more often it results in gibberish.   Minor rearrangement of two words or lines can completely destroy a poet's creation.

Table 4-3 *Structural Factors of*
Information Transmitted by Signals

Signs and symbols—space and time
Code—space and time
Language, alphabet, words
Spelling, grammar, syntax
Redundancy
Ordering in space and time

Ordering has other aspects. In space, photographs and texts are ordered on the page of a newspaper or magazine. Advertisements, editorials, feature articles are also ordered in the makeup.

Information is also ordered in time. Magazine articles about Christmas gifts usually appear in December. Political and policy announcements are "timed" to produce wanted impacts.

Table 4-3 lists structural factors in some forms of information of great importance in human communication. Included are manufacturing and other drawings, handwritten, typed, and printed manuscripts, and spoken communications. Every system designer must use all of these forms in doing his job.

All the factors of Table 4-3 do not apply to all forms of information. The minute amount of information-carrying energy from a distant star is but one of many examples where some factors do not apply.

Measures of Amount of Information: Units

To measure the amount of information in a message or signal, *three different kinds of units may be necessary.* These *three* units are measures of the unexpectedness, the structural complexity, and the precision. In the literature most attention is directed to the first measure. Despite their importance, the second and third are almost ignored.

Measures of Unexpectedness

Messages and signals may be either discrete or continuous functions of time. It can be shown that the same unit may be used for either case. The applicable theorem (the Sampling Theorem) is included in a later section.

To measure an amount of information using the unexpectedness concept, the communications engineer considers a particular amount of information as selected from a set of possible alternative amounts. Thus, with a true die, the chance of rolling a five is $\frac{1}{6}$—the value given by probability theory. In fact, much of the mathematical theory of information is closely akin to certain aspects of probability theory.

In a classical paper, Hartley showed that when a particular amount of information is chosen from a set, the logical choice of the measure of information produced is logarithmic.

If the base of the logarithms is 2, the unit for expressing a quantity of information may be called a "binary digit" or simply "bit." If the base is 10, the unit is called a decimal digit (sometimes called a "decit").

The amount of information or information content of a message is the number of bits in the message.

The number of bits per unit time (frequently per second) is called the information rate, that is:

$$\text{Information rate} = \frac{\text{signs} \times \text{bits/sign}}{\text{time}} = \frac{\text{bits}}{\text{time}} \qquad (4.1)$$

With more than one source, the amounts of information from the sources are added.

Measure of Structural Complexity

Logon-content is the number of logons in a representation. A logon, the unit of structural information, enables one new distinguishable group or category to be added to a representation.

The number of logons provided by apparatus per unit of coordinate-space (cm, cm², sec, etc.) is called its logon capacity. For example, in a microscope, logon capacity is the measure of resolving power in logons/cm, etc. In the time domain, a channel whose bandwidth permits n independent readings per second has a logon capacity of n.

Measure of Metrical Information

One unit of metrical information, a metron, supplies one element for a pattern. For a numerical parameter, it is a measure of the "precision" with which it has been determined.

Each metrical unit may be thought of as associated with one elementary event of the sequence of physical events which the pattern represents. Thus the amount of metrical information in one logon (its metron content) can be thought of as the number of elementary events subsummed or "condensed" to form it.

These elements are indistinguishable to the extent that their number is not the number of bits to which the logon is equivalent. Precision increases *monotonically* with metron content, but few quantities are linearly related to metron content. Power and energy in the classical sense are among the few exceptions.

The number of metrons per unit of coordinate space is called the metron capacity or metron density of a physical system.

The number of logical elements in a group or pattern is termed its metrical information content.

Changes in Amount of Information

The output corresponding to the input to a device may have (1) the same amount of information as the input, (2) less information, or (3) more information.

In (1) the input is merely encoded into the output by a one-to-one transformation.

In (2) a device deletes some unwanted or unnecessary information according to a built-in table or rule. The transformation is not one-to-one.

(3) If the output of a device contains more information than the input, then the output information is increased over the input information by a built-in table or rule. By this process, over a short time interval more information can come out of the device than goes in. But—and this is important—before the input reached the device, the information contained in the table was put in to be used later.

Shannon proved that over a long time interval the amount of information from the output of a device must always be equal to or less than the amount of input information. For this reason, *over a long time interval no device can increase the quantity of information put into it.* This is an extremely important fact.

Properties of a Particular Message

Typically, a signal generator is used to send different messages from time to time. In every case, the same zero-entropy generator is modulated, so the signal energy form is always the same.

If changes are made in the space domain, as in successive frames of a motion picture film, then the change from one frame to the next can be described in terms of the location or locations and their extent in space.

Within the changed location(s), the changes may involve few or many of the elementary areas. Thus the spatial density may vary.

The efficiency of the changes occurring in a particular message

Table 4-4   *Properties of a Particular Message*

Space domain
   Location and extent of changes conveying
      the information
   Density of changes
   Efficiency
Time domain
   Start-end, duration of the message
   Rate of conveying information
   Efficiency

may be described by the ratio of the actual change in density to the maximum possible change in density over the zero-entropy energy flow.

In the time domain, a particular message has a start in time and an end in time. Successive messages can only modulate the zero-entropy generator sequentially, never simultaneously. There may or may not be time intervals between messages. Each message has its own extent or duration in time.

The efficiency of information handling may be described by the ratio of the actual information rate to the maximum possible rate allowed by the zero-entropy source.

Table 4-4 presents a summary of these properties of a particular message.

Signal Path and Receiver: Compatibility

The signal path or medium from the signal source and receiver has only one function: to convey the signal energy between the two locations in space, as far as feasible without change or interference. To do so, its properties must be compatible with both the source and receiver. And of course, the receiver must be compatible with the source. Otherwise, unless devices are added to make it compatible, some—even all—of the information will be lost.

The medium carries the form of energy put out by the signal generator and delivers it to the receiver input.

In the space domain, the receiver has a location. Its location may or may not vary with time. For example, the receiver may be on a ship underway at sea.

The ends of the medium are determined: one is at the signal generator output; the other, at the receiver input. The direction or directions in which the signal energy flows and from which the receiver can take its input are also known. Thus the length of the shortest signal path and the directional requirements are also determined. For some simple cases, the path can be described mathematically by a vector.

Some media (such as a pair of wires or a wave guide) can be used to transmit energy in either direction. For such media, energy may either be transmitted in one direction, or in both directions as in local telephone conversations, or in one direction for a time and then in the other (as reversible transmission used over some telegraph circuits, and one-way mountain roads).

A path between a signal generator and a receiver may always be available (full-time availability). It may be available only part-time or occasionally. Or it may be made available upon request when information is to be sent.

Similarly, a receiver may be available always, or sometimes, or only upon request.

The signals from the generator have an extent in space. If none of the information is to be lost, the available extent in space in the medium and at the receiver input must not be less than that at the source.

The receiver must be compatible with any modulation method that may be used to vary the space structure of the information and with that used to vary the time structure. The medium must be able to convey the modulated energy.

In a practical communication system, the maximum information rate may be limited by the source, the medium or the receiver.

For one example, take a communication system using semaphone signals. With normal daylight, the transmission medium imposes no restrictions on the transmission rate. And possibly the signals can be read faster than they can be sent. Then, the *source* sets limit on the information rate.

Now suppose a telephone dial can send twenty pulses per second. Conceivably, the telephone channel imposes no speed limitations. But the receiver can only accept ten pulses per second. The information rate is limited by the *receiver*.

Finally, a newsboy delivering papers can carry only so many, and move only so fast. For maximum overall efficiency, every time he returns to the printing plant, just enough papers should be ready to keep him busy delivering until the next batch is ready—and no more. The newsboy-*channel* is the limiting factor.

By proper planning, the information rate of a communication channel can be made a maximum. This idea of maximization is a central result of Shannon's information theory concepts.

In the design and maintenance of telephone and some other signal paths and receivers, the transmission performance is usually described in terms of the frequency band location and the bandwidth, the phase variations over the band, the range of signal powers that can be accommodated, and the unwanted distortions and interference. The medium or receiver may not exactly match the frequency location of the source or may have a frequency bandwidth less than the source. Similarly, the medium or receiver may contribute phase variations across the wanted band. Unwanted signal distortions may be contributed by either the medium or receiver or both.

The medium always attenuates the signal energy, so the receiver input is always less than the signal source output. The loss of energy may or may not be important.

The medium may set an upper limit on the signal power from the signal source. The receiver always sets an upper limit on the acceptable power input from the medium.

Interference in the medium or in the receiver or both may set a lower limit on the useful signal power at the receiver input. The power of interfering sources may be measured in the same units as the signal power. The signal to noise ratio, sometimes written S/N, is an important dimensionless number used to describe the performance of a medium or a receiver. The S/N requirements differ for different signals. High-fidelity reproduction of music requires a high S/N ratio. Otherwise, the interference is annoying when the music volume is low. Telephone communication can be satisfactorily carried at a somewhat lower S/N ratio. With very complicated receivers, radar signals can be detected even though the interference power exceeds the signal power, so the S/N ratio is less than unity.

The transmission performance of some kinds of media used for communication may vary over wide ranges with time. Some kinds vary over such wide ranges that under adverse conditions, no useful path exists. For one example, short-wave radio communication is possible at times between points separated by thousands of miles while using only modest signal power; at other times, communication is impossible over far shorter distances.

In a similar manner, receiver performance may vary with time.

However, receiver performance is under design control—at least to some extent.

Receivers are often designed to accept a range of signal inputs, such as variations in signal level. In fact, receiver adjustments are quite commonly provided to compensate for variations in the medium. For example, the volume control of a radio receiver can be changed as the signal fades in and out.

In some other signaling applications, and particularly in radar and space signaling, the performance of a part of the path such as the medium is described mathematically in terms of the correlation of its input and output signal, or of the cross-correlation of the transmitted signal with its output signal.

The importance of understanding the need for compatibility of source, medium, and receiver can hardly be overemphasized. If they are not compatible, then either no information is received, or what is received is either incomplete or wrong.

Appropriate devices can sometimes be added to patch up an incompatibility, but not always. For example, a television picture requires that much more information be transmitted and received than does the voice. Telephone channels are designed to handle electrical signals suitable for carrying the voice information. They are completely inadequate for television. For this reason, new broad-band channels had to be built so that you may enjoy your favorite programs. These new channels represent a world-wide investment of hundreds of millions of dollars.

Of course, any devices added for reasons of compatibility cost money. The Bell System has grown enormously over the years. Yet the first step-by-step and panel-type dial offices must work with the latest No. 5 crossbar and electronic central offices. Many different kinds and vintages of offices have been installed over the years. Many signaling languages are in use. All the offices—the new, middle-aged, and the old faithfuls—must work together compatibly. To achieve the necessary compatibility many kinds of matching devices have been added. Some are simple; some are very complicated. Many are imbedded in the already complex dial central offices so their true (or matching) function is obscured. Although great care has been exercised to keep the costs down, nevertheless, their aggregate cost is many, many millions of dollars.

Table 4-5 on the following page summarizes the properties of paths and receivers.

Table 4-5   *Signal Paths and Receivers: Compatibility*

Form of energy
Location and direction of energy flow of signal source and receiver
Path: Length
        Transmission—one-way, two-way, reversible
Availability of each source, path, receiver—
        Full-time, part-time, by request only.
Compatibility of Signal Properties
        Extent in space
        Structure in space
        Density per unit area
        Extent in time
        Structure in time
        Information rate
Transmission Performance of Paths, Receivers
        Amplitude range
        Frequency band location and bandwidth
        Phase variations across the band
        Distortions
        Interference

Multiple Sources, Paths, Receivers

Many systems have multiple zero-entropy energy sources; many have multiple signal sources; many, multiple signal receivers; many, multiple paths. Some have many of each. The telephone system with 70 million customers, well over ten thousand central offices, and billions of miles of paths in cables and other media is only one example. A naval task force consisting of many vessels takes in information from hostile aircraft, surface vessels, and underwater craft by radar, radio, visual signals, and sonar. The information inputs are processed. The task force sends out antiaircraft shells, shells from main and secondary batteries, missiles, and torpedos as well as radio and visual signals. The amount of information received, processed, and transmitted is enormous.

To describe such complex systems, each *kind* of zero-entropy generator, signal source, receiver, and transmission path must be known. Table 4-1 gives the factors which serve to differentiate the different kinds of power sources. Tables 4-2 and 4-5 cover signal sources and receivers and paths.

Further, the *number* of each kind is important. Also, remember that a zero-entropy power source must always be suitable for the signals to be generated; a receiver must be compatible with any signal generator with which it is to work; and an appropriate path must convey the signal energy from its source to the appropriate receiver. A medium provides a path or paths between locations in space. As an example of such restrictions, a knowledge of the number of appropriate paths between each information source–receiver pair may be important. Four different methods can be used to provide multiple paths.

The first method simply provides identical multiple paths in space. For example, a telephone cable in the local plant may contain two thousand or even more pairs of wires in one sheath. The two wires of each pair are separated from each other and from all the other wires by a very thin layer of insulation.

The other three methods all use one medium to carry multiple messages by multiplexing. These possible methods can be described mathematically

The second method uses a separate frequency band in the medium for each signal. Radio and television signals are examples. You tune your receiver to get the station you want. A coaxial tube may carry six hundred or more one-way telephone messages simultaneously. Tuned wave filters separate them at the ends of the cable. Six or eight space-separated tubes are commonly assembled in one sheath. Half of the tubes are used to transmit in each direction. A coaxial cable thus combines space separation and frequency separation. The multiple paths—even thousands of them—in such a cable may transmit many different signals simultaneously. The signals may also differ in kind; for example, they may be telephone, telegraph, and data signals as well as the many kinds of signals used during the setting-up and taking-down of connections.

The third method uses one medium to carry multiple messages by using pulses at different relative phase positions of a single ac carrier wave. Commercially available phase multiplex systems can send four telegraph or data messages simultaneously in one direction over one space-separated path. Voice or television signals are not multiplexed by this method at present. More than one space-separated path in a cable can carry such multiplexed messages.

The fourth method uses one medium to carry multiple messages by time division. Assume there are four message sources. First information from source 1 is carried, then from source 2, source 3, source 4, and back to source 1 again. The information from the four sources is interleaved in time. If the interleaving operation is properly implemented, all of the information from all of the sources is carried without interference between the four signals. Time division for telegraph signals is more than 50 years old. In the recent past, systems have been developed to put 24 one-way voice channels on a pair of wires in a telephone cable. Many (but not all) pairs in a cable may carry such time-division multiplexed messages.

For two-way transmission between two locations, different methods may be used for the two directions. For example, one way may be over space-separated paths; the other, over frequency or time-separated paths.*

Many multiplex systems require an appropriate combiner at the input end of the medium to combine the signals from the separate sources and a divider at the output end to separate them so they can proceed to the proper receivers. But radio and television broadcast signals are simply sent out. It is up to you to tune your receiver to the program you want.

Examples can be found where multiple paths exist between a source and a receiver because of the nature of the medium. Multipath transmission is frequently observed on long-distance short-wave radio circuits. On occasion, it may be a nuisance. Sometimes it can seriously affect the performance. Such unwanted multiple paths are not to be counted as separate paths.

The *location* of each source, receiver, and path is important as well as the *relative locations* with respect to each other. If a location (and therefore a relative location) varies with time, this fact must be known. For some purposes quite exact information about all the positions in space is necessary, as well as the variations with time. For other purposes, such as some design studies, distribution curves may be adequate.

For each source, path, and receiver, the *number of kinds of messages* (see Table 4-2) and the *number of each kind* tell how much information traffic is generated, transmitted, and received. The *time distribution* of the starts and ends of the messages and their extent or *duration* in time may be important in some cases. Such traffic data may be plotted in the form of distribution curves showing the average number of messages per source, average message length, variation of traffic with time of day, and so on.

Availability involves two separate concepts. Thus, two telephones with separate lines to the central office may be used *simultaneously* by the customers. Two telephones on a party line to the central office must be used *sequentially* by the customers. If one customer is using the line, the other must wait because it is not available for his use. This is an example of *spatial availability* in the medium—or lack of it.

* U.S. Patent 1,974,090, I. G. Wilson.

Table 4-6   *Multiple Sources, Paths, Receivers*

Number of kinds of each multiple source, path, receiver
Number of each kind
Location of each functional unit
For each source:
    Variations with time of location, direction, extent
    Number of kinds of messages originated
    Number of each kind
    Time distribution of starts and ends of messages
    Distributions of durations in time
Availability of each functional unit of each kind:
    Simultaneously with others; sequentially
    Full-time; part-time; by request only
Efficiency or occupancy measures

Sources, paths, and receivers may be available only part of the time. A radio relay satellite can provide a path from the source to the receiver only when it can be "seen" by both. Post offices are closed on Sundays so no mail is handled. Business offices are the sources and also receivers of many messages. Almost all are closed on Sunday; many are also closed on Saturdays. These are examples of lack of complete *availability in time.*

The occupancy or information-handling efficiency may be stated in the form of a ratio:

$$\frac{\text{Actual information handled per unit time}}{\text{Maximum possible information per unit time}}$$

The ratio applies to the use of zero-entropy generators, signal sources, multiple paths, and receivers. The unit of time may be seconds, minutes, hours, or days. The peak load over a few seconds or minutes may be very important in some systems; in others, a high long-time occupancy is the goal. The efficiency may be evaluated by taking into account the actual working hours or the theoretically possible working hours.

Table 4-6 summarizes the additional properties of multiple operation.

Importance of Message and Signal Properties in System Design

Once the properties of a zero-entropy energy source and the information structure are listed, it follows that any information-handling device can only change one or more of the listed properties. Information-handling systems to change one or more of the listed properties can be interpreted as special cases of Fig. 2-4. Appropriate and more-detailed block diagrams to make the possible kinds of changes can be drawn and will be presented later. Moreover, the possible kinds of changes in objects can be listed.

An understanding of information handling and of the physical changes of objects is an essential requirement for understanding the principles of system design. Furthermore, all phases of system planning, system design and manufacture, and system operation and maintenance involve information handling and processing.

In 1950, 40% of the labor force was performing paper work, in other words, processing and handling information. By 1960, the figure had risen to 51% where it remained in 1962. The lack of a further rise shows the help rendered by computers.

Any new system requires learning by and training of *people*. Information must be passed along. New ideas must be accepted all along the line—not just by those who do the planning and the research and development. New skills are needed, and those who are to provide them must learn them rapidly. To train these people, information must be prepared and absorbed so that it can be applied.

All possible kinds of information handling and information-processing operations can be described in terms of changes of signal properties. However, much classical information theory is concerned with the problem of transmitting signals over a noisy channel with a low probability of error. Noise may be less of a problem in many aspects of systems design and operation. Near-perfect information transmission is possible by using accurate drawings and diagrams and clear typing and printing on good paper. Progressive organizations provide plenty of light for reading such drawings and papers. Telephone and face-to-face discussions facilitate exchange of information between human beings. Do-it-yourself projects can minimize the need to put accurate information down on paper. Many engineers prefer building a first working model themselves to preparing adequate and accurate information for its construction by someone else.

5

Time-varying Systems

The Model

In a time-invariant or fixed molecular system, the operation of the system that changes the input wave (or waves) into the output wave (or waves) or the input object into another object is always the same.

In a time-varying system, the operation differs at different times. To change the operation, some change must be made within the system. A block may be changed or removed or a block may be added.

Figure 5-1 represents a molecular system modified so that the operation can be varied in some way with time. The molecular-system output depends on:

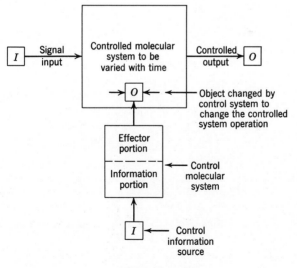

Figure 5-1

1. The information input
2. The components and the built-in connections
3. Some components or built-in connections (or both) which are made to vary in some way with time.

Thus the output depends on the state existing when the input is applied.

There are two separate sets of information: one from the (I) source and one from the "control (I)" source.   The word "control" is defined: to exercise an influence over something; to guide, correct, manage or restrain it; to check.   The effector in the control system changes an object to vary the molecular system's performance.

In Fig. 5-1, the added information source and molecular system cause the change in the controlled system.   But note particularly, that no new kinds of functions are necessary to make the molecular-system operation time-varying.

The control system requires all the component blocks of a time-invariant molecular system.   Hence, time-varying operation is always more complex because of the control system.   In practice, since some systems must give different performance at different times, changes or "adjustments" in components or connections must be possible. But much effort is expended in the design of technical and consumer goods to reduce the number of necessary changes or "adjustments." When possible, the components and their connections are made in the factory and not changed later.

Time-varying Arrangements

Time-variable arrangements all involve combining and dividing, because an information source is necessary to cause the time variation. The control information may be arranged to control several systems.

The existing or built-in conditions plus the control result in a new or regulated performance.   Any component or built-in connection or even combinations of a fixed block or blocks may be arranged to be regulated or adjusted and thus changed with time.   Any variable used to describe the energy wave or the object may be controlled.

Some important kinds of changes with time are: regulation or adjustment, selection in space, and feedback.

The change or changes with time may be made continuously or discontinuously (i.e., on-off).   A change may occur intermittently or only occasionally.

The tuning of a radio or a television set to a wanted station is an example of a continuous adjustment or control over a range. Turning the energy flow on and off is an important function in many systems. Fuses, valves, control switches, and faucets perform such an operation. The control may be on-off (fuses and switches) or continuous (valves and faucets).

Stepping switches and switching networks composed of crosspoints are examples of combining-and-dividing arrangements used to select and set up different paths in space at different times. They find important applications in telephony and computers.

Feedback arrangements and servomechanisms are discussed below.

Random Variations with Time

If the control-system information source is made unpredictable with time, then the operation of the controlled system is also unpredictable. Random noise generators are examples of unpredictable sources.

Unpredictable operation is useful in studies of the operation of certain systems with random inputs and also in cyptographic systems used to encode and decode secret information.

Three Sources of Control Information

The external information source of the control in Fig. 5-1 may be a human being. But a program of changes may be stored for future use. A bank vault time clock is an example. A key to open a lock is another. Complex sequences of changes can be made by a computer-type control.

External control is sometimes called open-loop control. For some situations it may not be a satisfactory method. For example, an automobile might have several marked positions for the accelerator. With the accelerator set at a certain mark, the nominal speed would be exactly 50 mph. Even if the car always ran on the level, this would be unsatisfactory (e.g., it would take a long time to get to 50 mph).

Figure 5-2 shows reflexive control. The control information is derived from the output of the controlled system via a divider. The control path forms a closed loop or feedback path.

In the automobile acceleration example, the driver obtains information visually about his speed from the road or the speedometer.

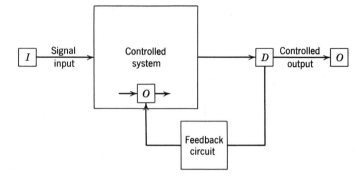

Figure 5-2

He then applies more power until he reaches the desired speed and then reduces power to maintain the speed.

In any feedback system

1. a wanted output performance reference is supplied;
2. some function of the controlled variable is examined to see how closely the output performance agrees with the reference;
3. the difference between the wanted and actual performance generates an error signal;
4. power is applied under the control of the error signal to reduce the difference so that it approaches zero.

Any variable used to describe the output may be controlled.

Two common types of feedback control arrangements are called regulators and servomechanisms. In a regulator, the controlled variable or the output is kept nearly equal to the desired value despite a changing load or outside disturbances. In the steady state, the error signal is constant. Generally, a regulator contains no integrating elements.

In a servomechanism, the change or rate of change of the output with time is kept nearly equal to the desired value. The feedback loop must contain integrating elements.

In a servomechanism for position control (i.e., a zero-displacement-error arrangement) the controlled variable is a position or a velocity. The reference is the desired position or displacement. The error signal indicates a departure for the desired value. Load disturbances may be present but are secondary factors.

For acceleration control (i.e., a zero-velocity servomechanism) the controlled variable is an acceleration. The error signal indicates a departure from the desired speed.

Since the pioneer work of H. S. Black, H. Nyquist, and H. W. Bode, there have been many publications dealing with the theory and design of feedback and servomechanism systems.

The basic principles were used in antiquity, but understanding of these principles and their widespread application dates from about 1930. It was the privilege of one of the authors to design and build some of the first feedback amplifiers.

In Fig. 5-3, the control information is obtained from the *input* information of the controlled system via the divider. The control path forms a closed-loop or "feed-forward" path.

Combinations of external, reflexive, and feed-forward control are also possible. Figure 5-4 shows a simplified block diagram of a feedback amplifier designed to be used in multichannel telephone systems. If the feedback path were held fixed with time, the amplification would be constant within extremely narrow limits. But the cable temperature and hence its power transmission efficiency changes during the year. The temperature change is measured and the feedback path is changed as the temperature of the cable changes, so that the amplification changes to compensate almost exactly for the cable efficiency changes with temperature.

In feedback and servomechanism arrangements, the input and feedback waves are almost always continuous. In a few systems, feedback occurs only intermittently, but such examples are exceptions. In "sequence" circuits, the input waves are pulses on one or more input leads. Figure 5-5 represents such a feed-forward system. When certain predetermined pulse or digital information appears on the input leads,

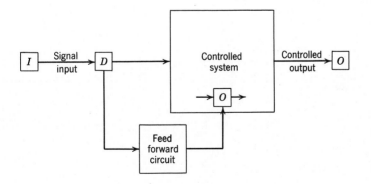

Figure 5-3

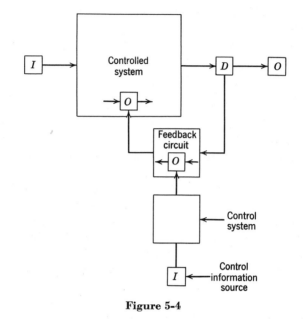

Figure 5-4

the output of the logic blocks provides information so the internal configuration of the translator is changed by the operation of an effector or effectors. A submerged mine that counts the passage of four vessels and then explodes when the fifth passes is an example of such a time-varying performance.

Figure 5-6 represents a feedback system. The pulse or digital information is taken from the output leads instead of the input. Otherwise, the operation is much the same as in Fig. 5-5. An extensive literature

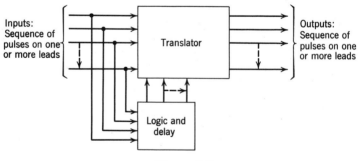

Figure 5-5

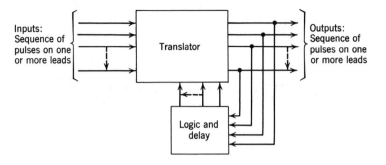

Figure 5-6

is devoted to the problems of analysis and synthesis of systems represented by Fig. 5-6. Such arrangements are widely used in telephone
switching systems and digital computers. In switching systems the
operation is usually asynchronous; i.e., the operations occur in the
wanted order, but the operating times may vary. In computers the
input pulses and system changes are synchronized with a control
"clock" wave.

A combination of feed-forward and feed-back control is also
possible.

6

System Building Blocks

Introduction

A logically developed set of functional building blocks can be very helpful to anyone involved with any phase of system design. In an actual system, these blocks can be realized by physical components.

Existing systems can be broken down into a particular collection of the fundamental blocks. New systems can be synthesized by suitable collections of the blocks to perform wanted functions. Rules can be formulated for doing either analysis or synthesis.

Because the blocks are logically necessary, it may be possible to use computers for at least some aspects of systems analysis and synthesis. And, by further work, the approach can possibly (perhaps even probably) be applied to situations involving human beings in their behavioral and social relations.

To illustrate the approach, the "molecular" model can be broken down into a few different kinds of component blocks or "atoms" (Fig. 6-1). Each kind of component block has a name and performs only one kind of function. A standard language for the various kinds of functional blocks is believed to be an important step. In Fig. 6-1 the necessary media (however short) between blocks are indicated. Thus a molecular system is a particular aggregation of functional blocks.

For the electrical portion of a system, the "atoms" are electrical generators and inductances, capacitances, and resistances. For a mechanical or other kind of system, the "atoms" are the appropriate analogs of these.

The Information Source

In a physical system, the information supplied by the source object (I) must be in the form of energy in space. This is true because

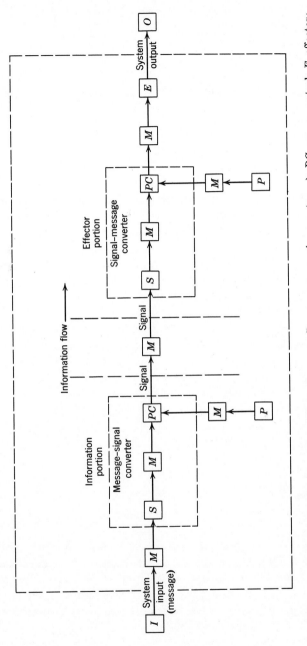

Figure 6-1 *I*, information source; *M*, medium; *S*, sensor; *P*, power source (zero–entropy); *PC*, power control; *E*, effector; *O*, object changed.

information can be transported between space-separated objects only by an energy flow.

The concept of unexpectedness requires that the energy pattern in space vary unpredictably with time.

The information source must have energy and other characteristics compatible with the system input. The information source must either:

1. emit energy;
2. reflect energy from a power source; or
3. control a power source.

Radiation from the sun and human speech are examples of emitted information. Echoes in a cave and reflected light from a scene are examples of reflection. A radio transmitter is a controlled power source.

In many systems, the information source is a human brain. It directs the power furnished by muscles. The muscular actions may result in the almost continuous sound waves of speech or in discontinuous actions such as playing a piano.

The information from (I) is assumed to contain no errors. But received signals may contain errors caused by some improper operation, by noise, or by a trouble in the transmission medium. Even when the signal contains errors if the information it carries has some redundancy, some errors can be detected and corrected so that they do not interfere with the accuracy of the information received at the destination.

Sensors

Figure 6-1 shows a message-signal converter in the information portion of the model and a signal-message converter in the effector portion.

The input block in each converter must be a sensor that recognizes the unexpected variations of the input energy with time. Sensing recovers the information-carrying variation of message or signal energy. Obviously, the sensor must be compatible with the input waves. If the waves are electrical, the sensor must respond to electrical waves; if they are acoustic, it must respond to acoustic waves.

To recognize the unexpected variations, the sensor performs a measurement function. In systems work, measurements are made for at least three purposes:

1. To gather information about some unknown phenomenon. Some information-gathering is done as pure research to add to the store of human knowledge without any immediate application in mind. But information-gathering about a particular phenomenon is frequently necessary before the design of a new system can even start or during subsequent stages as the design proceeds. Many man-years of measurements of all sorts of reactions of the human body to conditions encountered in space flight were necessary before a man could make his first journey into outer space in a suitable capsule. Each subsequent step in space travel will require many, many more man-years of measurements.

2. To test the functioning of the first model of a new design, of the parts of a system as they are manufactured, and of the complete assembly when it is first put to use or after it is modified. A new design of an automobile goes through exhaustive tests before it is released for manufacture. The parts are measured during the manufacturing process so that the quality of the product is kept at a satisfactory level. A completed car is test-driven by the factory, or by the owner, or both to make sure that it is working satisfactorily.

3. To monitor the operation of a working system. Literally hundreds of measurements are made continuously in a complex chemical plant, in an oil refinery, or in an electric utility generation and distribution network. Your automobile instrument panel allows you to monitor the minute-by-minute operation of the car.

The Measuring Operation

To make a measurement, the object or system to be measured must first be modified in some way to insert or apply the measuring equipment. Clearly, the modification is an example of a variation with time of the object or the system to be measured. For this reason, an external information source and system is necessary to attach some measuring device to the object or energy flow to be measured.

After the measuring device is attached, the object or energy flow being measured becomes the information source. If the object is a part of a system, then its changes with time can furnish information about changes in the system.

Methods of Measuring

The process of measuring some property or properties of the input information consists of:

1. Comparing the value of the input property with an appropriate scale.

2. Deciding on the nearest division, i.e., quantizing.

3. Counting the number of divisions.

4. Expressing the count as a number and recording or otherwise using it.

These four steps must be performed in making any measurement.

Many variations in methods are possible. For step 1, the comparison between the property to be measured and the scale may be indicated by a null device, e.g., a galvanometer in a bridge circuit.

The need for quantizing in step 2 arises because a continuously variable quantity may have an infinite set of values, but the scale has only a finite set of numbers.

Measuring devices may perform step 3 by several methods:

1. By counting. For example, the number of units can be counted out one-by-one until the residue is less than one unit.

2. By comparison with one digit value after another proceeding from the most significant digit to the least. Each time the digit value in question is subtracted if that value is smaller than the quantity remaining from the previous subtraction.

3. By comparison with a set of scaled values. The actual counting of divisions may be eliminated by having each scale division numbered.

An example of method 1 is measuring length by stepping the unknown along a ruler marked with unit steps and counting the required number of steps.

An example of method 2 is measuring a mass with a balance. The unknown is placed on one pan and known masses are added to the other. If the known mass is less than the unknown, it is left on the pan. In effect, this subtracts mass from the unknown. The process is continued until balance is indicated within the smallest digit. The known masses are then totaled. Handling the most significant digits first is the economical procedure, but the least significant digit may be handled first. Servomechanisms using feedback magnitudes corresponding to digit values fall into this class.

Method 3 includes all the devices where numbers are associated with the divisions on an established scale.

Sensor Output

The sensor supplies an output suitable for operating the power control that varies the output of the zero-entropy power source.

Thus the sensor and power control by their joint action convert message energy into signal energy (or vice versa).

The sensor output changes an impedance (i.e., the power control) and thus varies (modulates) the output of the power source with time. In this way, the input information is mapped on the zero-entropy output of the power source. The mapping process may be called power conversion if no frequency changes occur (e.g., a dc supply source such as a storage battery is used); otherwise modulation is probably a better word.

Ideally, a sensor operates instantaneously.

Different kinds of measuring devices provide different amounts of output information:

1. The simplest kind indicates that the input is or is not present. If the indication is visual, such devices rarely need a dial.

2. A more informative type indicates whether conditions are satisfactory, and if not, the direction in which they are off. Visual gauges of this kind need not have numbers. For example, an automobile temperature gauge may tell whether the engine is too hot or too cool, but not whether the temperature is 130° or 150°.

3. A third kind gives precise quantitative readings.

4. In the fourth kind, the precision varies with the input. Thus, an altimeter may give only rough values for higher altitudes and more precise values for low altitudes. At high altitudes, a pilot need know his position only approximately. But while landing he must know exactly how far he is above the ground.

Predictable Power Source

Ideally, the power source should furnish zero-entropy power. By definition, zero-entropy power is completely predictable and therefore conveys no information. In other words, there should be no "unexpectedness." Any unpredictable noise or jitter is an imperfection.

The energy may be mechanical, electrical, acoustical or some other form.

In some cases the exact power source may be hard to identify precisely. For example, the rays of light shining on a picture may come from many sources having differing intensities and located at different places.

The energy from a power source need not vary with time. Thus, dc power may be controlled (modulated) to generate time-varying and hence information-carrying energy. For example, a steady (i.e., a dc) power source is controlled (modulated) in a telephone transmitter by voice waves to create a time-varying electric current.

A continuous sinusoidal wave is also completely predictable. Sine-wave power sources find wide application in communication systems.

The output waves of "discontinuous" power sources contain abrupt changes, but may be completely predictable. A train of on-off pulses is an example of such a wave. In a physical system, changes cannot be "perfectly" abrupt: a finite time is always required for any change. So even "discontinuous" waves are in fact continuous—the difference is one of degree.

The space or time structure (or both) of a power source may be quite complex. For example, recurrent ramplike waves, electrical noise, white light, or even smoke from a fire may be controlled (e.g., turned on and off) and thus used to convey information. These sources vary with time and yet they can be used to signal.

Power Control

The word "control" is defined: to exercise an influence over something, to guide, direct or restrain it. In a converter, the power control controls or modulates the energy from the zero-entropy power source.

A power control does not change the form of the energy from the power source: so the power source and converter output energy are of the same form. Of course, the converter output must be completely compatible with the next block in the system.

The modulated output depends on the instantaneous values of both the power source and the power control. Hence, if both the information-carrying input and power source waves are continuous, then the converter output wave is continuous; if *either* is discontinuous, then the output wave is discontinuous.

To produce information-carrying energy, a power control can only change one or more of the variables describing the zero-entropy power source. It can change either the space or time structure or both.

The number of dimensions in the space structure may be one, two, or three. Of course, time is always one dimension. Any change that can be sensed to recover the information can be used. For example, the energy output amplitude may be varied (AM or amplitude modulation). In an important special case, on-off keying, the controlled characteristic is in either one of two conditions.

A particular power control changes the energy flow from the zero-entropy source by varying an impedance. In electrical circuits, the variable impedance may be a resistance, inductance, capacitance, or some combination of these; with other forms of energy, an appropriate analog of the electrical impedance.

Ideally, at one extreme of the power control the power source delivers full output to the converter output; at the opposite extreme, no power to the converter output.

A power control contains no storage and hence operates in real time.

Effector

The effector causes the wanted change in the object in response to its input energy from the converter. To make the wanted change, energy must be expended on the object.

The energy forms at the input and output of the effector may differ. For example, a telephone receiver has an electrical input and an acoustical output.

An effector contains no storage elements and hence operates in real time.

An effector may control the presentation or display of an information output to (1) a human eye or ear or (2) another system.

Object

The wanted change made in the object may be mechanical, electrical, magnetic, chemical, or thermal in nature—in fact, any possible change whatever.

The changed object may be a human brain. Exactly what changes are made in this case is not completely understood.

Media to Transmit Energy between Space Locations

In physical systems, the components are separated in space. In the operation of the system, it is necessary to transmit energy between the space-separated components.

The energy transmission is carried out by some sort of carriers moving through a medium.* As information-carrying energy, electro-

---

* The blocks represent delay and loss that are independent of frequency. Other kinds of delays and losses are considered to be imperfections and are discussed a little later.

magnetic waves are particularly well adapted. For by using such waves, transport is made much faster and a path may be better controlled than with heat waves (for example).

Nevertheless, many results of the transmission theory developed for telegraph, telephone, and television can be applied to other forms of information-carrying energy.

Component Imperfections

Practical or nonideal molecular systems exhibit performance departures from an ideal system. The departures arise because the components themselves are not ideal. For example, every inductance dissipates energy in the form of heat. In a particular practical system, the departures from the ideal (i.e., "imperfections") may or may not be important, but the consequences of departures should always be understood.

The possible kinds of component departures from ideal performance may be classified as energy transmission effects, distortions due to unwanted nonlinear effects, and interference.

Energy Transmission Effects

Loss. Any physical component, such as a transmission medium of finite length, dissipates or "loses" energy in the form of heat. Because of this "loss," the output power is always less than the input.

Pass-Bandwidth. Below a low-frequency cutoff, and above a high-frequency cutoff a physical component may transmit energy poorly. Some components do not exhibit a low-frequency cutoff; all exhibit a high-frequency cutoff. Between the two cutoffs (the pass-band), energy is transmitted more efficiently than in the cutoff regions (see Fig. 6-2).

Finite Transmission Speed. Energy cannot be transmitted faster than the speed of light (roughly, 300,000 km per second). Radio transmission can occur at the speed of light. Electrical waves, such as those used in telephony, can be transmitted over certain kinds of open-wire and cable circuits at speeds only moderately lower. However, the speed of acoustic waves is only a few hundred meters per second. Heat waves in solid media travel even more slowly. So the range of transmission speeds is quite wide.

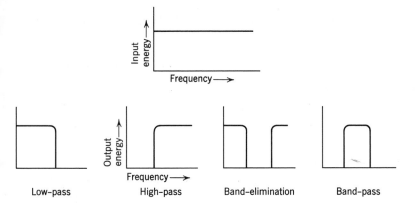

Figure 6-2 Input-output energy relations.

The transmission time through a component is often called the "delay."

Variation of the energy transmission with time may also be an imperfection. Rather rapid variations are sometimes called "jitter"; somewhat slower variations, "fading."

In a particular application, energy transmission imperfections may be relatively unimportant. For example, media always depart from ideal performance. But if components are close together so that the medium is short, its presence and therefore its imperfections may be quite tolerable, if not completely unimportant. On the other hand, in many important situations, media losses and delays must be taken into account. Long-distance telephone connections are just one example.

Distortions

Amplitude Distortion. A change in the relative amplitudes of the input waves may be present when they emerge from the output of a component because of unwanted nonlinear input-output relations that are independent of frequency.

Attenuation Distortion. Frequency deviations from a desired amplitude-frequency characteristic of a complex wave-form over the wanted pass-band.

Phase or Delay Distortion. A change in the relative phase of the signal-frequency components in the wanted pass-band caused by a change in the relative transmission times of the various frequency components.

Harmonic Distortion. New frequencies produced by a nonlinear input-output characteristic. They are integrally related to the input frequencies.

Intermodulation or Cross-modulation Distortion. New frequencies produced by a nonlinear input-output characteristic. They are not integrally related to the input frequencies.

Sensors, power controls, and effectors may produce unwanted amplitude distortions so that the actual input-output curve differs from the desired curve. The distortions may vary with time in a systematic or random manner. Such distortions—or even partial failure to function—can be caused by marginal operation. Amplifiers and modulators usually produce harmonic and intermodulation distortion. Distortions can also be caused by malfunctions due to a trouble condition.

The importance of an imperfection depends on the performance objectives that must be met by the component if the overall system is to perform satisfactorily.

Interference

The outputs of a system are wanted by some person or persons. Other persons may not want them. The unwanted effects can be called interference or "noise" by such people.

In an information sense, there is no such thing as "pure noise." Radio static may give information about the ionosphere or about the stars, as in radio astronomy. In any case noise indicates something about its cause and thus can give some information about its source. Thus the distinction between information and interference is whether the observed effect is wanted or not.

Unwanted noise may be classified as follows:

Random
Cosmic, in radio media
Impulse, such as interference from sparking contacts
Static, from thunderstorms and other atmospheric disturbances
Signal frequency or tones, due to leaks from or unwanted exposures to various signal generators
Crosstalk (sometimes called crossfire by telegraph engineers), from other transmission paths in the same or paralleling media
Echoes due to reflections from objects in or nonhomogeneities of the medium.

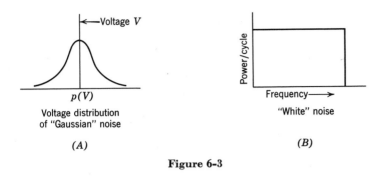

Voltage distribution
of "Gaussian" noise

"White" noise

(A)

(B)

Figure 6-3

Random noise is not localized in time or frequency. A common source of such random noise in electronic systems is the "thermal" noise due to the random movements of electrons at temperatures above 0° Kelvin. Sometimes the word "noise" is used loosely to mean thermal noise.

Random noise is sometimes loosely referred to as "Gaussian" noise or "white" noise. Actually, the word "Gaussian" specifies the voltage distribution in terms of probabilities: $p(V)\,dV = 1/p\sqrt{2\pi}$ (Fig. 6-3A). "White" noise has equal energy at all frequencies. "Band-limited" white noise has equal energies at all frequencies within the specific band, and zero energy elsewhere (Fig. 6-3B).

Impulse noise is highly localized in time but covers a broad frequency spectrum.

Single-frequency noise is highly localized in frequency but lasts a significant time.

In impulse noise, the phases of the spectral components are correlated; in single-frequency noise, they are not.

Failures (Lack of Reliability)

A failure is any component is an imperfection. The wanted performance is sometimes expressed in terms of a reliability objective by a time interval without failure or between failures.

Combiner

A combiner merges two or more space-separated inputs to form one output (Fig. 6-4). The inputs may be energies or objects or both. The inputs may be continuous or discontinuous in time, or both.

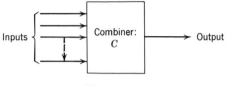

Figure 6-4

By definition, a combiner does not store energy. Hence, the common output must carry the instantaneous sum of the energy from all the inputs. One example of combining is several power generators feeding a common bus.

In combining, the form of energy supplied to all inputs may or may not be the same. In some systems, all of the proposed inputs to a particular combiner are not of the same form, and suitable conversions are made before the energies are combined (see Fig. 6-5). For example, in a telephone system the acoustical waves are all converted to electrical waves. The converted waves may then be combined for multiplex transmission. On the other hand, some permanent magnets are made by applying a strong magnetic field while the material is being heated in a furnace. Thus two forms of energy are applied to the object at the same time.

There are two kinds of combiners: the reversible and the irreversible. The inputs to a reversible combiner can later be recovered. In multiplex telephony, separate input waves are combined and later recovered to be delivered to their proper destinations. The inputs to an irreversible combiner can not be recovered. A water faucet which mixes streams of hot and cold water is an example because recovering the original streams would be almost impossible. For

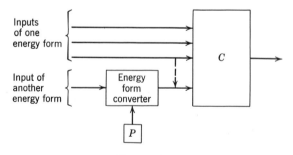

Figure 6-5

another example, take a number which you know to be the sum of two or more other numbers. There are an infinite number of possible inputs that would give the same sum. In the absence of further information, rational selection of the input numbers is impossible.

Divider

A divider divides its one input among two or more space-separated outputs (Fig. 6-6). The input may be energy or an object.

The input and output energy forms are the same. When input energy is divided among the several outputs, the energy in some or all outputs may be so weak that amplification or reinforcement is necessary.

A combiner has only one output; a divider only one input. In combining and dividing, the inputs and outputs are always space-separated. If certain conditions are met, combining and dividing may be made inverse operations. Combiners and dividers contain no storage and hence operate in real time.

With suitable arrangements of combiners and dividers the number of inputs and outputs may both be greater than one (Fig. 6-7). Furthermore, the number of inputs and outputs may be the same or different. Either may be the larger number.

By dividing, one generator may feed (or "fan-out") to thousands

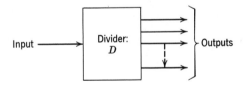

Figure 6-6

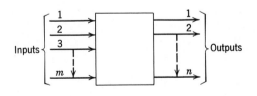

Figure 6-7

of incandescent lights, motors, toasters, and other appliances; a radio or television station may send its program to a million receivers.

A divider input may be divided with no intent of reconstituting it (e.g., a water main supplying many homes). On the other hand, information may be divided among several outputs in such a manner that it can be put back together.

Uses of Combiners and Dividers

Some important uses of combiners and dividers are:

1. To provide two-way transmission of information. Figure 6-8 shows a "four-wire" arrangement to provide separate channels for the two directions. The divider and combiner may employ "hybrid coils" or frequency-, time-, or phase-selective arrangements. Some media and devices, such as a pair of wires, transmit energy equally well in either direction. They can be used for two-way energy transfer. Figure 6-9 shows an arrangement for using the two wires of a customer's loop for two-way transmission.

2. Multiplexing and demultiplexing several signals for transmission over a medium (Fig. 6-10A).

The separate signals may be differentiated by frequency, time, or phase (Figs. 6-10B, C, and D).

In a multichannel carrier system, the signal of each channel is transmitted on a separate carrier wave. All the separate waves are

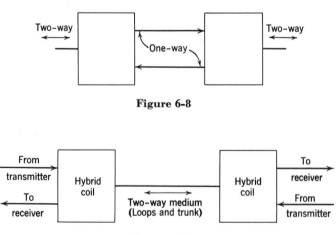

Figure 6-8

Figure 6-9

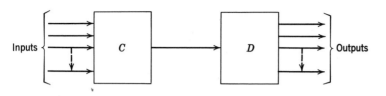

Figure 6-10*A*

superimposed or added to form a single signal wave. At the receiving end of the medium, the channels are separated. In this way, a single medium (such as a coaxial cable) may be used to carry telegraph, telephone, data, and television signals simultaneously.

Objects may be divided and combined in the space domain (Fig. 6-10*E*).

3. Translation. In the present context, the word "translate" means: to interpret; to render into another language; to express in words of a different language. Translation is an important function in con-

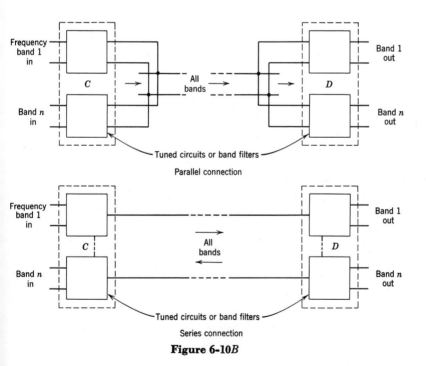

Figure 6-10*B*

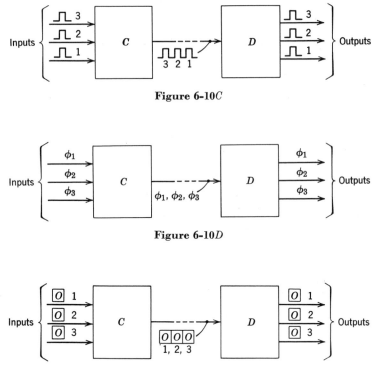

Figure 6-10C

Figure 6-10D

Figure 6-10E

versions from one language to another and also between different codes such as those used in telephone switching systems.

In a simple translation a particular input causes a particular output: an input is merely relabeled to give the corresponding output as in Fig. 6-11 which shows a wired translator. There need be no time delay in the operation.

Language translation is much more complex. A Russian word or phase might be translated into quite a few different English words or phases. Context or other information must decide the most appropriate choice. A block diagram for more complex translators is given later.

The information flow is always one way. For two-way translation, two sources and two outputs are necessary. The input and output blocks may be interchanged by suitable switching arrangements.

4. Arithmetic computation to determine a number, amount, or other answer. Such computation implies a determinable precise result.

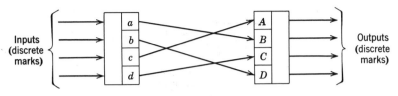

Figure 6-11

In arithmetic operations, two inputs are combined according to some rule (e.g., a rule for addition) to give an output or answer, or their equality or un-equality is sensed.

5. Logical operations that involve the logical relations of propositions to one another such as affirmation-negation, inclusion-exclusion, and particular-general. Such relations may be expressed by the words is, is-not, if-then, only (none but), and, or, some, all. As examples, in Fig. 6-12*A*, an output occurs only if all inputs are present: an AND arrangement; in Fig. 6-12*B*, an output occurs if any input is present: an OR arrangement.

In practical systems, such logical arrangements are used for many purposes. For example,

a. To govern the information flow through switchable media, and to interchange connections

b. To process information to derive new information

c. To control information flow

d. To make decisions

e. To alter the program of a time-variable system

We now consider two other important logical functions.

Comparison is setting or bringing (things) together in fact (or contemplation) and examining the relations they bear to each other

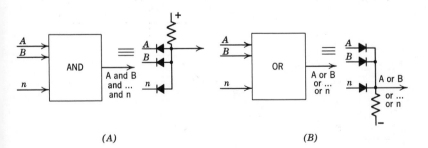

(*A*)   (*B*)

Figure 6-12

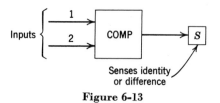

Figure 6-13

especially to ascertain their agreement or disagreement or the points of resemblance or difference (Fig. 6-13). Comparison depends on some non-constancy or non-linearity of response to the measured quantity. Frequency or phase comparison may use linear elements to give the required non-linear response.

Figure 6-14 shows more details of a particular arrangement for comparing the two sets of digital inputs $(a, b, \ldots k)$ and $(A, B, \ldots K)$. If both inputs are 0 or 1, there is an output to the corresponding OR circuit. If all the OR circuits provide outputs to the AND circuit, the AND circuit gives an output to the sensor to indicate the match.

Level setting is the inverse of comparison. At a given time, equality

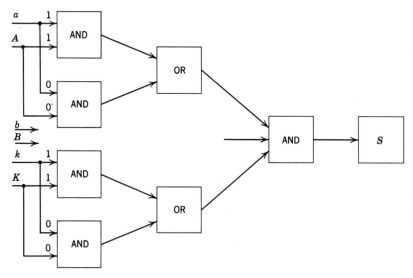

Figure 6-14

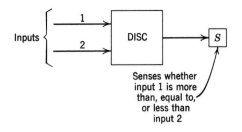

Figure 6-15

of amplitude, frequency, or phase is achieved.   Level setting is important in sensing or demodulation.

Discrimination is the act of distinguishing; the act of making or observing a difference (Fig. 6-15).

A comparison or discrimination may be made with an appropriate fixed reference or measure, as in Figs. 6-16*A* and *B*.   The reference takes the place of one of the inputs of Fig. 6-13 or 6-14.

Everyone is familiar with the operations of comparison and discrimination from his daily experience with objects, money, and time intervals—and even abstract ideas.   These operations are also of great importance in information-handling systems.   For example, information structures and rates of messages and signals can be compared. So too can the waves from zero-entropy generators and from signal and message converters.   Later, comparison and discrimination will be shown to be extremely important in system design.

Multiple comparison and discrimination operations are possible. Two comparisons can indicate round *and* red objects; two discriminations, inputs greater than one value and less than another, i.e., values within a "tolerance" range.

Comparison and discrimination circuits are widely used in radar

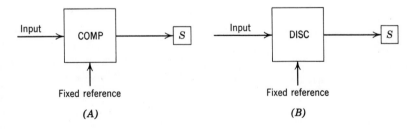

(A)   (B)

Figure 6-16

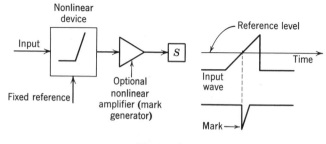

Figure 6-17

and other equipment employing very fast electronic waves. A few examples are next described.

Mathematically, *amplitude comparison* is the determination of the abscissa of a wave, given the ordinate. In physical terms, amplitude comparison indicates the instant of equality of two waves. A marker may show whether the approach is from a larger or smaller value. See Fig. 6-17 which shows an approach from a smaller value.

Time comparison determines the amplitude of a wave at a given instant. It gives the amplitude corresponding to a given value of the wave abscissa. A detector gives a constant output. Time comparison can be thought of as a special case of time selection (discussed later) in which the selected interval is very short to give the instantaneous amplitude.

A *reference* is a precise position of a waveform on a voltage, current, or time axis. The mean level may be specified or a certain part may be held at a particular level or time. For operations on the time axis, the reference may be a portion of the wave itself or a separate wave such as a pulse train.

Amplitude discrimination (Fig. 6-18) determines the equality or inequality of two objects or energy flows and the sense and magnitude of the differences. It thus is akin to a subtraction. The objects or energy flows may be continuous or discontinuous.

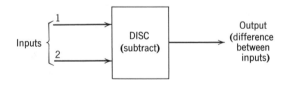

Figure 6-18

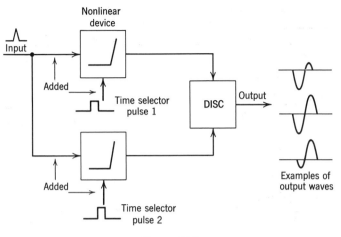

Figure 6-19

Time discrimination (Fig. 6-19) indicates the relative time of occurrence of two events by an appropriate output if they are simultaneous. If not simultaneous, the sense and approximate magnitude of the time difference is indicated. Two operations, time selection and detection, are required.

Some Complex Arrangements

Certain complex multiple input-output arrangements of the basic blocks occur frequently in existing systems and during a system design. These arrangements perform the functions of selection, connection, storage, sorting, and identification.

Selection

Selection is an important operation. It is the act of choosing and taking from a number of alternatives; a taking from another by preference. The selection may be from either a continuous spectrum of possible alternatives or a discrete set of alternatives. Measuring and counting are particular (but frequently used) examples of selection.

The selection process in space is used in steering an object or energy to the selected one of the set of locations or objects from which the choice is made. Unselected locations or objects are not

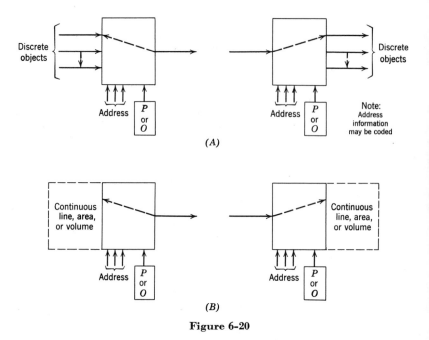

(A)

(B)

Figure 6-20

affected (Figs. 6-20*A* and *B*). Selection alone causes no other effect on the object. The selected object is merely located.

Positioning always involves selection of a location in space for the object.

To perform a selection, suitable information is necessary:

1. A start signal to initiate the operation
2. Locations of the objects from which the selection is to be made—such information is often called the "addresses"
3. An access path to each object
4. An order of examining the objects
5. A signal from each object when it is examined
6. A comparison or discrimination arrangement to receive the signal and to recognize a suitable object
7. A rule for acceptance or rejection
8. A signal to stop the operation

In Fig. 6-21 the address is provided over space-separated leads. The access to the objects is via a binary tree in which each of n choices gives access to one of 2^n locations.

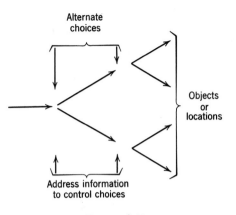

Figure 6-21

In Fig. 6-22 the address is provided by two sets of space-separated leads from two sources. A location is reached by a coincident choice by the two sources.

The methods shown in Figs. 6-21 and 6-22 are frequently called *random access* because the objects may be reached in any sequence. A program is therefore necessary to determine the order of examination. The program may actually be "cut-and-try" without a plan. Several "search" programs for locating an object (such as an enemy submarine) are described in operational research literature. Clearly, the time required for success depends on the search program, barring a lucky guess. Fundamental research is still going on to find effective search strategies.

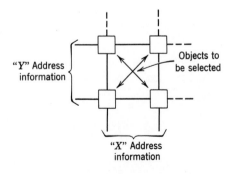

Figure 6-22

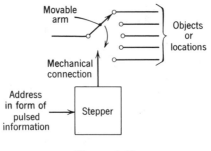

Figure 6-23

The order is fixed in *sequential access*. As an example, Fig. 6-23 shows a self-stepping switch that gives access to a new location for each bit of address information (such as an input pulse). The stepper or counter mechanism moves the arms to each location in its turn. Phonograph records and strips of movie film are also examples of sequential access arrangements.

As each location is reached, the comparison arrangement (i.e., a logic arrangement) indicates: (1) a successful match, (2) a failure to match, or possibly (3) a partially successful match. The information to be examined may be in the form of numbers or letters or both and may be coded or not.

The program for selection may examine all possible objects and classify them into these two (or possibly three) categories.

Selection may be made in two or more stages. Figure 6-21 shows a simple example. In the general cases of multiple stages, any number of choices can be used for a stage. Furthermore, the numbers need not be the same for the various stages. An appropriate number of stages and the number of selections to be made by each stage are chosen by the designer. Depending on how the address information is supplied, the selections in the various stages may be made sequentially stage-by-stage, simultaneously in all stages, or even by a combination of the two methods.

In "hunting" and "allotting" arrangements used to select an idle link in a telephone central office, the program specifies: Take an available object (i.e., an idle trunk) in the group of objects (trunks) to the wanted office. First the wanted group is selected from all the groups of trunks.

Hunting arrangements, such as Fig. 6-24, then make an examination of the objects according to a second program that specifies: Test in sequence and take the first available one. If there are none, so

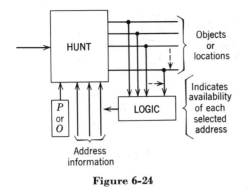

Figure 6-24

signal. Thus hunting arrangements select after the start signal initiates the operation.

Allotting arrangements (Fig. 6-25) also examine the objects according to a second program. This program specifies the object to be taken when the group is next selected from all the groups of objects. The "allotment" is made before the selection of the group, and may provide that objects are used in order rather than taking the first available one as in hunting.

With either hunting or allotting arrangements, a *lockout* information source may be added so a selected object is made unavailable for another selection until it becomes idle again.

Scanning (Fig. 6-26) arrangements look over a group of objects to find any that may be generating a particular information mark. A sensor observes whether the mark is present or absent at each address.

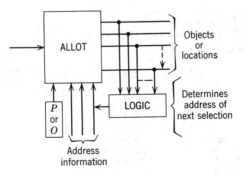

Figure 6-25

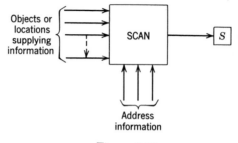

Figure 6-26

Identification (Fig. 6-27) gives the address of the source of such a mark and hence one object or location. It involves both selection and translation.

Figure 6-28 shows a *finding* arrangement involving identification and then selection. One object among a group starts the operation with a request to be "found." This object might be a telephone line originating a call. The selection is ended when the object is found.

Selection of waves may be performed on the basis of amplitude, frequency, phase, or time. In pure selection, the selected portion is undistorted.

Amplitude selection involves a portion of a wave lying above or below a boundary or within two bounds. In *rectification,* the useful output is greater than some value, usually near zero (Fig. 6-29). In *limiting* (clipping), the useful output is either (1) above some lower value, or (2) between a lower and an upper value. Case 2 is some-

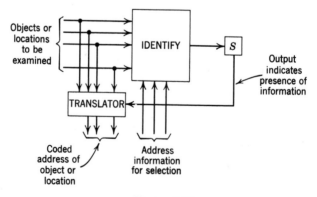

Figure 6-27

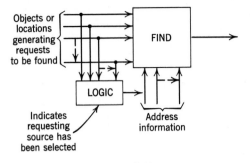

Figure 6-28

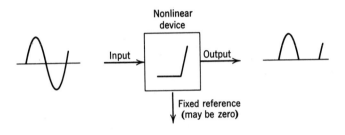

Figure 6-29

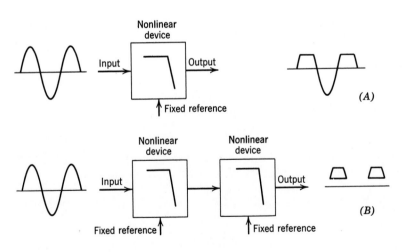

Figure 6-30

times called "slicing" (Fig. 6-30*A* and *B*). Amplitude selection may be used for amplitude modulation of a zero-entropy wave (Fig. 6-31). In some electronic applications, *quasi-selection* above or below a reference amplitude is followed by a distortion of the selected wave into a step or a pulse (Fig. 6-32).

Frequency selection involves waves with frequency components below or above a certain frequency called the cut-off frequency, or with components between upper and lower cut-off frequencies. Figure 6-2 shows the several possibilities.

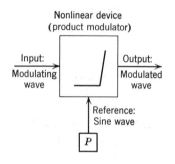

Figure 6-31

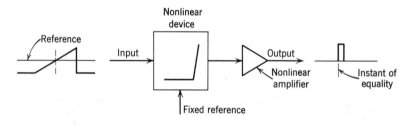

Figure 6-32

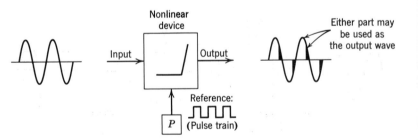

Figure 6-33

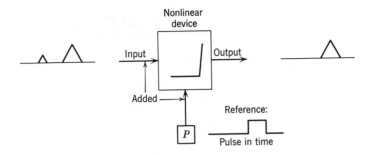

Figure 6-34

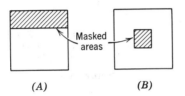

(A)   *(B)*

Figure 6-35

Phase selection selects waves with a particular phase relation to a reference wave (Fig. 6-33).

Time selection selects a portion of a wave that occurs within a given interval or before or after a given time relative to a repeated time reference (Fig. 6-34).

Selection of areas *in space* is also possible. Figures 6-35*A* and *B* show examples.

Connection

By definition, selection alone causes no other effect on the selected energy or object. In most practical situations, the reason for the selection is to change the object in some wanted way by either applying energy to it or changing its relation with respect to another object.

To apply energy to a selected object, a path must be established from an energy source to the object; i.e., the energy source must be "connected" to the object. The selection operation must give information about (1) when a suitable object has been selected and (2) the location of the object. These two pieces of information can then be used to close the path. Figure 6-21 shows a simple "tree" arrangement that can provide a path to a selected object. Figure 6-36 shows the arrangement for changing the gate from one of its two conditions to the other.

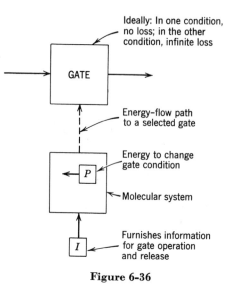

Figure 6-36

Similarly, to bring an object to a fixed object after the selection, information must specify the path. If two movable objects are to be brought together, information about both paths must be furnished. Such control operations are performed in assembling objects in manufacture. The movement of the human hand toward an object is another example. In this case, the eye can monitor the movement, and provide information to the brain to direct the hand to the object. This is an example of feedback controlling the steering of the hand in space. Once the object is reached, the brain can then direct the grasping of the object (as an example of "connecting" the hand to it).

Storage

Storage may be defined as a change in the time location of an amount of energy or of an object. Ideally, no other changes except the time location should occur. The stored energy may be zero-entropy or information-carrying. Stored information may be "retrieved" or read out soon after it is stored or sometimes years later.

Storage of either energy or an object *always* occurs at a location in space. Storage *always* requires the expenditure of energy. The stored energy or object *always* tends to deteriorate or disappear with the passage of time. Energy stored in a storage battery must be regenerated from time to time by recharging the battery. A trunk stored in the attic also tends to deteriorate over the years, as does a book sitting on a library shelf for many decades. Rates of deterioration may differ—but deterioration is certain. Besides the deterioration, stored information may undergo distortion or interference (noise) during storage or removal from the store.

In a sense, an energy wave traversing a medium is "stored" in the medium because of the finite velocity and hence the time delay between the input and output. Media called *delay lines* are actually used to store information. Because of their comparatively low velocity, acoustic waves in a mercury or quartz medium offer relatively long delay per unit length of line. In the line, the energy is stored serially in space, and emerges at the output in the same sequence as at the input. By tapping a line at appropriate places along its length and examining the energy at all the taps simultaneously at the right time, a delay line can be used as a time-space information converter (Fig. 6-37).

A delay line always attenuates the input energy, so that the output energy is less than the input. In practice, it may be far less. However it may be regenerated as in Fig. 6-38, so that the information may be recovered after many trips.

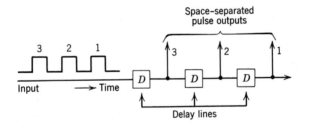

Figure 6-37

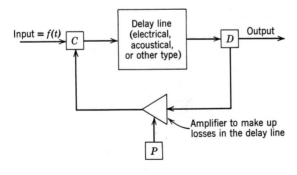

Figure 6-38

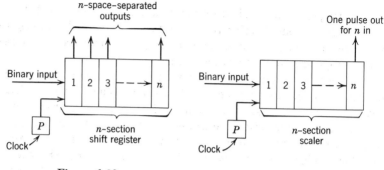

Figure 6-39   Figure 6-40

Another form of *time-space converter* widely used in digital computers and other digital systems is the "shift-register" (Fig. 6-39). Previous binary-pulse information is shifted by the clock power one stage along the register to make room for each new input bit as it arrives. The contents of the shift-register may be read out on the space-separated leads.

Clearly, a shift-register can be used as a *counter* of the number of pulses that have arrived prior to the readout.

A shift-register can also be used as a *scaler* or *pulse-divider*. As represented in Fig. 6-40, a scaler gives one pulse out for a fixed number of input pulses.

In another arrangement, a shift-register can act as a *space-time converter*. Binary information is put into the register via space-separated leads and pulsed out in the corresponding time sequence under control of the clock power source (Fig. 6-41).

The effects of applying energy to an object to change it in some

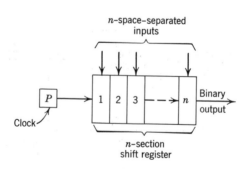

Figure 6-41

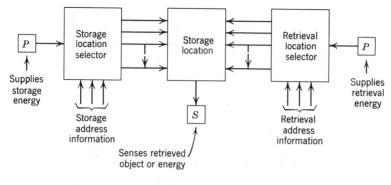

Figure 6-42

way may be *stored* so that the effects may be observed or retrieved at a later time. Any form of energy may be used, for example, mechanical, electrical, thermal, magnetic, or acoustical. Warehouses, books, newspapers, phonograph records, photographs, and magnetic tape are familiar examples of storage of objects or information.

Storage involves two operations (1) selection of a space location at which the object is to be changed and (2) application of energy to make the change.

Retrieval involves three operations (1) selecting one or more space locations at which there are suitable objects, (2) applying energy to the object or objects to determine their state, and (3) sensing the readout energy.

Figure 6-42 shows the essential building blocks of a storage and retrieval arrangement.

The readout of stored information may or may not destroy the information: "destructive" and "nondestructive" readout, respectively. In some destructive readout stores, auxiliary arrangements immediately replace any information read out.

Besides deterioration during the storage interval, distortion, damage, or interference (e.g., by noise) may occur during either the storage or retrieval or both.

Translation Using Storage Look-up

Earlier in this chapter, a simple form of translator was described. In such simple translators (Fig. 6-11) each input is merely relabeled to give the corresponding output. More complex translators are required for many applications. An unabridged dictionary is only one example of such a translator. You enter the dictionary with an input

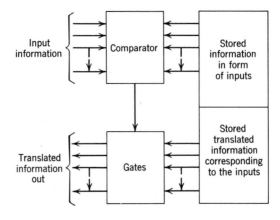

Figure 6-43

word for which you want a definition. Words are stored in the dictionary in alphabetical sequence. When the wanted word is found, the corresponding definitions can be read out. The same operations are necessary if the input word is in one language and the output is in another, as in language translation. Figure 6-43 represents the functions in the form of a block diagram.

Sorting (Pigeon-holing)

Sorting of objects or information is another widely used operation. There are two important forms:

1. True sorting, for example, post-office sorting. All letters put in a given box have same address. Order in each box is irrelevant. First the appropriate box is selected by a rule (such as a person's name); then, mechanical energy is applied to the letter to place it in the box.

2. Reordering (sequencing), for example, arranging a pack of cards in sequence. The end result is an ordered pack. In many cases, the objects or information may have some order before the sorting. Cards, such as IBM cards, can be directed into boxes according to the value of a decimal digit in a particular column. By collecting the contents of the boxes in sequence, the sorting operation is turned into a reordering.

Reordering can also precede sorting. Thus, if many packs of cards are mixed up, and are to be sorted into 13 groups—aces, twos, etc.—then one method reorders the cards so that the aces are together, as well as the twos, and so on. Dividing the pack at the correct places results in the sort.

Set-up and Tear-down

It is necessary to assemble or "set-up" a new system and to make the built-in connections that distinguish the system from a collection of components. Assembly can be considered a special case of time variation. As Fig. 6-44 shows, assembly requires planning and programming of the responses to information inputs. The wanted input-output relations depend on the existence of appropriate information and object inputs as well as a program for the physical arrangement and the connections.

It may be necessary or desirable to disassemble or "tear down" a system after completion of the wanted mission— perhaps to reuse the components. Tear-down can also be considered as a special case of time-variation. Just as in assembly, tear-down requires information and a program.

In theory, assembly and disassembly are reversible functions. In practice, disassembly may be impossible. For example, if components are welded together, an attempt at disassembly may destroy them.

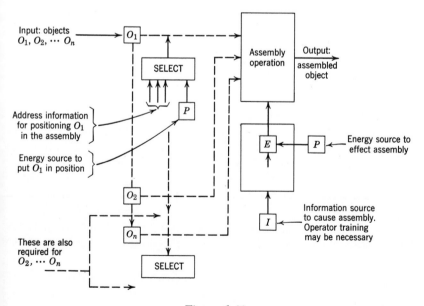

Figure 6-44

Transducer Functions

Other kinds of complex arrangements called transducers may be put in a transmission medium carrying signals. A transducer changes signal information from one representation to another. The representations may differ in any of the properties of messages or signals.

A particular transducer may change the signal form in some way. For example, if the input to a medium and the receiver are incompatible in some way (such as in form of energy), a transducer "matching" device can be added to make them compatible. Or, it may restore some signal change made by another transducer or the medium. Finally, it may change the information itself (e.g., change the code or language).

The input and output waves of a transducer always differ in some wanted way. Otherwise, the transducer would perform no useful function. The difference may be fixed or vary with time.

Transducers can never be 100% efficient: the energy output is always less than that at the input. The difference between the two energies (sometimes called the *loss*) may be so great that regeneration (e.g., by an amplifier) must be provided. Moreover, if the energy output of the transducer is to exceed the input, the transducer must contain a power source.

Reasons for Using Transducers

Transducers may be added in a medium to improve some aspect of the overall transmission or make it possible for information to be transmitted in an advantageous manner.

To receive information correctly, the receiver must be compatible or be made compatible with the generated signal in many different properties. An error in setting up a channel between a particular origin and a particular destination can be fixed only by providing a different and suitable path. Control of the start, duration, and end of a message may be taken care of by special signals or by waiting for the longest possible message. All other kinds of incompatibilities require transducers to match the properties of the source and receiver. Thus, the input information to a sensor must be in a suitable form or a transducer must be used. Otherwise, if the information is received at all, it will be mutilated. Even worse, in multiplex operation over a medium an incompatibility may cause undesirable effects in other channels.

The transducer complexity depends on the requirements for a match.

For a particular message, the possible number of kinds of incompatibilities is the product of the number of ways the signal generator and the sensor may differ. Some combinations may not occur (e.g., because of the design), but the possible number of kinds of incompatibilities is still very large.

Transducers are widely used in telephone systems to match up (or patch up) incompatibilities between central offices of different kinds and vintages so that they can work together.

Location of Transducers

Economics or expediency (or both) determine where transducers are located with respect to the medium: (1) at the sending end, (2) at the receiving end, or (3) divided between the two. With one or a few transmitters and many receivers, the logical place is at the sending end (as in radio broadcasting); with a single receiver and many transmitters, at the receiving end.

Transducers are frequently used in pairs, as in Fig. 6-45. The input information is carried by mechanical energy, but electrical energy is preferred for transmission over the medium. Furthermore, the information is a continuous wave in time, but transmission over the medium is by pulses (digital transmission). Two transducers at each end of the medium make the necessary conversions. When

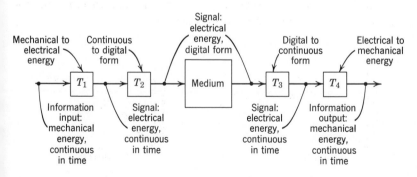

Figure 6-45

pairs of transducers are used, a change in one transducer of the pair may require a change in the other transducer.

Passive and Active Transducers

Transducers may be described as passive or active. A passive transducer may be defined as one whose output waves are independent of any sources of power controlled by the actuating waves. An active transducer is one whose output waves depend on one or more sources of power apart from that supplied by any of the actuating waves, which power is controlled by one or more of the input waves.

Possible Kinds of Transducers

The properties of information-carrying signals have been described in an earlier chapter. The possible kinds of transducers must match all possible kinds of inputs with all possible kinds of outputs. Many kinds result.

In a general way it is clear that for a particular signal a transducer might effect a change of:

Amplitude relations in space and time
Energy form
Type of modulation
Frequency band
Space location and direction
Time location (delay)

or some combination of these.

In practice one transducer usually changes only one variable; multiple changes are made by several transducers.

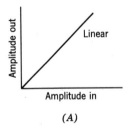
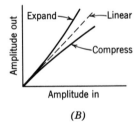

Figure 6-46

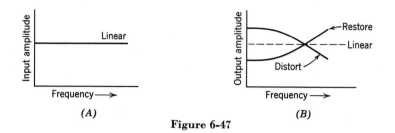

Figure 6-47

The signal amplitude can be increased by a suitable amplifier and decreased by an attenuator.

Figure 6-46*A* represents the operation of a block when the output amplitude is a linear function of the input amplitude. Figure 6-46*B* represents the operation when the input-output relation is non-linear and higher amplitudes undergo *expansion* or *compression*. Two such transducers may be used in tandem: a compressor and then an expander. In the telephone system, such a combination is called a *compandor*. Compandors are used at the ends of certain telephone systems to minimize unwanted effects when a noisy medium is used for a transmission channel. A linear amplifier may be used at the output of a compressor or an expander to compensate for the unavoidable energy losses incurred in performing their functions.

In Fig. 6-47*A*, the input amplitude of a block is represented as invariant with frequency. In transversing the block, the relation may be changed so that the output wave is distorted, as represented in Fig. 6-47*B*. A compensating transducer with the inverse characteristic may be added to restore the relationship existing at the input (Fig. 6-47*B*). Such a transducer is often called an *equalizer* by telephone engineers.

Figures 6-48*A* and *B* represent an analogous situation involving

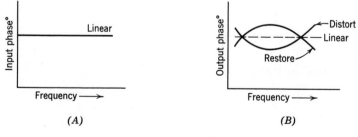

Figure 6-48

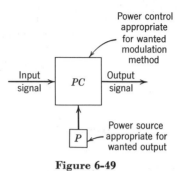

Figure 6-49

phase distortion and compensation by a *phase equalizer*.

To make certain kinds of changes in the input signal, such as:

1. The type of energy
2. Any space or time variable of the power source
3. The modulation method or index

the original information must be recovered from the input wave and a new wave created using an appropriate source and modulation method (Fig. 6-49).   For example, to change AM to FM or vice versa, or AM to or from phase modulation, the original information must be recovered and used to control a new power source to produce the wanted change in the output.

Changes in Information Structure

An important class of transducers can change (1) the information transmission rate, (2) the amount of information contained in a signal, or (3) the information structure itself.

These changes can be made only by transducers operating on the signal energy.   Hence, they cannot be made until the original message energy is converted to signal energy.

Transmission Rate

If during an interval of time, signals are generated faster than they can be used, the excess must be stored and sent later or some information will be lost.   Over a sufficiently long interval of time, there can be no excess.   When the rate of generation is lower than

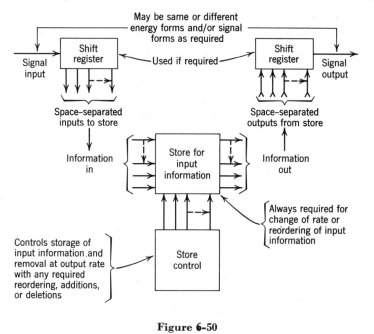

Figure 6-50

the receiving rate, information can be stored and then sent to the receiver at a higher rate during a shorter time interval.

If the transmitting and receiving rates differ, a rate converter can be used to match them. Any rate converter must (1) sense the incoming signals, (2) store them, (3) select them from storage, and (4) use them to control an appropriate zero-entropy power source at the output rate (Fig. 6-50).

Amount of Information

A transducer cannot increase the amount of input information. An apparent exception can exist: input information can be combined with stored information available to the transducer, or noise having known properties that is present in the input can be removed. In either case, a built-in set of rules or a program must select the stored information to be used. The transducer must contain arrangements to combine the input information with that selected from the store. Thus the total amount of information available to the transducer includes both that contained in the store and in the program.

A built-in program can compute an unknown value using built-in rules and then use the result or it can make a decision based on past experience weighted for time (e.g., with more recent experiences given most weight). For example, an integrating alarm can count troubles in a given interval; if a predetermined number does not occur, it can cancel the record and start over.

A transducer can delete information from or reduce the input information appearing at the output according to a built-in program. The program information is not added to or superimposed on the input information.

A suitable transducer can disregard unwanted input information without decreasing the total amount of useful information; for example, an initial pulse preceding a pulse train may be ignored.

A transducer can add noise, crosstalk, or modulation to the input signal. If the interference structure is unknown, then the disturbance cannot be removed, and some or even all of the input information is irretrievably lost.

Complex arrangements are necessary to change the amount of information. That shown in Fig. 6-50 can either increase or decrease the amount of output information compared with that in the input, since rate conversion is possible. With information deletion, rate conversion is not necessary if the space area or time interval is simply left unfilled.

Language, Code, or Efficiency

Input and output symbols can be in different alphabets and different languages. Moreover, either the input or output efficiency (or redundancy) may be the greater.

At least in theory, a transducer can be built for any one-to-one code change (translation) or change in efficiency: if item A is received, item B is sent. In this way, the input information can be changed from one code to another. With the elements of a rate converter in addition to a translator and a built-in program, information can be added or deleted or the order changed. Because of differences in sentence structure, such an arrangement is needed to translate English into German or the reverse.

Changing can involve:

1. Substitution of information such as changing $CH3$ to ABC.

2. Deleting some input information and substituting either more or less information in accordance with a built-in program.

3. Changing the order either in space or time. Because of differences in sentence structure, reordering is often necessary in translating from one language to another (e.g., English into German). Also, the letters

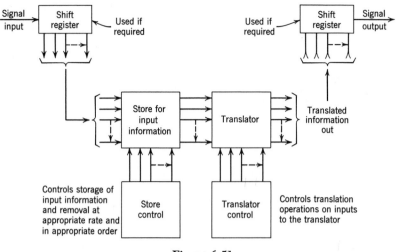

Figure 6-51

of a word may be rearranged in space so the word is read vertically instead of horizontally.

The most complex arrangements of all are necessary to change the information structure in any way. In Fig. 6-51, the original information is recovered and stored so that it can be rearranged. It can then be removed from the store according to a program that selects the stored information so as to create the new structure. Translation can be made either before or after storage. The program can change the order. Finally, a new signal is generated and the operation is completed.

Conditions for Information Recovery

In Fig. 6-52, the transducer output is merely the signal input acted on by the transducer in a particular way.

For complete recovery of the input information of one transducer

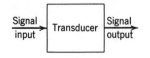

Figure 6-52

Table 6-1

Input Transducer Effect on Information	Recovery by Second Transducer
Deleted	Impossible
Partially changed in some way	Possible if: 1. enough information is left and 2. operation known and 3. inverse operation exists
Added to	Possible if: 1. operation known and 2. inverse operation exists

by a second transducer, the operation of the two transducers must be exact inverses.

Clearly, if some input information to the first transducer is destroyed and hence does not reach the second transducer, then recovery is impossible. These conditions may be expressed as in Table 6-1.

7

A Classification of
System Building Blocks

Table of Functional Blocks

This chapter presents in compact form the different kinds of functional building blocks adequate to synthesize any complex system. It has already been shown that any wanted system operation can be performed using only a few different kinds of blocks. It is shown in this chapter that all possible kinds of blocks can be put into one of five classes. These concepts have far-reaching theoretical and practical consequences.

Table 7-1 lists the names and functions of the set of functional building blocks and also a modest number of frequently used combinations of the basic blocks. These combinations are marked with an asterisk.

The number of kinds of blocks is modest so a search of the table to find a wanted function can be brief.

Two or more functions may be performed by one physical device. Also, a particular function may be performed by a combination of devices. Thus, the number of actual devices may either be more or less than the number of functions.

Furthermore, all possible arrangements of the functional blocks are not useful. The useful arrangements of these blocks are discussed later in the chapter.

Table 7-1 and an understanding of the useful arrangements together are preparation for the presentation of the "Canonical" complex system in the next chapter.

Table 7-1   *Functional Building Blocks*

ONE INTERNAL STATE (TIME INVARIANT)

1. Message Power Supply $\boxed{I}\!\rightarrow$

2. Zero-Entropy Power Supply $\boxed{P}\!\rightarrow$

3. Noise or Interference Power Supply $\boxed{N}\!\rightarrow$

4. Object Changed by Energy Input $\rightarrow\!\boxed{O}$

5. Medium to Transmit Energy in Space $\rightarrow\!\boxed{M}\!\rightarrow$

6. Effector to Change an Object $\rightarrow\!\boxed{E}\!\rightarrow$

7. Transducer to Alter Energy Input Relations $\rightarrow\!\boxed{T}\!\rightarrow$
    Amplitude Relations
        Compression or Expansion
        Amplitude-Frequency
        Amplitude-Time
    Phase Relations
    Frequency Relations
    Space Relations
8. Combiner and Divider $\Rightarrow\!\boxed{C}\!\rightarrow$

    Multiplex—Demultiplex $\rightarrow\!\boxed{D}\!\Rightarrow$
        *Space-frequency domain
        *Space-time domain
        *Space-phase domain
        Space domain
    Computer $\Rightarrow\!\boxed{}\!\rightarrow$
        Arithmetic operations
            $+$, $-$, $\times$, $\div$, $\sqrt{}$, exponent
        Logic operations $\Rightarrow\!\boxed{AND}\!\rightarrow$ $\Rightarrow\!\boxed{OR}\!\rightarrow$ etc.
            AND, OR, NAND, NOR, etc.
        * Comparison of two inputs or one $\Rightarrow\!\boxed{COMP}\!\rightarrow$
          input and a reference
            Amplitude, frequency, time, or space $\rightarrow\!\boxed{COMP}\!\rightarrow$
            domain $\uparrow$ Reference

        * Sensing: an important special case of $\rightarrow\!\boxed{S}\!\rightarrow$
          comparison with a reference value $\downarrow$ Reference

        * Reference setting
            Amplitude, phase, or time domain

MORE THAN ONE INTERNAL STATE (TIME-VARIANT)

9. Control
    Control Power Flow $\rightarrow\!\boxed{PC}\!\rightarrow$
    Regulate or adjust: $\boxed{I}$

Table 7-1 *Functional Building Blocks (Continued)*

9. Control (*continued*)
    *Gate, connect or change between two states
    *Vary continuously over a range
    *Feed-forward arrangements
    *Feed-back arrangements
    *Feed-forward sequential arrangements
    *Feed-back sequential arrangements
10. Generate Information-carrying Energy
    *Modulate a zero-entropy power source
    *Change energy form
    *Change type of modulation or index
11. *Selection:
    Space
        *Hunt; *Find; *Allot; *Lock-out
        *Connect
        *Scan
        *Identify
    Frequency
    Phase
    Time
12. *Store and Retrieve Information
13. *Alter Information Structure:
    *Rate; *Ordering
    *Language; *Code; *Redundancy

Classification of Functional Blocks by Number of Inputs and Outputs

The set of functional blocks can be divided into five classes on the basis of the number of inputs and outputs. Only five classes are possible, so the list is exhaustive.

1. No inputs *or* outputs—the null case included for completeness, but of no obvious practical importance.

2. One input *or* one output. This class includes zero-entropy power sources, information and interfering energy sources, and objects.

3. One input *and* one output. This class includes effectors, media, and transducers.

4. More than one output and one input, or vice versa. This class includes combiners and dividers.

5. More than one input *and* more than one output. Such arrangements can be considered as combinations of class 4 blocks.

Of the five classes, class 1 can be neglected—at least until some theoretical or practical value appears. Similarly, class 5 can be analyzed in terms of class 4 blocks. Hence, only classes 2, 3, and 4 contain useful fundamental functional blocks.

The One-input or One-output Class

This class includes all forms of energy sources and all objects upon which energy is expended and which are therefore sometimes called *energy sinks.*

A zero-entropy input or output wave can be described mathematically by a generalized vector which includes space and time variables (among others).

Information-carrying waves can be described mathematically by an even more complex generalized vector which includes (1) all the variables describing the zero-entropy generator, (2) all the variables necessary to describe the information structure in space and time, and (3) variables describing how the energy flow from the zero-entropy source is modulated to create the information-carrying signal.

The One-input and One-output Class

This class operates on an input energy wave to form an output energy wave. Mathematically, the function can be described by an operator that changes the input vector into the output vector.

Many variables are necessary to describe a zero-entropy energy flow. An appropriate operator can change any one of these variables. The input-output relation may be linear, but in practice it is frequently nonlinear by design or by necessity. Thus there are a number of possible kinds of such operators. Actually, and perhaps surprisingly, the number of kinds is rather modest, as will be demonstrated later.

As noted above, even more variables are necessary to describe an information-carrying energy flow. An appropriate operator can change any one of these variables, however—including those describing the information structure itself or the modulation method or both. Again, the number of kinds of such operators is surprisingly small.

More-than-one Input and One Output, and Vice Versa

In the more-than-one input and one output class are found the power control, multiplexing, and computing functions.

The output of a power control at any instant depends on the values of both the input vector and the zero-entropy power vector. Only variables describing the zero-entropy energy vector may be changed by the power control. Mathematically, a suitable operator can relate the output to the two inputs and thus describe the modulation process.

In multiplexing, the space-separated input signals may be in the time, frequency, phase, or space domains. Objects may be combined in the space domain. In some commonly used multiplexers, the inputs are simply added directly or superimposed to form the output, and in some demultiplexers, in effect the inverse operation of subtraction is performed. Such blocks may be described mathematically by linear operators if certain conditions are met. In other multiplexers and demultiplexers, the operations are more complicated and a nonlinear operator is necessary for a mathematical description.

Computing may be further divided into arithmetic operations and logic operations. In performing the arithmetic operations of addition or subtraction of two continuous waves, a linear operator may be used. Multiplication or division always require a nonlinear operator. Arithmetic operations on waves representing numerical digits always require a complex nonlinear operator. Two digits may be used to select an answer from a table (e.g., a multiplication table) or a set of rules can direct an appropriate combination of the basic building blocks to furnish the wanted result.

In logic operations such as AND, OR, and so on, the input waves to the combiner and the output waves are discontinuous. Many practical logic networks use pulse waves shapes with only two states: ON or OFF. To describe the operations mathematically, nonlinear operators are required.

Mathematical Descriptions of Building Blocks

At least in theory, the waves of energy flowing from sources and into sinks can be described mathematically in terms of vectors.

Any block with one input and one output can only change the input vector into the output vector. Again, in theory a mathematical operator can describe the change. In practice, some innocent-looking changes pose formidable mathematical difficulties if an accurate numerical answer is wanted.

Any block with more than one input and one output can only combine the inputs to form the output. And any block with more than one output and only one input can only share the input among the outputs. Here again, a mathematical operator can describe the combination or division. But completely satisfactory procedures are not now available for numerical solution of some important practical problems.

To sum up, in theory, mathematical descriptions of all the kinds of functional blocks can be set up. In practice, major difficulties are present. Undesirable approximations are necessary and used. Replacement of a nonlinear operator by assuming linear operation is not infrequent—and in some cases the possible inaccuracy is not apparent to the inexperienced system designer.

Surely, much mathematical research is essential before mathematical models of complex systems will be completely satisfactory.

Useful Combinations of Functional Blocks

A few observations can lead to a list of useful arrangements of the building blocks but which comprise less than a complete system.

1. The input block must be a sensor, because the input information-carrying energy must be sensed to show that the operation is wanted.

2. A power control must follow a sensor. Other possibilities can be ruled out. The sensor output cannot be an input to a zero-entropy power supply, as in Fig. 7-1; the information would be lost, since

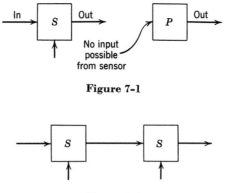

Figure 7-1

Figure 7-2

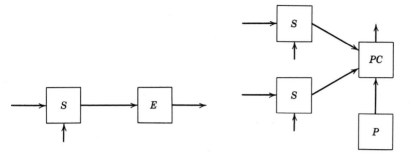

Figure 7-3   Figure 7-4

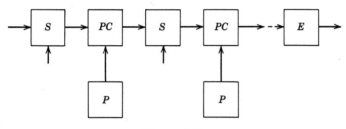

Figure 7-5

the only output of P is zero-entropy energy. The effect of the two sensors in tandem as in Fig. 7-2 would merely be that of a single sensor. Finally, suppose an effector followed a sensor, as in Fig. 7-3. Now an effector requires a particular form and structure of input energy. If the input energy to the sensor could operate the effector, then the sensor would be unnecessary. A single power control may follow two or more sensors (Fig. 7-4). This arrangement is used in logic circuits (AND circuits, for example).

3. If a sensor follows a power control, then a second power control must follow the sensor, and so on, as in Fig. 7-5. Many converter units may be used in tandem as in Fig. 7-5. Ultimately, an effector must follow a power control.

4. A power source cannot follow a power control as in Fig. 7-6 because then the only output would be zero-entropy power.

5. Two power controls can be used in tandem, as in Fig. 7-7. One might give a coarse control; the other, a fine control.

6. The information source of a molecular system may be a part of some larger system as in Fig. 7-8. Further, the output object may be a part of some other system, as in Fig. 7-9.

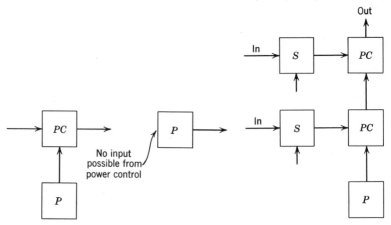

Figure 7-6   **Figure 7-7**

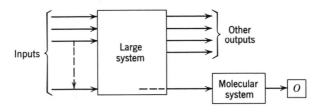

Figure 7-8

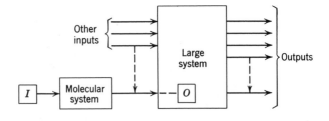

Figure 7-9

8

Examples of Complex Systems

Introduction

Any complex system can be represented by a collection of the functional building blocks described in Chapter 6 and summarized in Table 7-1. Useful arrangements of blocks are also discussed in Chapter 7. These ideas are very helpful in dealing with complex systems. To illustrate the point, a number of examples of complex systems are now given.

For the present discussion, the minimum number of blocks in a complex system may be considered to be at least a few score. The maximum number? Not infinite—but still very large. Thus, a combination of blocks to perform a selection function or an adder or a register in a computer are not here considered to be complex systems.

Sooner or later, almost every adult encounters two systems that meet the above criteria of complexity. One is the family automobile (or automobiles). Certainly a system with 2500 or more moving parts is complex. The other is the family residence, with its coal, oil, gas, or electric furnace, its electrical fusing, wiring, and outlets, its hot-water heating, its plumbing, its cooking and laundry facilities, its dozens of electric motors, a TV or so, its radios—but why go on?

Inputs and Outputs of Complex Systems

Since any complex system can be represented by a collection of functional building blocks, it follows that the possible kinds of inputs to such a collection are:

1. Zero-entropy energy
2. Information-carrying energy
3. Objects

The possible outputs are also limited to these three kinds.

Other authors have used other words for the three kinds of inputs and outputs: for example, "energy" for "zero-entropy energy," "information" for "information-carrying energy," and "materials" for "objects." The words used here were chosen to make clear the important ideas that information theory and elementary physics can contribute to our thinking about system design.

The inputs may be further classified as wanted and unwanted. Unwanted inputs may be either energy or objects. Examples of unwanted input energy may be heat, light, or mechanical shock and vibration; of unwanted objects, iron and steel in aluminum scrap, or meteorites striking a space vehicle.

Similarly, the outputs may be classified as wanted and unwanted. Examples of unwanted output energy may be heat or acoustical noise; of unwanted objects, scrap from a manufacturing operation or slag from a steel mill.

Acquiring a complete list of the inputs and outputs is a first step in system design. The useful arrangements that can follow each input and can precede each output can then be added, and so on, step-by-step.

Canonical Model of Any Complex System

In mathematics, the term *canonical forms* refers to the simplest and most significant forms to which general equations may be brought without loss of generality, for example, the *canonical* equations of dynamics.

By using this meaning of the word "canonical," it is now possible to present a canonical model of a complex system. Figure 8-1 represents such a model.

All systems must have an input of information-carrying energy—if only to start the operation.

All systems must have an input of zero-entropy energy because by definition information-carrying energy is modulated zero-entropy energy.

All systems must have an information output. This may be either in the form of the information-carrying energy or of observable changes in an object or objects.

All systems must have a zero-entropy energy output. This statement is true because all systems have unwanted losses. No system can be 100% efficient. But remember that unwanted losses *can* be observed. Hence, these losses *may* convey information to someone.

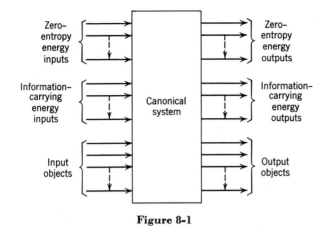

Figure 8-1

When examined closely, all systems have an input and an output of objects. To create zero-entropy energy some fuel must be used, whether it be fossil fuel, falling water, or fissionable or fusionable material. Even in nuclear reactions, material objects cannot be completely changed into energy. The coal, oil, gas, water, or uranium input to a power plant results in an unavoidable output of ashes, soot, water, or radioactive waste.

Thus, if viewed broadly enough, all complex systems have both inputs and outputs of zero-entropy energy, information-carrying energy, and objects. It follows that differences between systems more or less depend on the interests of the system designer and the system user.

By their very nature, in some systems certain kinds of inputs and outputs are very important; other kinds may be of only minor importance; some may not even be given a passing thought. A few examples of particular kinds of systems will bring out such differences in emphasis.

Example 1: Electric Power Plant

The purpose of an electric power generating plant is to produce a maximum amount of zero-entropy (perhaps 60 cycles per second) power per unit amount of fuel. The efficiency is sometimes expressed as kwh/lb of fuel or kwh/dollar. Some plants are arranged so that they can switch between competing fuels (such as coal, oil, or gas) to hold costs down.

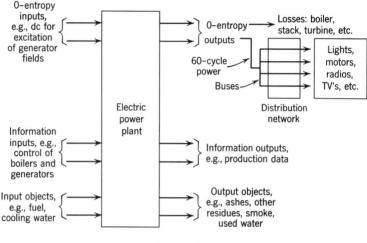

Figure 8-2

Figure 8-2 represents an electrical power system in a greatly simplified form. Input objects include fuel and the cooling water for condensers. Zero-entropy power is necessary for such functions as excitation of the fields of the generators, for lighting and for modulating to create information-carrying energy. Suitable supplies may be furnished by auxiliary generators within the physical plant. Information-carrying energy is necessary to control all of the boilers, machinery, and switches. In some recent plants, some of these controls have been automated.

Of course, the wanted output is zero-entropy power in the form of electrical energy. As represented in Fig. 8-2, energy is distributed over a network to the lights, motors, clocks, TVs, radios, and appliances so necessary in our modern cities. The energy flow through the plant and network is one-way and, of course, is not reversible. You cannot put electrical energy into the network and have the fuel come out of the power plant.

Examples of information outputs are the meters and lights of the load dispatcher's control board. These give him data about how the plant is functioning. If anything is wrong, he can take corrective action based on the information presented to him and thus keep the plant running at high efficiency. The instrumentation and control can represent a sizable fraction of the initial cost.

Unwanted zero-entropy energy outputs include the many forms of heat losses: Boiler, stack, cooling water, and exhaust steam, and the turbine generators, transformers, and bus-bars all contribute their part to the total loss.

Finally, unwanted objects, such as ashes, soot, and smoke, are produced and must be disposed of.

To sum up, a power plant's primary function is to convert the zero-entropy energy contained in the fuel input into the zero-entropy electrical energy output. But, clearly, other kinds of inputs and outputs are also present.

Example 2: Information-transmission (Communication) System

The purpose of a telegraph system is to transmit information from one location in space to another location. If the distance is great, repeaters may be necessary at intervals to regenerate the signals. The performance may be measured in bits per second or perhaps in words per minute transmitted. A design problem is to maximize the words per minute per dollar of cost. A typical study might compare the relative costs of a line with few repeaters and large conductors and a line with more repeaters and smaller conductors.

Figure 8-3 represents the system inputs and outputs. Input and output objects are not shown. As shown by Example 1, zero-entropy energy generation always requires the handling of objects, but the communication system designer may merely assume the existence of power sources, and leave the details to a power engineer. As Fig. 8-4 shows, zero-entropy energy is modulated at the input by the information-source energy and also at repeater (regenerator) stations. The wanted output is acoustical energy which affects the ear and then the brain of the human receiving the message.

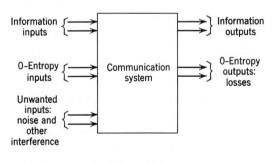

Figure 8-3

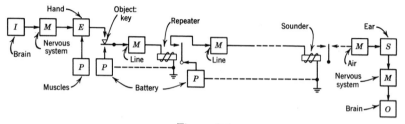

Figure 8-4

Unavoidable zero-entropy losses occur in the repeaters because of their inefficiencies; as heat losses due to the resistance of the line conductors; and in the energy conversion from electrical to acoustical by the sounder. While the designer may try to hold such losses down, he must always remember that the message must get through. For this reason, he must use enough energy to override the unwanted interference represented in Fig. 8-4. Minimizing or combating unwanted interference (or both) is a very important part of the system design.

Figure 8-4 illustrates another important point. The information generated in the brain directs the hand to generate the signals. The signals traverse the system and energy to affect the human ear and then the brain. The information-handling system is also inherently one way. Thus we talk with our mouths, and listen with our ears—not the other way around. For full-time two-way operation complete and separate systems are necessary for the two directions. Long ago, a courier carried a message from the King of England to the King of France, waited for the reply, and carried it back with him. Today, the courier's speed is far surpassed by modern communication systems. But they still require a one-way trip, the wait while the reply is composed, and the trip back. The transmission times today are very small fractions of a second. Sometimes it takes a much longer time (even days or months) to compose a suitable reply to a question.

Example 3: Telephone Switching System

The primary purpose of a telephone switching system is to set up wanted connections between two or more telephones so that information-carrying energy can be exchanged over the connections.

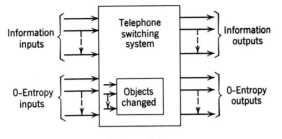

Figure 8-5

Other necessary but auxiliary functions will only be briefly mentioned or omitted to concentrate attention on the primary purpose.

Figure 8-5 represents the block diagram of the system. In a large central office, information may flow in and out over many customer lines. Zero-entropy energy sources are necessary so they may be controlled to create information-carrying energy and to change the switching network to set up and take down connections.

The switching system designer is intimately concerned with the changes in the switching network and its control. He seldom worries much about the zero-entropy power he uses. Such details are left to power engineers.

Among switching system engineers, measures of performance such as connections per second are seldom used. For a particular office, the connections per second for which the office is engineered depends on the calling rate during the busy hour of a busy month. The habits of the customers generating the calls can only be studied statistically. Furthermore, each customer must be provided considerable equipment—even though he may seldom make or receive a call. For such reasons, cost in dollars per line is the usual measure.

Because it shows the importance of information flow in one kind of complex system, Fig. 8-6 represents a canonical model of a telephone switching system. Note that information flows from the calling party, for example,

1. A request for service when he lifts the instrument
2. The wanted number
3. An indication he no longer wants the connection when he replaces the instrument

Information flows from the central office to the calling party:

1. The office is ready to receive the wanted number—number please by an operator; dial tone by a dial office

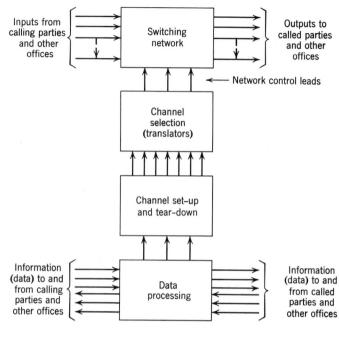

Figure 8-6

2. Progress reports about the call: the called line is busy; all trunks are busy; the called line is being rung

Information also flows to the called party:

1. You are wanted, your telephone is being rung

And information also flows from the called party:

1. An answer signal to the central office that may be used to charge for the call
2. An end-of-call signal when the instrument is replaced

Coin boxes also send coin denomination information and receive coin collect and return information.

The information made available to the central office when a call is initiated is used by the network control to identify the calling line and to set up a suitable connection between the calling and called lines. To do so, it is necessary to identify the calling line—perhaps by scanning or finding. Then a suitable path to the wanted line is found by hunting and selection. Block diagrams for these basic functions have been given earlier. The control also directs the connection of appropriate information sources (tone generators) to the calling and called lines to tell about the progress of the call.

The operation of the network control conforms to a built-in program for any type of call the office is designed to handle. The program contains instructions on how to perform each step and alternate actions to be taken under any condition. In essence, the program is merely a succession of very simple logical steps. But every contingency must be foreseen—no matter how improbable.

Modern switching systems perform many of the operations formerly handled by human operators; many—but not all. For example, no machine yet available can handle calls for "Information." However, new techniques may well enable future central offices to diagnose and report many of their own infrequent troubles.

Example 4: Information Processing by Digital Computer

The purpose of a digital computer is to take input information, process it in some way such as by additions, subtractions, and rearrangements, and deliver the result in a suitable form at the output. For "research" computers, the quantities of input and output data may be rather small but the processing may be long and complex. For "business" computers, the amounts of input and output data are enormous but the processing operations are relatively simple. The amount of business data may be so enormous that machine-reading of documents (such as bank checks) is advantageous.

Figure 8-7 represents the inputs and outputs of a digital computer. Figure 8-8 gives somewhat more detail about the general organization but is not intended to represent any particular computer.

Information-carrying energy is necessary to start the machine, and

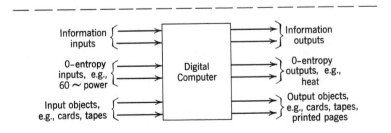

Figure 8-7

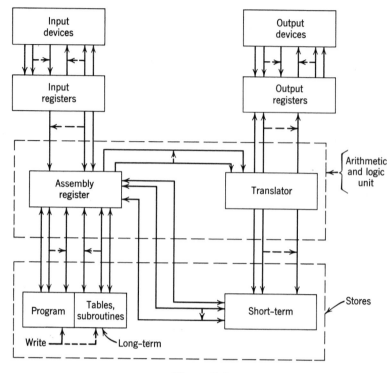

Figure 8-8

to override its actions on occasion. Information output is provided (perhaps at a console) to permit monitoring the operation.

Zero-entropy electrical energy is necessary for the information-processing and transfer operations. On the other hand, heat-energy input is usually not wanted. In fact, in some large computers, so much unwanted heat energy is generated that air conditioning must be provided to remove it.

Although some information may be put into the computer by an operator, the usual input is in the form of information-carrying objects such as punched cards, teletype tapes, and magnetic tapes. The computer is programmed to read the input information. After the information is processed, the results are delivered in the form of information-carrying objects. Teletype tapes, punched cards, magnetic tapes, printed paper, and visual displays are some of the methods used.

The performance of digital computers may be measured in a form such as operations (e.g., additions) per second or operations per second per dollar. The information input and output rates may be measured in bits or digits per second. Other performance figures frequently quoted are punched cards read in per minute or punched out per minute or magnetic tape characters read or printed per second.

Example 5: Information Processing—Language Translation

The purpose of a language translator is to change input information expressed in one language such as English into another language such as Russian. In the translation, the exact meaning of the input information should be preserved.

In theory, translation is merely the processing of input information to change it into the target language. If items A, B, C go in, then items D, E, F, come out properly ordered. Thus, Fig. 8-9 can represent the inputs and outputs of a language translation system because it can perform the necessary operations.

In practice, it takes (or better say, it will take) a very advanced digital computer to do an even passable job of translation. For the system must take in the words and the idiomatic expressions, and must know the rules of declension and conjugation and the rules of grammar and syntax of the input language. It must deliver the words and idiomatic expressions and comply with the rules of the

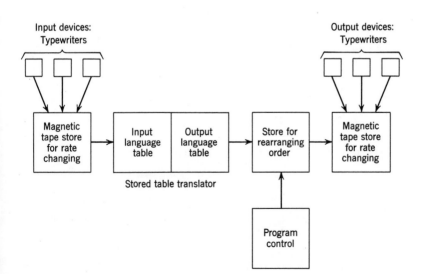

Figure 8-9

target language.   This is a tall order indeed!   For example, the output of the translator may be *more ambiguous* than the input, or the output may be unambiguous but contain *errors*.   Either is a *distortion* of the input information.

A particular distortion may be lexic or syntactic.   A lexic distortion is caused by lack of exact correspondence of the dictionary entries in the input and target languages.   A syntactic distortion is caused by an incorrect or ambiguous ordering of the translated words or phrases.

To meet the requirements, the translator must have storage units for the dictionaries and rules of the two languages.   These stores must be so large that their cost—even if they could be built and searched—is a major problem today.   Certainly, the capacity required is much larger than today's computers can offer.

Figure 8-9 represents the basic blocks required for a language translator.   The information inputs and outputs can be typewriter or tape units.   In the future it may be possible to read documents such as magazines mechanically.   Some limited progress has been made on such machines, but much remains to be done.

Today the data processing required for accurate language translation is done by men and women using their brains.   The problem of building a machine to translate documents is being attacked, but a trained person can still do a more accurate job and do it faster.   About 1915 certain radio operators in the tropics received messages in English in the radio (Continental) code and sent them out over the land telegraph line in Spanish in the telegraph (Morse) code.   Besides, the incoming radio messages were interfered with by tropical static.   The delay between input and output was only a few words.   Today, nearly five decades later, no machine can translate so rapidly.

Example 6: Changes in Objects—Manufacture

The purpose of manufacture is to produce changed objects by applying effectors to them.   The overall change in an object may be accomplished by an ordered set of smaller changes.   For each change, alternative methods may be available.   A collection of processed objects may be assembled into a larger object.   The larger object may be the final product or it may be a subassembly in a still larger assembly.   Figure 8-10 represents a manufacturing process.

Objects, or in other words, raw materials, are an important input.   Manufactured objects are the wanted output.   Unwanted output ob-

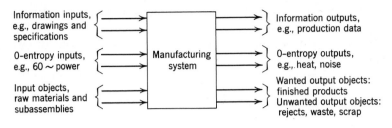

Figure 8-10

jects include scrap material created by the processing and partially or completely changed objects rejected because they do not have all the wanted properties. Some factories produce other unwanted outputs such as smoke, odors, or chemical wastes.

Zero-entropy energy is necessary so that it can be modulated by information sources to perform the operations. Large amounts of power may be required for such operations as forming, cutting, heating, cooling, and transportation of objects. Unwanted zero-entropy energy output may take such forms as heat or noise.

An input of information-carrying energy is always necessary to control every process changing an object. Information must also be furnished on what is to be made, how, and when. One output of the factory is always information. The amount may be meager—limited to the number of changed objects. For a large fac-

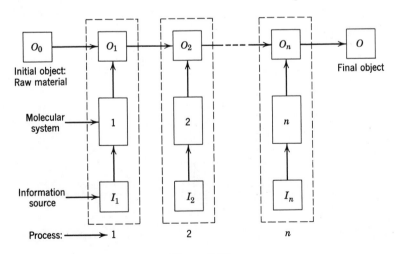

Figure 8-11

tory, the immense quantities of information produced daily give data about every phase of the production.

The measure of a production process may be the amount of object change per minute, objects per minute or objects produced for one dollar. For example, in some metalworking, production may measure inches (or cubic inches) removed per minute by a machine.

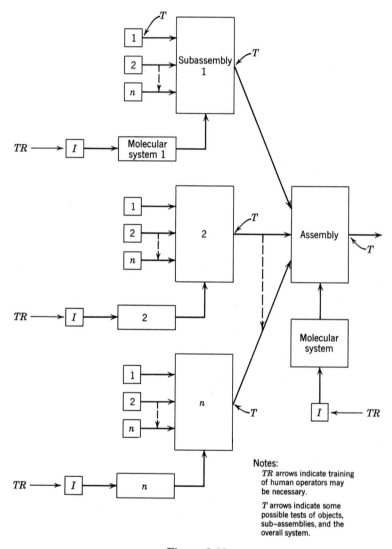

Figure 8-12

Figure 8-11 represents an ordered sequence in time of operations on one object. Each information source provides the information necessary for one operation—information such as when to start, how much to cut, and when to stop. Zero-entropy energy is supplied to the effector to produce the wanted change.

After an operation is completed, the object either is transported to the next station or the next effector is brought to the object (as in a turret lathe). In any case, the transportation involves a change of an object in space, and therefore another molecular system.

For efficient use of tools or operators, it is frequently expedient to store a partially completed object. The functional diagram for storage and retrieval of objects has already been covered. Appropriate information sources are necessary to control the transportation and storage of objects.

Figure 8-12 represents the assembly of several objects. Assembly requires the objects to be brought together in space. Accurate positioning may be required, in other words, accurate selection of two or more locations in space. The operation of selection in space has already been covered.

The assembly operations may also be ordered in time. For example, before a nut is tightened on a bolt, the bolt should be put in place.

In assembly, just as in production of parts, information is necessary to direct every detail. Energy is furnished to the effectors to cause the assembly and joining together of the objects—perhaps by welding.

The building up of small subassemblies and finally of the finished product follows exactly the same pattern.

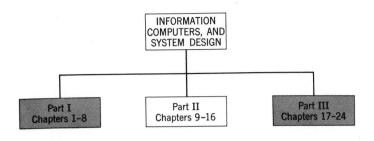

PART II

This part applies the information and building-block concepts presented in Part I. The exposition is nonmathematical.

The necessary steps in the life of a system and the functions performed during each step are put in the form of block diagrams. The necessary inputs and operations for each kind of step can then be easily grasped.

A logical argument points out the sixteen kinds of system design problems. Familiar examples of the nontrivial kinds of problems are given.

A step-by-step procedure for the design of a "new" system is given. The mathematics appropriate for each kind of step are pointed out. Logic, algebra, and calculus are useful for certain steps; linear programming and queing theories for others. No form of mathematics is suitable for all of the kinds of steps.

The step-by-step procedure makes it possible to divide the design tasks into those that a computer may do; those that a human must do; and those that either may do. This is an important result.

9

Life Story of a New System

Introduction

In Chapter 1, a system was defined as a set of components arranged to perform some wanted operation or operations. Of the several meanings of the word "design" given in the same chapter, two are particularly pertinent here. Design refers to the adaptation of means to an end (i.e., use of available means to perform the wanted operation); the coordination of parts or separate acts to produce a wanted result. Taken together, the two definitions clearly describe what must be accomplished by a system design. Further, the possible kinds of functional building blocks have been tabulated. Thus, any system consists of a coordinated set of the functional blocks to produce the wanted result.

A very good way to explore the implications of the words "wanted result" is to consider the life story of a new system. The description is made general enough so that the pattern can be made to apply to many different kinds of systems. For a particular new system, some of the steps may be of little consequence, or even missing. For another particular new system, possibly some steps must be added. Certainly, the importance of certain steps can vary widely for different systems. These facts are brought out by a few examples.

As one example, some of our contemplated military systems are enormously complex, and are installed and operated at a modest number of widely separated, sometimes almost inaccessible locations. Only one or at most very few such systems are ever designed and built. There is only one customer: the contracting military service. Where national security is involved, dollars must be considered but they are not the most important factor.

Now, take the telephone system in the United States. It, too, is enormously complex. Central offices are installed and operated at 10,000 or 15,000 locations. Telephones are installed on the customer's premises when and where he wants them. The telephone system grows. Every year, hundreds of new central offices and thousands of new PBXs and hundreds of thousands of new telephones must be added. These additions must work with all the existing central offices, all the existing PBXs and all the existing telephones. Hence, the compatibility of new and existing telephones must always be maintained. The 70 odd million customers buy a service—the ability to communicate with each other at any time. Most of these customers see only their instrument. They know little and care less about the network of outside plant wires and cables and the complex central office equipment that make their communications possible. Today, all but a very few communities have only one telephone company. In a sense, competition is very limited. But each customer always has the option of buying telephone service or some other commodity with his money. For this reason, competition for his dollar is very keen. The company must give good service today and tomorrow, and must maintain good public relations. Rates are regulated by many agencies of government. Yet the telephone company must make profits and pay adequate dividends to its stockholders.

Finally, take a major automobile company. It sells a product and service for that product. In one year, it will mass-produce a million cars, more or less. Yet, because of the large number of customer options, at least in theory each car could be different from every other car produced that year. And yearly model changes make sure that cars produced next year will differ from those produced this year. The complex system that we call an automobile is owned and operated by the customer when and where he wants it to go—in hot weather and cold, in rain and sleet and snow and sandstorm. He cares a great deal about how it runs. Thousands of mechanics must know how to repair it if anything goes wrong. Stocks of repair parts must be kept available in suitable locations for the life of all of this year's models as well as for last year's. Competition for the customer's dollar in the automobile industry is intense not only between different companies but also between divisions within a company. General Motors competes with Ford, and Chevrolet with Pontiac, Buick, Oldsmobile, and Cadillac. Prices are regulated almost entirely by this competition and only to a small extent by government agencies. A successful company must redesign its products every year, retool to make the new model, distribute the cars to the dealers who sell them. It must make a profit, pay taxes to the government, and have something left for the stockholders.

Major Steps in the Life of a New System

The life story of a new system starts with a conception—a thought n someone's mind. It may be (and usually is) just an idea in is mind. The first idea of a complex new system is never complete n every detail any more than a human embryo is.

The life story of a new system ends with the complete removal f every physical system that resulted from the original conception nd the replacement by something more up-to-date and therefore ewer and better.

Long life is an outstanding characteristic of even a reasonably omplex system that meets a real need (not a Rube Goldberg system). Take the family car as an example. A "completely new" design s started to incorporate advances such as important engine, transmission, brake, and body improvements. From the time management pproves the new design until the last survivor is scrapped, twenty r more years may pass. Some Model T Fords are still in use. The life span of major household appliances such as refrigerators, reezers, and dishwashers is also twenty or more years. The DC-3 vas the workhorse of the airlines in the 1930s. Many are still lying in the 1960s. Magneto telephones are still in use, although lial systems have been available for more than a half a century.

The life story of a new system can be broken down into many imple steps. The various kinds of steps and their arrangements and equences in time are conveniently presented in the form of block liagrams. Such a presentation makes several points clear. Among hese are:

1. It shows the sources and kinds of information necessary at each tep. The tremendous role of information generation, storage, retrieval, and communication becomes obvious.

2. It shows that many different people are involved in the various teps. Information transfer between these people is not only essential out the information must not be likely to be changed by the transfer. To avoid possible changes, graphic forms such as blueprints and printed papers are widely used to convey instructions and other information.

3. It shows appropriate uses of various mathematical tools and echniques during the life span. Many new names have appeared n the literature in the last ten or fifteen years. Linear programming,

decision theory in management science, and operations research a
only examples. Where these concepts may be usefully brought
bear is clarified.

Before going into too much detail, some major steps in the li
of any new system are presented in Fig. 9-1.

Since the new system does not exist it must be designed on pape
Almost always, because of possible human fallibilities or insufficien
knowledge, the paper design must be developed and proven befor
management will risk money and resources on production. In tl
development, one or more engineering prototype models are built an
tested. If the first try is not satisfactory, modifications must b
made until the performance is acceptable. Necessary and desirabl
changes and improvements are then incorporated in one or more pre
duction prototype models.

Since a new system is assumed, some new production methods an
tools very likely must be developed as well as testing methods an
equipment. Before production can start, the necessary resources mus
be available: drawings and instructions, floor space, tools, raw ma
terials, and people.

In production, parts must be made, then subassemblies, and finall
the complex system put together. Spares must be made for futur
maintenance and repairs. Tests must be made on parts, subassemblies
and the overall assembly to ensure the quality of the manufacture
product. For some systems, one or only a few are ever produced
for others, millions. Production may require only a few weeks o
a decade or more.

The systems must be transported to the location where they ar
to be installed and used. For some systems, a suitable site mus
be selected and made ready. Many simple and most complex system
are shipped "knocked-down" so that assembly is completed at o
near the point of use.

As pointed out earlier, the useful life of many complex system
is measured in decades. During the life, the performance must b
tested, and necessary maintenance work done and repairs made.

In the final step, systems are removed from service. When th
last one is gone, then that generation of the new system is no more.

Figure 9-1 shows two more blocks labeled "Advertise the System"
and "Sell the system". These steps may extend over a large portio
of the life. Military systems in particular may be sold before th
design even begins. Sometimes the results are less than spectacular
the system simply cannot be designed, built, and made to work satis

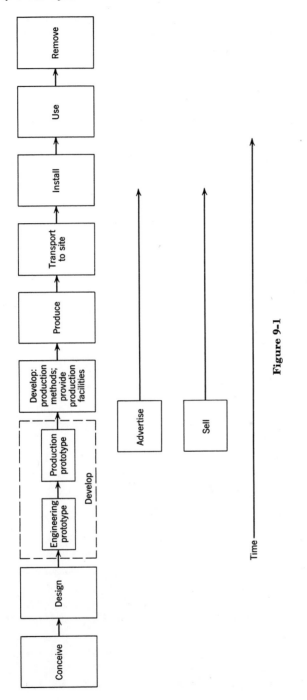

Figure 9-1

factorily. Thus, hundreds of millions of dollars have been spent on a few pre-sold systems. Once produced and sold, the advertising of military systems is usually done on only a modest scale to help create a favorable image of the producer in the minds of engineers who might be recruited and in the minds of the general public. The practicing electronics engineer is flooded with advertising material for components and small systems. Inquiry sometimes brings out the fact that the advertised items are not yet available.

In Fig. 9-1, advertising and selling are shown as starting after the production preparation is well along and volume production is about to begin. Thus the selling effort helps to create a demand for the initial production. The effort continues until the end of the useful life can be established. This is the usual pattern for systems intended for the consumer market, such as automobiles, refrigerators, freezers, and other major appliances. The manufacturer decides when to introduce a new model and uses this information in making his plans for advertising and selling.

Ordering of Steps in Time

In Fig. 9-1, the steps are not completely ordered in time—only partially ordered.

Some steps must occur before others and hence must be ordered in time. For two examples, a system must be produced before it can be used; and components must be produced before thay can be assembled.

Other steps need not be ordered in time. Some parts of a particular system may be designed either before or after others; some may be produced and made into subassemblies at any time before they are needed for assembly of the complete system.

Finally, some steps may overlap in time. Mention has already been made of the relation of advertising and selling efforts to the other steps. For some systems (e.g., automobiles) production, transportation, installation, and use may all be going on at the same time.

The possible alternative orderings of steps and overlaps depend on the particular system, and also on the value of time. Thus, production may start before the design is complete. If all goes well, the first system may be made available sooner than would otherwise be possible. But if an unforeseen design difficulty arises, time may be lost, money wasted in production of components that cannot be used.

10

System Design

Figure 10-1 represents the design step in the life of a system. Its purpose is to develop information so that management can make a sound decision as to the wisdom of committing resources necessary to develop and market the system.

The various steps shown on Fig. 10-1 are little affected by the size and complexity of the system to be designed. Each must be performed or trouble—even disaster—may follow. On the other hand, the time required to execute a step may vary greatly between systems. The activities are divided into two categories: management activities and design activities. Time flows from left to right, i.e., from start to end of the step.

The functions performed during the design step of a new system can be represented by block diagrams. The inputs to a block list the various kinds of information that must—or at least should—be available. The output represents the result of the information processing operation.

Such a representation shows very clearly why the design steps are at least particularly ordered in time: a step can not be started until at least some, or even all, of its required input information is available.

Preliminaries

Organization and Planning

Before design work can begin in earnest, and particularly work on any large project, an organization must be set up. Also, a detailed plan should be prepared. When a project is first conceived, the wanted operations can be stated only vaguely and in general terms, such as "Wouldn't it be a good idea if we did so and so? It would put us in a better position to meet competition from XYZ. I think we ought to act PDQ."

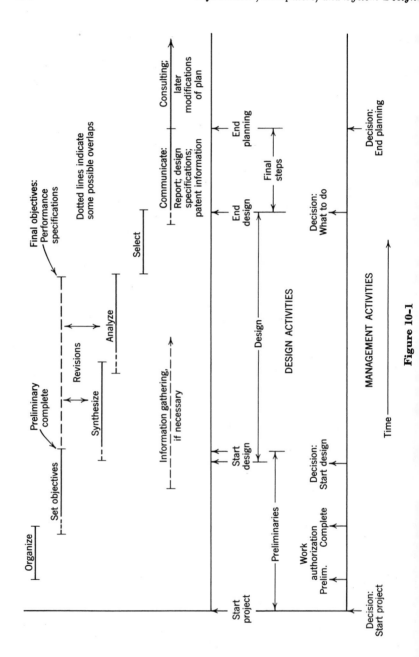

Figure 10-1

The design phase cannot start until (1) a decision is made to start the project; and (2) personnel, money, and other facilities such as work-space and tools are made available. Naturally, the decision must be made by a management person or persons with adequate authority to commit the necessary resources for the project. Many a proposed design never gets started because one of the two conditions is not met by management. A preliminary authorization may be given to start work, with a second and larger authorization following.

Before and during the design, setting up time schedules, evaluating the progress of the design activities, and monitoring the expenditures are other management responsibilities.

Even after the decision is made to go ahead with the design, some time must elapse in getting the people, work-places, and tools together and organized.

A necessary preliminary to actual design work is setting up a performance specification for the new system. The specification defines the system problem to be solved. This step changes an unclear situation into an information pattern that describes the preliminary design objectives. These first objectives may be (and usually are) amplified and clarified as design work proceeds. The continuing work on the specification is indicated in Fig. 10-1. It is also necessary to have a set of decision rules for judging alternative proposed designs. These rules are sometimes called a value system. They are used in selecting the particular physical system to be produced and used. Figure 10-1 indicates that work on the specification and the decision rules may start before the organization is completed.

The information inputs to the block representing the organization (Fig. 10-2A) can be classified as follows:

Resources. 1. Total resources available for all projects. Resources include personnel, money, and necessary supporting facilities such as floor space and equipment. Personnel should be classified according to job capability. Thus, the talents and skills of a physicist and a machinist are not interchangeable for all phases of design work.

The total available resources may include those already at hand and those that may be acquired if the proposal shows a great deal of promise. Thus, more people might possibly be hired, money might be borrowed or stock sold, building space might be added, more equipment might be bought.

2. Resources already committed to other projects and therefore not available for the new project.

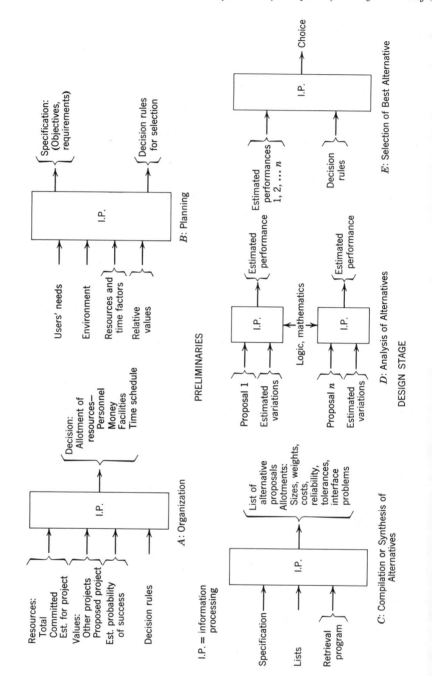

I.P. = information
processing

PRELIMINARIES

A: Organization

B: Planning

C: Compilation or Synthesis of
Alternatives

D: Analysis of Alternatives

E: Selection of Best Alternative

DESIGN STAGE

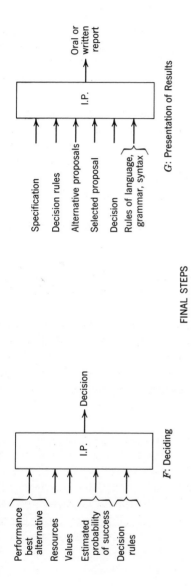

FINAL STEPS

Figure 10-2

3. Resources and time required for completing the proposed project. Obviously, only an estimate is possible before work has begun.

Values to Users and to the Company.   1. For the user the urgency and extent of his need may be a most important factor. New military systems are frequently proposed because of political or military requirements. In time of war, the very existence of the nation may depend on the immediate design and day-before-yesterday production of a new countermeasures system.

The user value may be purely economic and measureable in dollars. Diesel engines for railroad trains, computers for business operations, and automated machine tools for factories are just three examples.

Finally, the user value may be largely or entirely subjective and not measureable at all. It is difficult to put a figure on the prestige value of owning a Rolls Royce or a Cadillac, a private airplane, or a 3,000-ton ocean-going yacht.

2. The company may be faced with a pressing need for a new design because of competition. Time may be very important. The introduction of transistors into digital computers forced all companies who wanted to stay in business to follow suit—and quickly. Color television has taken a long time to gain acceptance, but the handwriting is on the wall.

Next, a new proposal may be cold-bloodedly looked at in terms of dollars. Almost always, the $64,000 or $64,000,000 question is: How much can we make on this proposal? In many practical situations, management must choose between alternative proposals—not merely evaluate one new proposed system. The company resources may not be adequate to pursue all possibilities, even if all of them would be desirable.

However, in some situations, social and prestige values may be important. Sometimes an organization may design and produce a top-of-the-line product largely for the prestige of making the best. The Bell System has produced many devices for the handicapped. The profit, if any, could only be minute. Artificial larynxes, special telephones for the hard-of-hearing, and PBXs for the blind show that social values are not always neglected by the management of a profit-making organization.

Estimation of Probability of Success

Nothing is certain in this life except death and taxes. In a very real sense the authorization by management of a proposed project is a gamble. Very real resources that might be employed in some other way are given up in return for the hoped-for values that may result from a successful design. To evaluate the possibilities realistically, an estimation of the odds for and against success must be made.

Decision Rules. Decision rules for balancing relative values and chances of success and failure are obviously an essential information input.

The Decision. The several information inputs are processed to generate an information output: a decision. The decision can take only a few forms:

1. Drop the proposal. This conclusion can be reached either because the odds for success are insufficiently high or the potential values or time intervals do not justify using resources for their creation—or both. If the estimates of odds or values are in error, the situation may be compared to that of an ostrich with its head in the sand. Some steam-minded railroad executives scoffed at diesels for too long.

2. Authorize all of the necessary resources to begin the design. Sometimes, existing projects have to be robbed of resources and, therefore, slowed down or even stopped altogether to get a new top-priority crash program going.

3. Authorize some resources to start the design work and to check carefully for major troubles. The check may well improve the estimation of the odds for success. However, the improved information costs both resources and time. Sometimes, the cautious course pays off, but sometimes it results in disaster if the enemy or the company competition is wide-awake and takes advantage of the delay.

Necessary Information for Planning

Figure 10-2B shows that to prepare a meaningful plan to guide the design at least four kinds of input information are necessary:

1. *User's Needs and Values.* The user's needs and wants should largely determine the system performance requirements. Besides performance, the user is always interested in the price he will have to pay. In some instances, he will pay more for better performance; in others, he will not. Also, he may specify upper limits on such properties as size and weight. He may have strong ideas about appearance. Simplicity of design, or ease of operation and maintenance may be important to him.

Sometimes, an attempt is made to find out the needs of potential users by a market survey. Opinion polls can sometimes give reliable information about user motivations and preferences between alternative designs to meet their needs. Sometimes, simulated models of a proposed new item are actually built to test users' reactions. A new product may be offered in a limited market area as a test.

Unfortunately, these methods check only a selected sample of the proposed market. Cost considerations often dictate a modest-sized sample. But the indicated results of a market survey or opinion poll based on too small a sample may be grossly misleading, and the consequences of a gross error can be disastrous. The optimistic estimate of the potential of the Edsel automobile reportedly cost the Ford Motor Co. a quarter billion dollars.

2. *Environment.* Information about the environmental conditions under which the system must operate must be determined. Temperature and humidity ranges, pressure range, shock and vibration exposure, weathering due to such things as sun, rain and salt spray are some environmental conditions to be considered. In this connection, the environment encountered during transportation and installation may cause adverse effects. These may be more severe than the conditions encountered in actual use. Transmission media may limit the choice of signal characteristics factors. Available kinds and capacities of power supplies and wiring may need to be taken into account.

3. *Resources and Time.* Company needs or company policy may put constraints on the design. For example, it may be necessary to use only certain available raw materials or only existing factory facilities. Work rules and abilities of available personnel may put constraints on an acceptable design.

Almost always, management sets upper limits on cost of the new system and on the total time until it will be available.

4. *Relative Values to Company.* In many system designs better performance can be had—but at a price.

Company policy may dictate that the product shall be advertised "None better at any price"; or it may be exactly the opposite, "We will not be undersold."

Information about such factors is very important in setting objectives.

These four information inputs are processed to produce two outputs: a detailed specification and a set of decision rules for evaluating proposed alternative designs.

The Specification

The specification spells out the objectives or requirements that an acceptable system must meet. Both the prospective customers' needs and company resources and policies must be taken into account.

Depending on the purpose of the system, it may, and often should, include such information as:

1. Wanted and unwanted inputs, outputs, and operations.
2. Acceptable performance and quality. Both maximum and minimum values may be included in the tolerable limits.
3. Permanence and reliability, perhaps including consideration of any failure to operate.
4. Limits on size and weight.
5. Environmental conditions under which the system must operate. Besides such conditions as temperature, pressure, and humidity, the environment may include power sources, signal characteristics, and existing systems with which the new design must be compatible.
6. Dollars—for example, manufacturing cost or expected profit. Depending on the system, the most important cost may be the initial cost or the total cost over a period of 1, or 5, or even 40 years. The important cost may be manufacturing cost, the purchase cost, the installed cost, or a total cost including such items as maintenance and operation.
7. Constraints. The use of particular materials or tools may be required. Personnel capabilities or work rules may restrict the possible design. Available resources or time required for development, test, and production may be important.
8. Other possible factors such as simplicity, adaptability for multiple uses, flexibility in meeting differing requirements, and safety.

The Decision Rules

The decision rules are to be used in two ways. First, they are to be applied to determine whether a proposed design is acceptable or not. Second, they are to be applied to order alternative designs from the most desirable to the least desirable.

In many designs better performance can be had, but will cost more; or conversely, money can be saved—but performance will be poorer. The decision rules should be able to resolve such questions.

The decision rules may not always be made explicit. And they may not always be reduced to writing. Sometimes *ad hoc* decisions are made by management or at a conference held after alternative proposals are worked out and presented for discussion. Nevertheless, decision rules are really an essential part of planning. This fact will become more clear later in discussing the role that computers may play in system design in the future.

System Design: Synthesis

Some design work may be started even before the specification and decision rules are completely worked out. As Fig. 10-1 shows, the first step is synthesis, the optimist's milieu, where everything is expected to work and nothing is impossible.

The requirements of the specification can be compared with properties of available systems (Fig. 10-2C). Preferably, a list or catalog of available systems and all their properties should be available.

For a really new system, no existing system meets all the requirements. Hence the new system must be synthesized out of a set of subsystems that together meet the requirements of the specification. A block diagram showing the proposed set of subsystems is often very helpful. The wanted and unwanted inputs and outputs and the functions to be performed by each subsystem may be shown.

The table of elementary functions of Chapter 7 and the information about useful combinations of the blocks can be of help in drawing one or more tentative block diagrams for the new system.

In the synthesis of a system, the overall requirements such as size, weight, and cost must be alloted to the subsystems. In effect, these allotments become part of the requirements for the subsystems.

Once a proposed combination of subsystems is found, one or more suitable sets of components must be selected to implement each subsystem. For some, or most, of the subsystems, suitable listings may be found in the catalog. The others must be further broken down into second-order subsystems and the comparison with the list of what is available repeated.

In the last analysis, any complex system is assembled from a set of subsystems. The more complex the system, the larger the number of subsystems is likely to be. But the *principle* of "search or synthesize" applies to either a small subsystem or a very complex system.

Clearly, a list or catalog of the possible functional blocks and another list of components must be available to permit a synthesis. The solution of the problem of the new system is thus broken down into a set of subproblems. The overall solution then depends on the solution of *all* the subproblems.

Further, the breakdown into subsystems results in numerous interfaces between two or more subsystems. Incompatibilities can result.

Hopefully, the synthesis step results in a block diagram of at least one set of subsystems that together can perform all the wanted functions. The putting together of such a set has been called *single-thread design*. The synthesis step may result in several alternative sets of subsystems that appear to meet the specification.

Synthesis always involves information retrieval. If needed information is not available or cannot be found for any reason, then that information must be acquired or the design is blocked.

The lack of an available list is most acute at the overall system level in the hierarchy. As the overall system is broken down into smaller and smaller blocks, usually more and more information is available from more and more sources.

Lists and catalogs of electronic and mechanical parts such as gears are free for the asking. The reason is quite clear. No company manufactures every single item of a large system. It purchases many raw materials, such as metal rods and sheets, many small components, and even sizable subsystems. A modern airliner is a good example of an assembly containing many purchased items. For another example, take the Western Electric Company, the manufacturing branch of the Bell System. It supplies all the telephone companies with their telephones, cables, and central office equipment. Yet, the Western Electric Company makes purchases from tens of thousands of other suppliers, large and small.

Thus, a complex system is an assembly composed of many things that are purchased from "outside suppliers." Additional operations are made on some of the purchased items to fit them for their functions.

The "list" of available systems and subsystems may not actually be a written list. It may be the accumulated and "stored" experience of a designer or a design team. It may be scattered through many articles and volumes in the library. The wanted information may be retrieved from the subconscious minds of the designers and the people with whom they consult, by long hours of lonely soul-searching contemplation, by informal meetings (perhaps during a coffee break or a lunch), by more formal conferences, or sometimes in free-wheeling, no-idea-barred "brainstorming" sessions. It may be retrieved from the library by tedious tracing from useless reference to even more useless reference—always hoping against hope.

The synthesis of most new systems applies known results and design rules. Gaps in existing information may sometimes be filled in by interpolation; extensions into unknown areas, by extrapolation. A new design is usually an evolution: it is seldom a revolution, even though it may be so proclaimed. The synthesis of a new electric wave filter or small power transformer is usually a routine procedure. The synthesis of a new turbine design to deliver 10% more output than any existing turbine may rely heavily upon extrapolation.

Particularly for the design of a system to perform some completely new operation or a known operation in a new way, adequate information may not be immediately available. Space travel is an example of a completely new operation; substitution of microwave relay for coaxial cable for telephone and television transmission is an example of performing an operation in a new way. In such cases, synthesis can only proceed on the basis of assumptions—or conjectures—not on facts. All needed information must be made available before the design can be considered to be sound. Development of a new system should not be undertaken until knowledge and techniques are available to meet the objectives without further research or exploration. This permits realistic development schedules and assurance that the design is realizable.

Pure research builds up the storehouse of human knowledge without an immediate application in view. This storehouse can be searched for information useful in the synthesis of a new system.

Experiments in a prescribed area may provide missing knowledge for a system design. For example, before a microwave relay system could be designed with confidence, thousands of measurements on the properties of the transmission medium were made under many different conditions. Such experiments to acquire missing information are sometimes called *applied research*. Another name might be *directed research* into the unknown.

If all the essential physical components assumed in the synthesis are not available, then they must be invented, or developed, and produced. Since the wanted properties are known, a tentative specification for the missing component can be prepared. For example, a color television set could not be built until a suitable picture tube was perfected.

A suitable component may exist but be "unavailable," because it is made or used by a competitor or because it is patented and the right to use it cannot or will not be negotiated. Sometimes much design effort is devoted to "designing around" unavailable components, perhaps by changing their proposed functions so that available components can be used.

If, for some reason, a system cannot be synthesized to meet the preliminary specification, the specification must be modified, or the design project must be abandoned as not feasible. Thus system design is often problem-solving by an iterative process. A not-uncommon management procedure is to set the initial sights high by making the preliminary system specification very difficult to meet. Sometimes the challenge to meet it results in a technical breakthrough. If the breakthrough does not occur, some modifications may be made. A nothing-ventured, nothing-won philosophy may bring rich rewards.

Today, relatively little mathematical help is available to guide the synthesis of complex systems. Brute-force tabulation and exhaustive examination of *all* possibilities is an obvious course. However, it is almost always impossible because of costs and time. An experienced designer chooses certain approaches as likely to be the best. These represent his evaluation of alternative breakdowns and his estimates of the likelihood of success. Sometimes he is right; sometimes he is not!

Heuristics is from a Greek word meaning "an aid or guide to discovery." The new discipline called heuristics is now being explored for solving certain mathematical problems. More is said later about heuristics and possible system synthesis applications.

System Design: Analysis

In Fig. 10-1, after synthesis comes analysis. Each alternative proposal should be carefully studied for its performance with various assumed inputs and estimated variations of the performance of the subsystems and environmental conditions. The consequences of choosing each alternative are worked out.

Searching and critical analysis can often disclose unanticipated weaknesses or even inoperative conditions in a proposed synthesis. Thus, analysis is the pessimist's milieu. He assumes that trouble lurks everywhere, ever ready to rear its ugly head.

Analysis examines carefully the operation under such conditions as multiple inputs, overload conditions, and enemy actions, if the system may be subjected to such effects. Analysis tries to estimate how the system will perform in extreme environments and with parts on the verge of failure.

Analysis takes into account various ways of breaking the system down into functional subsystems, possible ways of building each subsystem, and any interface problems involving two or more subsystems that work together. To study the performance under certain conditions, known or assumed probabilities must be used. An example of such uncertainities is the lack of knowledge of the possible number and kinds of system inputs at various times.

Analyses almost always involve a study of costs of materials, labor, and other resources to make, transport, sell, install, maintain, and even to remove each promising alternative.

Analyses may involve studies of how the new system can be introduced if it replaces some existing system or systems in whole or in part. How to phase-out manned bombers as missiles become available is an example.

Compatibility of the new with the old may be extremely important. A new type of telephone central office must work with every existing central office—even those installed in the eary 1900s.

Some systems are or should be designed to include provisions which enable future modification to accommodate new needs or technical advances. Adequate electrical and telephone wiring for a new office building is a familiar example.

Some results of the analysis are predicted values for such specified quantities as cost, size, and weight, as well as the expected performance. The predicted values and performances are compared with the objectives contained in the specification (see Fig. 10-2*D*).

The predictions resulting from the analysis provide information for necessary changes in the specification and hence information for modifications of the system plans synthesized to meet the specification.

Thus, the synthesis and analysis steps of design together provide information that changes the uncertainty of success or failure of a proposed system into certainty. They involve the finding, organizing, processing, and evaluating of information in the face of the uncertainties. Progress is made by changing a vague, often poorly stated abstract idea into one or more concrete, realizable proposals.

If no proposal meets the specification, the analysis may show that the proposed system is (1) physically impossible. (2) technically impossible, or (3) economically impossible.

The results of the analysis work are estimated data about the proposed alternative designs. These results may show that (1) none (2) just one, or (3) more than one alternative promises to meet the specification.

No actual system exists when the analysis is made. Obviously, actual experiments or tests can not be made on a nonexistent system. But what can sometimes be done is to perform some kind of abstract counterpart of experiments or tests. The combination of German and English words "Gedanken Experiments" (literally, "thought experiments") has been used to emphasize the abstract nature of such analyses. Logic and mathematical formulas are the tools used. In some cases, the system operation can be simulated by programming a computer; in many cases, it can not.

The value of the predictions depends on the quality and accuracy of the Gedanken Experiments, or simulation. Sometimes, the predictions later turn out to be overly optimistic or even completely wrong. Then disaster—even bankruptcy—can ensue for the unfortunate company that relied on wrong information resulting from an incorrect or incomplete analysis.

The rules of logic and mathematics are the only appropriate tools for the analysis of a proposed system, because no physical system exists that can be measured. For some systems, a mathematical model can set up. More or less extensive computations may explore the model's workings. A large amount of computation may not be feasible. Also, some designers trust experimental data rather than computed results.

For handling high-traffic input loads, probability, statistical, and queing theories can sometimes help the analysis.

Many systems, such as communication, transportation, and electric-power distribution systems involve a network configuration. Much mathematical theory is available for analyzing networks.

Boolean algebra, logic theory, and switching theory are useful in designing telephone switching systems and computers.

Information theory finds application in radar and certain communication systems in which the signal-to-noise ratio approaches one or less.

Feedback, cybernetics, and servomechanism theory underlie the analysis of highly linear amplifiers and many control systems.

If the system operation can be described by appropriate mathematical models, optimum operation conditions may be explored by differential calculus, the calculus of variations, linear or dynamic programming methods, or hill-climbing or steepest-descent methods. Nonlinear system operation usually offers formidable mathematical difficulties to any of these methods.

The system operation may be simulated on an analog or digital computer to gain insight into the response to various inputs and particularly those that occur at random. Here also, an appropriate mathematical model is a necessity.

Game theory deals with a few competitive situations involving unwanted inputs. It may or may not be helpful, depending on the system requirements.

Reliability theory can help to evaluate the consequences of some environmental stresses.

System Design: Compare and Select

If more than one of the proposed alternatives meets the specification, the final design step is to select the best one (see Fig. 10-2*E*). Based on the information from the analysis and the decision rules, the alternative plans can be compared with each other in the light of the specification.

Selection is easy if the choice is (or can be) based on a single measureable quantity. A frequently used measure is dollars (for example, dollars cost or expected profit). Selection may be more difficult if two or more important quantities (such as cost and performance) are involved in the comparison. Today, probably most such selections are based on someone's judgment or intuition or hunch. Such methods are occasionally—but not very often—supplemented by mathematical tools such as linear programming.

The comparison may show that none of the proposed systems is satisfactory in all respects. Need for the synthesis and analysis of new alternatives may be the inevitable conclusion. Often a new plan combining with the best features of several earlier plans results. Such studies are sometimes called *optimization*.

At this stage in the design, the best of the alternative systems has been selected or it is known that none is satisfactory. Unless further alternatives are to be explored, the design activites are completed.

Final Steps: Decide What to Do

The design resulted in the selection of the best proposal for meeting the specification. The next step is to decide what to do (see Fig. 10-2*F*).

Decision rules were one output of the planning done before the design was started.

Management now has to choose between three possible courses of action:

1. Drop the project. Many projects must be stopped because of unexpectedly high costs or unforeseen technical difficulties—or both. In some cases, although the proposed system may be feasible, not

enough money is available to go ahead. A bridge design may be completed but the bond issue voted down at the polls—a heartbreaking outcome for the men who have proposed and worked on the system. Yet, in the long run dropping the project may be the only sensible action to take. Lack of management courage can cost millions of development dollars. Examples are not too hard to find.

2. Authorize further design effort. Such a choice may not be made unless a promising new alternative turns up at the eleventh hour. The specification is changed and the necessary synthesis and analysis work carried on.

3. Proceed with development of the selected system. Of course, this is the hoped-for decision. To implement the decision to go ahead, the necessary men, money, and other facilities must be authorized.

Final Steps: Communicate the Results

The final stage in the design activities is the recording and communication of the results to management and all interested organizations (see Fig. 10-2G).

Almost always, a written report of the planning activities is prepared as a record of the work. A condensed version may be given orally to management people. Such a report should cover:

1. The system specification.
2. The decision rules for choosing the best proposal. In some cases, these rules are so well known to the people who will read the report that they may safely be omitted.
3. The more promising alternatives. Perhaps, mention of less attractive alternatives and their drawbacks should be included.
4. The estimated performances of the more promising alternatives.
5. The reasons for the selection.
6. The action decided on and the reasons for the decision.

An unattractive system alternative for today's objectives may be quite attractive if the objectives should change. Even if no suitable plan was found, the report might well be valuable for future reference.

The report (and particularly a well-written and complete document) is one of the most important products of the design phase. A file of such reports on various projects can be invaluable in helping set up objectives and decision rules for new systems.

Information about any ideas believed to be new should be furnished to patent attorneys for possible action. The designers of new systems frequently generate patentable ways to perform wanted functions.

In some companies, when the development of a new system is started, a prospectus is prepared that describes the system, its advantages, and possibly expected savings or profits from its introduction. Such advance information is useful to management, to the advertising, public relations, and sales organizations, and also to the people who will later manufacture the product.

Depending on company policy, one or more papers or articles may be prepared for learned societies or journals. These releases typically give technical information about the design and its expected performance. Some companies never publish such material because they regard it as "company secret"; others, publish only after the system has been manufactured and is in use; still others, and particularly companies designing military, missile, and aerospace systems, sometimes follow a policy of disclosure of projected systems while they are still in the synthesis or analysis stages of design.

When the selected system is to be developed, a specification gives a formal definition of the wanted physical system. It lists the wanted and unwanted inputs, outputs, and operation of the overall system, and also any size, weight, or other limitations. It also specifies the breakdown into the selected set of subsystems and lists their inputs, outputs, and wanted operations. The important findings of the analytical work are also included to make sure that the development systems meet the desired objectives. This information may form decision rules for choosing between alternate development proposals for building the system.

System designers should be familiar with the state of the art, including the latest pertinent discoveries. For this reason, reading published papers and attending meetings of technical societies are both very necessary to learn what is going on in other companies. Within the system designer's own organization, two-way communication with research people can sometimes be helpful, particularly during synthesis. The research staff can thus learn of system needs, and in turn convey up-to-the minute information about their work. For much the same reasons, talks with expert applied mathematicians during the analysis may be mutually beneficial.

During the design work, at least occasional two-way communication with management is essential. For one thing, the progress of the work must be evaluated in terms of the schedule. Management must also assess the economic value of the information being gathered and processed. After all, the gathering and processing require resources in the form of people, money, and facilities. The value of these resources must be balanced against the value of the evidence about success or failure of the design.

During the later stages, two-way communication should be maintained between the designers and the people who will develop the system. Then, the development people have a chance to contribute their ideas and knowledge while the analysis of alternatives is in progress. Also, they can become acquainted with the new system and its objectives at an early date. Even after the development work is started, two-way exchange of ideas is highly desirable to discuss any minor difficulties that appear.

For much the same kinds of reasons, two-way communications between the designers and the sales people should be set up before the design is frozen. Appearance and packaging questions are examples of items of mutual interest.

The communications of the designers with the research, management, development, and sales people may occur during rather informal meetings, rather than by full-dress formal conferences or by elaborate written reports.

End of Design Stage

The design actually ends when management decides to drop the project or the specification is completed so that development work can begin.

In practice, some of the people responsible for the study follow the development work closely. Necessary or advantageous changes in the plan or in the specification often turn up as the development proceeds. If the changes are acceptable, the design people can make them.

Management Activities

As Fig. 10-1 shows, the management or control activities are concurrent with all the system design steps. This situation is not peculiar to design. Management activities are necessary before, during, and at the end of every step in the life of a new system.

Management—not the designers—makes the initial decision to authorize a project and further decisions to get it under way.

The mortality of systems proposals is extremely high. Management may not agree to consider a new idea at all. Inventors and proposers have been known to take quite a dim view of what they consider

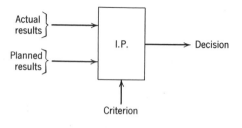

Figure 10-3

to be such a short-sighted attitude. Sometimes management is right—sometimes not.

Agreement to consider an idea means nothing unless the necessary resources are assigned. Resources may just not be available, even for a promising idea. Then, too, the design work may show that the system cannot be realized, or that it has an unforeseen operating difficulty, or that it is not better than other available systems on the market, or that it just will cost too much to make.

Many ideas are proposed; few are developed.

It is a management function to decide to speed up or slow down part or all of a project, or even to stop the effort entirely. Allocations of money or resources may be altered during the course of the work. Information gained can show that some problems are not as difficult as was thought at the beginning; others may be more difficult.

Figure 10-3 represents in the form of a block diagram the one or more kinds of information inputs to be compared with a reference input to produce the output information: a decision.

The initial management authorization covers resources for all tasks; personnel, money, and facilities. It also covers detailed schedules for all steps.

Three factors that management must always take into account are: resources needed for each task, total resources available, and resources allotted to or needed for other projects.

Management decides when to end the design. As Fig. 10-4 shows, such a decision involves comparing the cost of acquiring more information with the value of the information.

For a particular decision, the reference input may come from one or more information sources, for example, from a superior in management or a management policy, past experience stored in the brain, a personal philosophy of life, a personal set of ethics.

For most decisions, the information-processing function performed by the brain is difficult or impossible to analyze. Thus, to an observer, the decision process may be described by words such as automatic reaction, intuition, arbitrary and unreasonable thinking, or expediency.

A few important decisions may be reached by more formal or scientifically based methods such as classical Aristotelian logic (less often, symbolic logic may be useful), mathematical analysis, if the problem can be put into a suitable form, or statistical decision theory.

For help in planning large system projects, two techniques have been found to be useful: PERT (Program Evaluation and Review Technique) and Critical Path Programming. These are a graphical representation of the network of events to be achieved in the project and the tasks that must be done to achieve the events.

The network shows the logical sequence of steps by which the manager expects the project to be completed. Time estimates are used for each task. The total project time can be estimated by adding the times along all the series of tasks and events through the network. The series of tasks and events with the largest sum, the *critical path*, gives the total project duration.

The resources for all the tasks may also be estimated and from these estimates, cost estimates may be worked out.

More recently, a decision network with considerable similarity to a PERT network has been proposed. It also shows the sequence of events and the necessary tasks, but, it includes decision points in the project where two or more mutually exclusive possibilities exist. Thus, it shows where adequate information is available about how tasks may be performed but where there is insufficient information about which result will occur. The network may also show uncertainty in either tasks or end results if estimated probabilities are added.

Monitoring activities of management are concerned with the progress of the design and the results produced. They are also concerned with expenditures of resources and time. In system design it is neces-

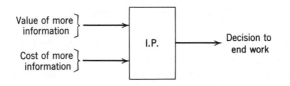

Figure 10-4

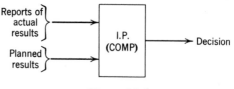

Figure 10-5

sary to evaluate the information generated by the work. The output of a production line can be measured in terms of units per hour or day. At the present state of the art, a comparable measure of information production rate is not feasible.

Monitoring can compare the actual expenditure of resources with the allotted amounts. The time schedule sets dates on which particular design steps are to be completed. Management can check to see whether the dates are met, and also whether expenditures of money and other resources are more than, less than, or equal to the allotted amounts for each step.

Figure 10-5 represents the monitoring function. Information from reports such as designers' time reports and reports from the budget director are compared with the results planned when the project was authorized. The comparison shows whether the progress meets the manager's criterion and is satisfactory. If it does not, and is therefore unsatisfactory, it is necessary to decide whether to take action or not, and perhaps what action to take.

Intermediate management transmits information about top-management policies and decisions to the designers and their supporting personnel. It also transmits information to top management about progress of the work, about results achieved, and about problems that require top-level decisions or actions. Typical problems involve personnel and other resources allotted to or needed for the design effort.

Time Scale of Design Stage

The time interval from the start of design effort to the end of the planning and authorization of development is seldom less than a few months. It may be many years. Management is—and must be—cautious about committing large resources unless the chances of success are believed to be excellent. Evaluation of the chances takes time.

Errors in Information-handling in System Design

System design is full of chances for technical error. And the consequences of an error can be so disastrous as to threaten the solvency of a company of modest size. Technical errors may be divided into errors in synthesis and errors in analysis. Management errors are also possible but are a separate category.

Errors in synthesis may be errors of omission or of commission. They can occur because of lack of information or improper use of available information. Possible subsystems may be overlooked or an inferior breakdown into subsystems assumed. Either way, the optimum alternative is not synthesized and hence it is not analyzed. As a result, a potentially sound system proposal may be rejected or an inferior design developed. If the system is intended for military use, the error gives the enemy an unnecessary advantage. If the system is for offer in the market, a competitive disadvantage can result.

Similarly, errors in analysis may be errors of omission or of commission. For example, a possible cause of overheating and resultant disastrous system failure may be overlooked. A not-uncommon error is extreme optimism about manufacturing and other costs. Such errors can lead to starting a development that should not be undertaken. Naturally, the company suffers because its resources are unwisely expended.

Because the penalties for design errors can be so great, management should use extreme care in the assignment of personnel to design. Imagination, objectivity, experience, and good judgment are all essential qualities. In combination in one individual, they are not easy to find.

11

Engineering and Production Prototype Development

Development of an engineering prototype of the new system begins with the decision to commit the necessary resources. The purpose is to develop information so that either a production prototype system can be built, if necessary, or the necessary steps can be taken to proceed with manufacture. However, complex systems seldom go into manufacture before a production prototype is built and thoroughly tested.

The purpose of the production prototype is to develop information so that the system can be produced and tested, transported safely, installed correctly, and operated and maintained.

A comparison of Figs. 11-1 and 11-2 shows that the functional steps performed during the development of the engineering and development prototypes are quite similar. Further, the two sequences of steps have much in common. Even more important, all the different *kinds* of functions have been discussed in earlier chapters. Where appropriate, references to these chapters are given. Naturally, the production prototype must not only work satisfactorily but also be capable of economical production. In this stage, emphasis is put on "Design for Manufacture."

Preliminaries

Just as in design, work cannot start until resources are made available and are organized.

Often, much of the organization (and facilities) responsible for the engineering prototype are also used to develop the production prototype model. Their background and experience can be of great value in changing the engineering model for the production prototype. Information gained from the engineering prototype should reduce the

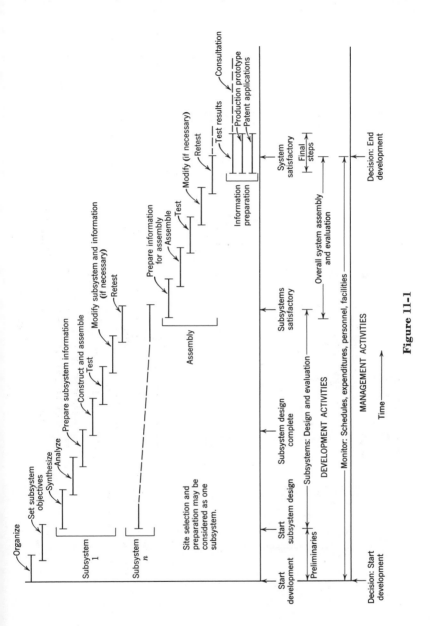

Figure 11-1

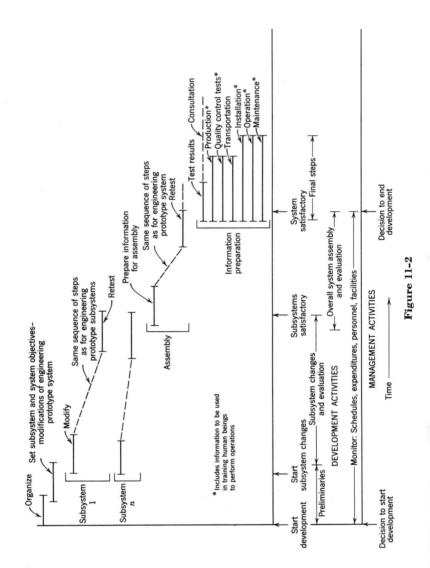

Figure 11-2

uncertainties of success or failure. Of course, new money must be available and new schedules must be set up. And, people familar with production methods and available factory facilities may be added to the team developing the production prototype.

For both developments, the organization function is quite similar to the corresponding function for system design (see Fig. 10-2*A*). In development, the inputs are:

1. Total resources made available for the project.
2. Resources and time estimates for each step in the development. Only estimates are possible before work is begun.
3. Decision rules for balancing uncertainties of chances of success or failure for each step.

The information inputs are processed to generate an information output: a decision. The decision allots the available resources of personnel, money, and facilities to the various development steps.

Every development should be carefully planned. Only by planning can the possibilities of costly mistakes be minimized.

The earlier work resulted in:

1. A specification spelling out the requirements an acceptable system should meet and the environmental conditions under which it must operate satisfactorily.
2. The selected proposal for meeting the required performance, including the breakdown into subsystems or possibly even smaller divisions. Thus the inputs, outputs, and functions to be performed by each subsystem are more or less completely specified. Tentative division of such design factors as size, weight, and cost among the subsystems has been made. But except possibly in a preliminary way, experienced planners do not go into the details.
3. Decision rules to determine whether a proposed prototype is acceptable or not. For the engineering prototype, these rules may not be completely determined. For the production prototype, they should be well worked out.

Just as in Fig. 10-2*B*, these information inputs are processed to produce two kinds of outputs: detailed requirements on each subsystem or possibly even smaller divisions and a set of tests for determining whether the prototypes of the divisions, subsystems, and overall assembly meet all of their requirements.

The engineering prototype of the new system is the first actual physical embodiment. To build it, every subsystem must be realized in actual hardware. A detailed plan for achieving each subsystem is the first step. Part of the plan may—and often does—take the form of a diagram showing a set of functional blocks that together can perform the necessary operations on the inputs.

Until the engineering prototype is built, measurements of the performance can not be made.

Unplanned or poorly planned tests can miss design weaknesses that should be removed. Properly planned tests of the subsystems can detect errors made in the synthesis such as the choice of inappropriate components. They can also check the analysis by showing up unwanted nonlinear performance or effects deliberately neglected or inadvertantly overlooked in creating the model. Remember that any model is a simplification of the actual facts. Therefore, tests of the subsystems are almost always essential. Furthermore, tests of the overall system can show whether the specified performance is achieved in all respects. Even if all subsystems test OK, interactions at the interfaces between subsystems can be troublesome.

To get the maximum amount of information from the measurement program at least cost, a well-thought-out set of experiments is certainly desirable, even though not always essential. The mathematical theory available for the "Design of Experiments" may sometimes be quite helpful.

Information gathered during the work on the engineering prototype indicates necessary or desirable changes for the production prototype. Planning activities determine the appropriate modifications of the engineering prototype subsystems, assembly, and tests.

Subsystems

As Figs. 11-1 and 11-2 indicate, all the subsystems may not be developed or delivered concurrently. In any case, all should be available when the complete system is to be assembled.

For systems requiring complicated and extensive preparation of the site for the overall tests, selection of the location and other necessary work may proceed simultaneously with the development of the subsystems. Missile test sites are an example.

The first design step, synthesis, is concerned with the design of each subsystem given the inputs, functions to be performed, and the desired outputs. The system planner usually is fairly certain that the subsystems are realizable.

For the engineering prototype, the available information may be somewhat sketchy. For the production prototype, it should be quite complete so that any shortcomings come to light before manufacture begins. Of course, the production prototype requirements contain the changes resulting from the engineering prototype development.

Given the subsystem requirements, the first design step is to find either an available arrangement or a collection of available components that together can meet the requirements. Whether the subsystem is to be purchased or constructed, a file or list of possible components and their performance must be available to the designer. One good source of information is manufacturers' catalogs.

The designer must have a plan for making the file search and any necessary computations. He must also know the decision rules for choosing between alternatives.

The problem is to match the inputs and outputs of each subsystem by a known transfer agent or function. If the system planner was overoptimistic, then innovations or invention may be necessary to work out a satisfactory design.

For any complex system, some objects or subassemblies are purchased from outside suppliers. The designer then must determine from published information or by other means the facts about such things as performance and cost. For some systems, outstanding performance is essential at any cost; for others, cost is more important than performance. The cost criterion may be only purchase cost or the total cost over a period of time such as one or five years. Again, the cost criterion may include not only the purchase cost but also the costs to install, maintain, and operate the purchased item. It may even include the losses when the item does not work. Generalities are impossible. But the designer must use the appropriate criteria and costs.

Other factors that may influence the designer's choice are serviceability and reliability. Finally, the delivery dates may be important so that the development schedule can be met.

Some designers must choose their components from the file or catalog on a take-it or-leave-it basis. Only certain sizes or performances are listed. Other designers are not quite so constrained. Within limits they can specify certain parameters. Take the design of an electrical network for a communication system. The wanted input and desired response are given. Several core sizes are available for inductances; several kinds of capacitors, with paper, mica, and air dielectrics; and resistances with different initial tolerances and stabilities with time. The required network components are specified to four or five significant figures. The exact inductance values may be realized in hardware by choosing a suitable core size with a winding of an exact number of turns. For more precision a trimming adjustment may be provided. Similar expedients may be used for capacitor and resistances. Power transformer designs follow somewhat the same pattern. A selection of standard core laminations is available, as well as standard cases. Wire sizes, number of primary and secondary turns, and insulations are at the designer's disposal. From such data he works out possible designs.

The synthesis of the subsystem involves information retrieval and often some computing. The techniques used for optimization may be useful. These were enumerated earlier in discussing system synthesis.

Several alternative possible arrangements for meeting the subsystem requirements are more desirable than is only one.

Broadly speaking, the synthesis is quite similar to the corresponding step in system design (see Fig. 10-2C).

Each alternative proposal can then be analyzed or examined for such additional factors as cost, size, weight, and sensitivity to component variations with the environmental conditions and with time. The engineering prototype development results are frequently helpful in analyzing the production prototype alternatives.

Logic and computations using estimated values are the tools used for analysis of each possible design. The analysis of electrical networks, transformers, motors, and generators has been extensively studied. For such items, mathematical studies can give quite useful results. Many other kinds of subsystems are so complex that mathematical analysis is not very rewarding.

The final design step is to choose the alternative that is to be constructed, if there is more than one possibility. In making the selection, the decision and evaluation rules worked out in the system and subsystem planning provide criteria for the choice. The resemblance to the functions represented by Figs. 10-2D and E seems clear.

Now, for the first time in the life of the new system, hardware is necessary. Hence, information must be prepared so that any necessary parts can be made and a preliminary model of each subsystem assembled for testing.

In large development organizations, construction of engineering prototype models is often done by versatile mechanics who can work from sketchy—even fragmentary—information. Sometimes, these master mechanics obtain some of the information they need by talking with the designer.

After the preliminary model of the subsystem is constructed and assembled, it is submitted to the planned tests. This is the moment of truth.

Not infrequently, information gained from one or more of the tests shows that modifications are necessary or desirable. Then, necessary modifications are made and the tests repeated. The drawings and any other information used in building the model are modified to include the changes. Again, if necessary, further modifications are made until the test results show the subsystem to be acceptable.

Each subsystem goes through the same sequence of test, modification, and retest.

System Assembly and Test

As Figs. 11-1 and 11-2 indicate, when all the subsystem performances are satisfactory, the assembly of the entire system can be started. In some cases, the assembly may be started before all of the subsystems are available.

The functions performed in producing the objects for and assembling the prototypes were discussed in Chapter 8. In particular, see Figs. 8-11 and 8-12.

The objects making up a subassembly are produced by operations performed on the input material. Transportation of objects between work-places and temporary storage between production operations are performed by appropriate systems.

The operator may require training so that he can supply the information input for particular operations. Special training may be required for a new kind of operation that he has never done before. More commonly, versatile operators with years of training and experience are used to produce prototype models.

As the objects are produced, they are tested to make sure that they will be satisfactory for their functions in the subassembly.

As the objects are produced and tested, first they are put together in subassemblies, and then the subassemblies are put together.

Not infrequently, tests show that subsystem modifications are necessary or desirable to facilitate the assembly. After this is done, all of the subsystems are known to be satisfactory.

For the prototypes, the operators who do the assembly work always require information about the operations they are to do. Perhaps they may require some special training for operations beyond their previous experience. The design information always implicitly assumes some degree of training and skill. Thus, it is almost impossible to determine how much information would really be necessary starting from scratch with untrained morons.

The assembly of the overall system can then begin. After the system is assembled, the planned overall tests are made to prove that all of the wanted system functions are achieved. If necessary, modifications are made to correct any unwanted or inadequate performance and the appropriate tests are repeated. The production prototype may be tested in the field under the expected operating and environmental conditions.

Information is gained about the performance, but the operators must be informed about what to do, when to do it, and how to record the results.

Some mathematical tools that may be brought to bear on the problems of measuring objects are: Design of Experiments and theories covering data reduction and analysis.

Changes or adjustments of certain objects forming part of the system may be made to vary the performance with time (Chapter 5). Such adjustments may be made by a trained human operator in response to observations of the performance. Some adjustments may be the result of the operation of a servo-control loop. But a human being is always involved, if only to turn the system on and possibly to turn it off.

Modification is another way to vary the performance. Modification of a system or subsystem involves gaining access to an object or objects within the system and removing, modifying, or replacing them. The modification function is always performed by a human being. For proper performance, he must have training and information so he can do the job properly. Otherwise, he almost certainly will end up like the little boy who takes an alarm clock apart but somehow cannot get it back together again.

Of course, after a modification the system is again operated so that the performance can be observed or measured to see whether the modification achieved its intended purpose.

A modification may be intended to correct some design shortcoming or operating malfunction. Such a modification may be necessary for satisfactory performance. Other modifications are made because of new ideas that appear to offer some advantage over the existing arrangement. They are not absolutely necessary—only desirable.

Modifications and then tests are continued until the specified performance is achieved or it becomes clear that it can not be.

At this stage in the life of a system, major modifications may actually cause or be the result of changes in objectives. Hence, they often represent changes in the earlier plans. For this reason, any major modifications should be approved by the system planners. Changes of plans made during the hardware stages can be expensive—even disastrous. To avoid such unfortunate happenings, planning should be both careful and complete.

Major modifications resulting from new ideas may require careful management consideration. Many engineers strive for better and better performance. As a result of their efforts for improvement, the original system specification may require reexamination. A management decision whether to stick with the original specification or to change it may be necessary. Not infrequently, the decision is difficult to make. Turning down good ideas may cause personnel problems; accepting them may affect costs and schedules.

Final Steps

If the performance of the engineering prototype is satisfactory, authorization to build a production prototype is likely to follow almost automatically. A less happy outcome means that the specification must be changed so that revised requirements can be met. If the change would give unacceptable performance, management must decide whether to stop the project or to re-examine the original plan.

Information Preparation

Information preparation involves reporting all the tests and the results, and making recommendations for changes to be incorporated in the production prototype.

It is also necessary to inform the patent attorneys of any ideas believed to be new, and also to inquire whether the organization has the "right to use" all the ideas incorporated in the proposed system. Unexpected infringement proceedings can be both unpleasant and expensive.

This engineering prototype effort ends with the decision to proceed with the development of one or more production prototypes. When the production prototype is satisfactory, then production can be authorized. However, the work of the development people is far from over. Many kinds of information must be prepared for the people who will be concerned with the later phases of the system. The development organization must supply all of the necessary information so that the system can be produced and used. Some of the kinds of information are:

Manufacturing Information
  Raw material specifications for each kind of purchased material
  Specifications for each kind of procured part and subassembly
  Inspection methods and tolerances for all purchases
  Production information for objects, subassemblies, and the overall system
  Quality control methods and tolerances for objects produced, for subassemblies, and for the overall system
Transportation Requirements
  Special packing information
Installation Information
  Specifications for site, floor layouts, floor plans, floor loads, power supplies, and environment control (if necessary)
  Assembly information
  Installer training material
  Test methods and limits for subassemblies and overall system
Operation Information
  Operator training
  Instructions for operating the overall system under normal working conditions
  Test methods and limits for checking for proper operation
  Information about conditions requiring adjustment or maintenance
Maintenance Information
  Maintenance craftsman training
  Instructions for performing corrective or preventive maintenance
  Test methods and limits for checking repaired or replaced subassemblies and for checking the overall system
Removal and (Possibly) Disassembly Information
  Craftsman training
  Conditions for removal (test or elapsed time)
Sales
  Technical information incorporated in sales material and advertising

After the system goes into production, the development people often are called on for consultation and advice.

Information Problems

Preparation

On Figs. 11-1 and 11-2, the function of information preparation appears quite a number of times. There are good reasons why.

As pointed out earlier, the engineering and production prototypes are working physical systems. They are made up of subassemblies of actual objects. The complete assembly performs all the wanted system functions. Every object is composed of raw material that came from some original source such as a mine, a farm, or a forest. Many, many operations may be necessary to change the raw material into the wanted object.

The designer—and only the designer—determines the requirements that each completed object must meet. Hence he must prepare the information for a series of operations so that the original raw material is changed into the object he wants. He must also specify all the requirements and limits or tolerances for an acceptable object.

In its simplest form, the information-handling and transmission chain is: Designer to another human who furnishes the input information to a system that causes one wanted operation. Thus, the information is passed from one human to another. In actual production of an object for a complex system, the chain has many human links between the designer and the wanted operation. The many links provide many possibilities of misunderstanding or error. Because such errors will result in unacceptable objects, the information must pass substantially perfectly through all the links in the chain.

The designer may delegate the performance of some preliminary operations to a supplier of semifinished objects. For example, instead of starting with the basic raw materials and specifying in detail all the operations and tolerances for steel making and fabricating, he may choose a particular size of steel bar or tube provided by a supplier as the raw material for the object he wants. He assures himself that the steel bar is satisfactory for his purpose by preparing information giving his requirements on such items as size, length, per cent carbon, grain size and orientation, and heat treatment. This delegation does not alter the necessity of someone preparing information for all the operations from raw material to finished object. It merely divides the preparation among two or more organizations. And, each supplier-user relation may require the user to prepare his specific requirements in detail so that any questions of unsatisfactory performance by the supplier can be resolved. Thus, division of operations between organizations can generate the need for more total information.

For a complex system the total number of objects to be produced may be in the hundreds of thousands or even millions. Even such a simple, everyday object as a table or chair contains a surprisingly large number of parts when every piece of wood, screw, tack, nail, and bit of glue is counted. Information must be prepared so that each kind of object may be provided.

Particular sets of objects are put together into subassemblies. Information must be prepared telling how each subassembly is made—perhaps the information must tell the order in which objects are added, the exact relations of objects to each other, and methods of temporary and permanent fastening to hold the subassembly together.

Finally, the subassemblies are put together to form the completed system. The necessary kinds of information are much the same as for each subassembly.

Storage and Retrieval

Because of the large number of objects to be produced, the lesser but still large number of subassemblies, and the complexity of the final system, an enormous amount of information must be prepared. It may be measured in the tens, or hundreds, or thousands of typed or printed pages.

This enormous amount of information is prepared and stored or filed because it has to be used. For efficiency, a user must be able to get what he wants without wasting his time. Thus, the very volume of information that is stored creates the need for an index so that any particular item may be found and retrieved quickly. For a company working on many systems, the problems of setting up a satisfactory indexing scheme for all the necessary information is far from easy.

Information Forms

The design information is conveyed by signs. With a few exceptions, the signs must be suitable for communication between human beings. Signs for communications between humans are one of the subjects considered in information theory.

The wanted objects and the operation for producing and assembling items are commonly described in the signs placed on "drawings" and in "instructions." Objects or subassemblies purchased from an outside supplier are described by "specifications." Engineering and architectural drawings and specifications use their own peculiar signs and conventions that are quite unintelligible to a person without adequate training. Signs, abbreviations, and conventions for the same information may be different in different industries or even in different companies in the same industry. The instructions may supposedly be expressed in the English language. Actually, so much of the text may be phrased in technical jargon and legal-sounding words that the information can not be fully understood except by the initiated. But after all, Washington has its gobbledegook; some systems have "instructions" for production and assembly that are just about as unintelligible.

In the past few years, some metal-working machines have been arranged to accept the information for producing complex parts from punched paper or magnetic tapes. This is a very important innovation. The amount of information required on the tape to make a particular part is relatively easy to determine. On the other hand, the amount of information represented by the conventional signs and text of the engineering drawing for the same part is very difficult—perhaps, even impossible—to determine. The ability to measure the amount of information makes it possible to compare different approaches to putting the essential information on the tapes. To say the least, new and interesting applications of information theory concepts are becoming possible.

The information provided for producing and assembling the engineering prototype may sometimes be incomplete. A designer may make a necessary object himself without even a sketch, much less a complete drawing. Some large development organizations have highly skilled mechanics who can work from the designer's oral instructions. Then the information chain is short: from one human to another.

Such informality is both undesirable and unwise in making the production prototype. Eventually, when the system goes into full production, the development people and the factory may be separated by hundreds or thousands of miles. The drawings and instructions should be complete and free from ambiguities and errors. Preliminary drafts of the information can be used in building the production prototype. Shortcomings that appear can be corrected with much less difficulty and cost during the development than when production is under way.

Some Necessary Kinds of Information

Figure 11-2 indicates that several kinds of information must be prepared during the final steps of the production prototype development.

A well-organized report of the test results is extremely important. Systems may be manufactured for many years. The original development people may be transferred to other work, become ill, retire, or go to work for another organization. After some years, the test report may contain almost the only available information about what went on during the production prototype development.   Should a modification of systems in the field or in production become necessary or desirable, a good report is an invaluable document.

The development organization must supply all of the necessary information so that the system can be produced and used.   Almost all of this information must be written, typed, or printed; only a small amount of supplementary information can be conveyed by oral communications, such as consulting or answering specific questions.

The input information for all the publications may come from many sources.

The overall system objectives
The chosen design plan and analysis results
The subsystem design objectives
Results of tests on the prototype subsystems and overall system
Production experience
Company policies

From the enormous amount of input information, a selection is made of items that will be useful to a particular group of people (for example, to the maintenance craftsmen).   Obviously, different groups may require different emphasis on particular aspects even though the basic information is almost identical.

Some of the information provided by the development people may be used to help train the people who actually produce, ship, install, operate, maintain, and sell the system.   Some may be used by the people who actually perform the function after their training period is over.

For uniformity of appearance, some companies specify the physical makeup of the publications in considerable detail.   A fairly standard outline may also be specified to help in the preparation and to ensure that all necessary information is included.   Other standards may define page sizes, and even page and column makeup, illustration sizes, and type faces.   They may even include a glossary of acceptable technical words with definitions.   Such careful attention to details is helpful in minimizing misunderstandings of the information the author intends to communicate.

Consulting is another aspect of development work that may go on for a long time after production of the system begins.   Questions are raised by the factory production people, by the installation forces, and by the users.

Answers (in other words, information) are given in response to questions that come up. Perhaps a question arises because the information available to the inquirer is not completely clear or because some new situation is encountered. Telephone calls are frequently used to get quick answers.

To come up with the right answer quickly requires good information retrieval. A good development man familiar with the system may "know" the answer. The wanted information is stored in his brain. Or he may be able to turn to the notes and measurements he made during the development. In some cases a question requires that tests be made on a system. To take care of such cases, the production prototype may be kept in working condition for many, many years after production starts.

Management Activities

As Figs. 11-1 and 11-2 indicate, management must make decisions and decisions—and still more decisions!

Various aspects of the decision-making function were discussed for system design. In prototype development, decisions must be made about resource allotments and about schedules. The progress must be monitored and compared with the planned use of resources, money, and time. Experience gained during the engineering prototype development usually makes it possible to allocate resources and set up time schedules for the production prototype with some confidence.

In the design phase, all of the human effort is directed to the processing of information. In prototype development, much effort is devoted to the production, assembly, testing, and modification of hardware. Some managers are more comfortable in evaluating progress in hardware than progress in handling information and ideas. After all, hardware can be seen, handled, and measured. To many people (including some managers) tests on actual hardware mean more than solutions of mathematical models of complex systems.

Management also must monitor the preparation of the necessary information about the system. Each kind of information must be ready when it is needed.

Management has the responsibility for releasing the system for production. This is an important decision because starting production means committing large amounts of resources, far more people and production facilities and larger amounts of money than are needed for development.

Time Scales

Development of an engineering prototype of a complex system is seldom possible in less than a year. Two, or even more years is not an unreasonable or infrequent interval.

The schedule for building and testing the production prototype of a complex system also may run from a year or less to several years. Information preparation may extend for another year after production is authorized. Good scheduling and careful monitoring of progress is necessary to insure that information is ready when it is needed for training people or for use by them in their work.

12

Production, Installation, Removal, Disassembly

Production, transportation, and installation are the major steps involved in getting a new system ready for use; removal and disassembly occur after it has served its purpose. In these phases, the actual objects composing the system are the focal points of the activities rather than any information gathering and processing. Information generated in the design and prototype steps tells what is to be produced by every operation. Information-handling is an important function in each of the five steps even though it is not the primary function.

The preliminaries for each of the steps follow the by-now familiar pattern of allotment of resources, organization, and planning.

At most, a modest number of prototype systems are made. In large-scale manufacture, thousands or even millions of systems may be built.

A constant worry of the development engineer: I have built one or two (or a few) prototypes of the new system. Manufacture involves large-scale production. How sure can I be that the manufactured systems will work satisfactorily? The rigorous answer is disquieting because any prediction involves inductive reasoning. That 1, 2, 3, . . . n systems have worked satisfactorily constitutes no proof that the $n + 1$ system will be satisfactory. Anyone with production-line experience knows that an operation apparently under complete control can suddenly go wild for no apparent reason.

In production, unit costs are very important because so many systems are involved. Production methods must be chosen for each object to minimize its cost. This means a selection of the best way to make the objects and to assemble them. Some manufacturing organizations, such as the Western Electric Company, have large groups of people that perform research and development work on new production methods. Free choice may not be possible because many tools are already available and must be used even though more suitable ones might be bought.

For large-scale production, some special tools may be necessary or desirable because they can keep costs down. The design of such new tools follows the usual sequence of the system design and the construction and test of a prototype. Seldom are many copies needed.

Special new jigs and gages may be necessary to inspect the product and insure its quality. Similarly, special testing equipment may be necessary for the installation forces, so that they can check the performance before the system is turned over to the user. The design of such equipment also follows the usual sequence.

For a new system, extensive personnel training may be necessary before production can start.

Management activities are also essential during each of the steps. No new kinds of activities beyond those already described are necessary. Moreover, the factors considered in making decisions are much the same. But the production, installation, and other people involved weigh the various factors quite differently. They are concerned with objects more than with ideas. They think and worry about rates of changing objects, about the numbers produced and assembled. They also worry about costs and schedules. For example, a lot of nonconforming parts from a supplier can be a minor catastrophe. A quick decision is necessary: shall we junk the parts, send them back to be reworked or repaired, or get permission from the development engineers to use them even though they do not meet specifications? Any alternative except the last is painful to the production man. Yet nonconforming parts almost surely will affect the performance. A production line shut down for lack of parts is visible to all. The overhead costs that go on despite no production output can spell trouble. Union relations may be far more important in the factory or at the installation site than in the relative calm of a research and development organization.

Production figures and schedules are sometimes easier for top management to understand and evaluate than any elegant mathematical model of a system. Costs and profits measured in dollars and cents are items on the balance sheet. Top management must be concerned with profits. New design ideas may be mentioned in the annual report, or they may not.

The production and installation organizations may be an important source of ideas and information about desirable design changes and improvements. These should be communicated to the development organization for action.

The problem of scheduling or balancing the diverse tasks of the workers on an assembly line has been attacked mathematically. Computer programs have been written for helping to solve some of these very difficult assembly-line problems. Also, inventory models can be used to determine the optimum batch sizes for parts made only intermittently rather than continuously as they are needed.

Clearly, an information input is necessary for the systems that change the objects. The information input may come from a measurement of the system. People may make some changes; others may be made by servomechanisms. The people must be trained; that is, they must be given information on how to perform their tasks and perhaps tested to be sure they understand.

Operating, Maintaining, and Modifying a Working System

Operation and maintenance are the activities involved in actual use of the system. Both involve *time variations of objects in the system.*

The mathematical techniques often grouped under the title of Operations Research (inventory theory, queing theory, game theory, linear and dynamic programming, among others) may be applied to obtain improved use of an existing system. If the system planning was well done, the attainable gains may not be large.

After they have been in service for a period, many systems are modified to incorporate improvements and bring them up-to-date. For example, the homeowner may change his heating plant from oil to gas or add air-conditioning. Information for the modification comes from outside the system.

Operation and maintenance require some allocation of resources. A new car requires a convenient place to park it when it is not in use. Some thought about the costs of gasoline, oil, and tires that must be included in the family budget is necessary. Some large systems require many thousands of operators and other thousands of maintenance people. Examples are the Bell Telephone System, airlines, and some missile complexes. Systems located away from populated centers such as radar system stations in remote parts of the world, may require that new housing be provided, and perhaps arrangements for feeding the personnel.

In planning the operation and maintenance activities, costs are almost always important. A management decision may be necessary whether to have the maintenance work done by the organization's own employees or by contract, or both. Plans must always be made for training the people who will operate and maintain the new system. As mentioned earlier, the basic training information is provided by the development organization responsible for the production prototype.

The time scales for operation and maintenance vary enormously. A missile is installed. It is then maintained in readiness for its mission for several or even many years. Hopefully, it will be removed without even being operated. If it should fly, its entire operating life is measured in minutes. A telephone central office has an operating life of thirty, forty, or even fifty years. Superb maintenance personnel and practices keep it in tip-top operating condition during the entire time.

Operation and maintenance require no new kinds of functions beyond those already described. Operation and adjustment of a working system was necessary during the development of the prototype systems. The maintenance function of testing and replacement of defective objects was also necessary during development.

Current Engineering and Updating

A new system design should be observed while it is in use to acquire information for improvements and for future designs. For example, the capabilities might be extended to meet new objectives. Then the system could furnish new services or tap new markets, or it might be adapted to changing or new environments.

Information might also be gained about unforeseen design weaknesses or faults that require correction. Sometimes the customer needs special assistance or consultation about some unusual operating or maintenance condition.

Based on the observations and customer's requests and comments, management can then consider whether an up-dating, a modification, or a new model is in order.

The automobile and a few other industries plan for yearly model changes. To a considerable extent the changes are really "face-lifting." Really major changes are made only at longer intervals. Enormous costs are incurred in making major changes, and these must be spread over several years of production.

In the major redesign, features of proven value can be retained. Known weaknesses can be corrected. Advances in the art can be exploited.

Questions of compatibility between the old and new systems can be troublesome. In the Bell Telephone system, every new central office must work with every existing office—a total of 15,000 or more. The two alternatives are:

1. Constrain the new design
2. Make reasonable modifications in the existing offices

The choice between the two is not always easy. Sometimes managers faced with the choice may envy automobile makers. After all, an epoch-making new 1968 model does not even have to work with a 1967—much less a 1957.

Often a "new" system replaces "old" systems over a period of time, perhaps measured in years. The old must be "phased out" and the new must be "phased in." How best to make such a gradual change may require study of possible alternative plans. The integration problem may be quite difficult if full service must be given during the changeover.

But sooner or later, a progressive management decides a new system is needed. Events have gone through the full cycle and we are now back to the system design step. We begin all over again and repeat each step in the life story of a new system.

13

The Systems Concept

History

As the word "system" is used in this book, systems are old indeed. They have been invented, planned, designed, and produced for many, many centuries. Men such as Archimedes and Leonardo da Vinci performed many of the functions of today's system planners and designers. True, some of today's systems are more complex. Some are spread over far larger areas. Some operate beyond the earth's atmosphere in outer space. But the fundamental design steps and functions are much the same today as they were in earlier centuries.

While systems have been used for centuries, the *systems concept* is only about twenty years old. This concept considers all the components of a bomber as one *weapons system* instead of separately as an airplane, an ordnance system, radars, bombing equipment, and many other systems. The system concept is useful because it integrates the separate requirements so that the resulting overall weapon system is optimized. Exactly what is included in a particular system concept is a question of definition. Thus a single bomber, a bomber wing, or even a bomber wing with all of its necessary ground support may be thought of as a weapon system.

Today's complex systems are assembled from objects obtained from many suppliers. For example, Western Electric Company is the manufacturing facility of the Bell Telephone System. It is an enormous organization with sales in the billions each year. Nevertheless, Western Electric purchases raw materials, parts, and subassemblies from several tens of thousands of supplies.

Partial Ordering of Steps in Time

The partial ordering of the several steps in the life of a system has already been pointed out. A somewhat similar partial ordering exists for the steps of system design, prototype development, and production.

Moreover, other activities such as advertising and selling are partially ordered. In every instance some steps must occur before others. For example, it is always necessary to go through the preliminaries of allotting resources and of putting an organization together or re-orienting some existing organization. Some planning must take place to give direction to the effort.

Management activities are also partially ordered. A decision to start precedes a decision to continue or stop.

Ordering occurs for two reasons:

1. The next step can not start until certain information becomes available. Plans can be held up because of missing data. Parts cannot be made without adequate drawings.

2. The next step can not start because of some physical reason. For example, some assemblies can not be welded together until all parts are available.

Ordering is not complete because some steps can either precede or follow others. Thus, the design of subsystems can often be carried on consecutively or simultaneously or some of each alternative.

To shorten a schedule, in some cases it is possible to start work before the organization is complete, or alternative plans are thoroughly analyzed, or all necessary objects are available for assembly. Such tactics are designed to "telescope time."

Telescoping may involve hazards. Of course, a selection between alternatives can be made before the facts are available by using human "judgment." Such a "judgment" is merely a special kind of decision. It certainly is not "prejudging" as described by the words "My mind is made up. Do not confuse me with facts." Judgment takes the alternative courses and estimates the outcome of choosing each one. Sometimes the right choice is made; sometimes, not. Taking chances can save time but it may be dangerous because a wrong choice can both lose time and increase costs.

Information and Systems

Design and management control functions involve information retrieval plus information processing. Both are information-handling operations. Objects are not important except when they are used to store or process information.

If necessary information does not exist or can not be retrieved, then it must be gathered by observing or measuring physical objects.

In other system functions, objects are involved. They are changed, assembled, transported, operated, and maintained. Every operation on an object requires an information input to an appropriate system to make the change.

In system development, the wanted result of the effort is information in the form of drawings, specifications, and instructions. In production, the wanted result is physical systems. But here also an information output is necessary: information about numbers produced, costs, and rates. The people who operate and maintain a system must have information about the way to perform their tasks.

Thus information gathering, information processing, and information communication play key roles in the life story of any system from its conception to its removal. More complex systems increase the necessary amounts of information. And as human knowledge increases, the problems will increase because our knowledge always lags behind our needs to know.

Clearly, large and complex systems are designed, produced, operated, and maintained by many different people. For even a rather small system such as a particular electric refrigerator model, the number may be in the hundreds of thousands. Person-to-person communication of the tremendous volume of information about a system is impossible for many obvious reasons. Yet the tremendous volume must be handled. Further, all the people who need particular information must receive it; for example, every purchaser of a Ford or Chevrolet receives an operator's manual.

Requirements for Error-free Information

Error-free reproduction and transmission are further requirements. These requirements are usually met by carefully checking an original or master copy in some graphic form such as engineering drawings and illustrations, or pamphlets, brochures, or books. Reproduction of graphic material causes relatively few errors due to smudges or broken type. Visual inspection can discard most poor copies. Hand-to-hand transmission of such copies can be used if it is needed to ensure delivery. An occasional copy sent by mail may be lost or mutilated. In such cases, another copy can be requested. The would-be receiver has to wait, but the transmission is error-free.

Training for System Planners

Today, a complex military or space system (such as a new missile system) is planned and designed by teams made up of our largest corporations. No one corporation has enough trained people with all the necessary kinds of knowledge.

It has already been pointed out that the life of a complex system from conception to removal of the last survivor may span several decades.

From these facts, it follows that few, if any, planners or designers have had the opportunity to be concerned in depth with all phases of the life of even one complex system.

What will the future bring? Today, most engineers and designers hold several different jobs during their careers. Even so, they come in contact with only a handful of systems during a working lifetime. Some engineers in the Bell Telephone Laboratories have spent the entire time from graduation from college to retirement working on one or two switching systems.

Organization charts show that for each system planner, hundreds—even thousands—of people are necessary in other tasks during the life of a system: management, development, production, maintenance, and use.

Yet, the success or failure of a new system concept depends on competence of the broad system planning—on skillful synthesis and careful, searching analysis. This need for competence means that severe requirements must be met by the people who do the planning. They must have or acquire familiarity with all the pertinent background information necessary to synthesize the new system. They must select the best alternative. To do so, they must be aware of the right set of values and know how to apply them

These requirements for system planners in turn set very high standards for their training and background. Few, if any, university graduates can meet these requirements until they have acquired experience with the particular kinds of systems they are called upon to plan. When it comes to foreseeing possible troubles, experience is the best teacher.

14

A Procedure for System Design

Definitions

By definition, a *system* is a set of components arranged for some wanted operation. In the systems under consideration, the wanted operation always involves changing a physical object or objects. The word *wanted* is significant, because it indicates that someone must conceive the wanted operation. Thus, conceiving the want is the first step in any system design.

A *problem* exists when someone desires a certain state of affairs and does not immediately know how to attain it. Some initial knowledge is always available, but with a real problem, the knowledge about how to proceed is imperfect or (at best) incomplete. There may be insufficient technical knowledge, or inability to visualize the relationships of all design variables, or inadequate data.

A problem-solving process uses the available knowledge to start an exploration, which discloses more knowledge, which causes more exploration, and so on, until a solution is discovered. Each step in the design process receives repeated attention.

But a satisfactory definition of *system problem* involves more than the separate meanings of the words *system* and *problem*. A system design problem actually takes the following form: Given a specification which lists the desired properties of the system, produce a document which describes an optimum (or close to optimum) realization of these properties.

The data specifying the set of inputs and outputs gives an abstract description of the desired system performance. These data should include any relevant information about the distribution in space and time of the inputs and acceptable tolerances for the outputs. The data may be in the form of curves, numbers or letters, words, or a combination of these.

Depending on the problem, the output or the system properties or both may (and preferably should be) at least partially ordered as:

1. Essential, e.g., certain system properties, maximum acceptable cost, or latest delivery time.

2. Desirable but not essential.

In practice, much more information must be obtainable than is included in the specification. This information often is drawn from relevant past experience.

The desired properties of the wanted system (i.e., the specification) may arise in at least three ways:

1. They may be chosen *in toto* by a man or men; for example, an appropriate specification may be determined by a survey of customer preferences.

2. Some may be chosen by a man or men, and the rest of the required information may be derived by computation or by a "hunch" or "feeling" of a man or men. This is a usual method for setting up a preliminary specification.

3. The source of the required information may be chosen by a man or men and the actual information acquired by information retrieval—perhaps executed by a computer.

The Sixteen Kinds of System Design Problems

Table 14-1 can be used to classify systems design problems. An initial object, the raw material, is to be changed into a wanted "final" object by the operation of the information source and the system. A system problem arises when one or more of the four items are given and the remainder are to be found.

Table 14-1 lists the sixteen possible kinds of problems. In Cases 1 to 4, one of the four items is given; in Cases 5 to 10, two; in Cases 11 to 14, three. Each of the sixteen cases can be shown to represent a familiar kind of system design problem.

Thus, Case 1 represents a "manufacturing" design problem. Stated in words, the problem is to find a suitable raw material and processes to make a wanted object. It may be divided into finding:

1. A suitable raw material. The choice may depend on the system available to process it, or vice versa.

2. A set of ordered changes to convert the raw material into the wanted object.

3. A set of effectors to make the changes.

4. A set of molecular systems to control the effectors.

5. A set of information inputs for the molecular systems.

Table 14-1

Case	Final Object	Initial Object	System	Information Source
1	G(iven)	F(ind)	F	F
2	F	G	F	F
3	F	F	G	F
4	F	F	F	G
5	G	G	F	F
6	G	F	G	F
7	G	F	F	G
8	F	G	G	F
9	F	G	F	G
10	F	F	G	G
11	G	G	G	F
12	G	G	F	G
13	G	F	G	G
14	F	G	G	G
15	G	G	G	G
16	F	F	F	F

Figure 8-11 showed an input object changed into the wanted object by a sequence of processes executed in time. The overall change may be broken down into a set of functional blocks. The set may have ordering or other constraints.

Assembly of two or more objects into a structure or the disassembly or tear-down of a structure can be considered as special examples of Case 1. Given a set of objects, the assembly problem is to combine them so they form the wanted assembly. In tear-down, the objects are separated. In either assembly or tear-down, an information source and information-handling arrangement must direct the operation.

When the input and output objects are specified, the only possibilities are:

1. Choice of functional blocks.
2. Method of executing each function.
3. Ordering of functional blocks.

For each function, the required amount of information can be specified, so that an appropriate information control can be drawn. Differences in the methods or the ordering may affect the information requirements and vice versa.

To solve the manufacturing problem it is necessary to have:

1. A set of possible raw materials, or available subassemblies.
2. A set of possible effectors to change the raw material.
3. Information about constraints on physical realizability. These may be ordering rules or other constraints.
4. Cost and reliability data for each possible raw material.
5. A set of decision rules to govern choices between alternatives.
6. A set of algorithms* for any necessary computations.
7. A program of ordered steps to be taken in the design procedure.

In a communication system, the input information is changed by a sequence of processes distributed in space and delivered to the destination. With some obvious changes in wording, the seven items necessary to solve a manufacturing design problem apply.

Case 2 represents the *utilization* problem. A process produces a by-product which is not immediately useful. The problem is to find a suitable use. Finding uses for blast-furnace slag is an example.

Case 3 represents the *idle-machine* problem. For example, a machine shop's lathe is waiting for any work it can do to convert a raw material into a wanted object.

To direct the work, appropriate information about the wanted objects must be supplied—perhaps in the form of drawings. Furthermore, a trained operator must set up the objects in the lathe, direct the cuts, and remove a completed object.

Case 4 represents the *information presentation* problem. Here, some phenomenon is to be measured and displayed on a meter scale or on an oscilloscope screen.

In the six cases 5 to 10, two items are given and two are to be found. Such problems may be easier than the first four cases, but only if the given items are suitable for producing the wanted result. Otherwise, a solution may be impossible, as when the raw material is completely unsuitable for making the wanted object. A silk purse can not be made out of a sow's ear.

In Case 11, the problem is to provide the information to direct a process—for example, to direct the successive cuts of a machine tool to produce a wanted object. An appropriate information format must be devised and the actual information to direct the tool movements must be provided. For cost reasons, it may be a requirement that the information or the machining time be a minimum.

In the three cases 12 to 14, three items are given and one is to

---

* An algorithm is an *effective* computational procedure.

be found.   The observations for Cases 5 to 10 apply with even greater emphasis.

Case 15 is trivial.   Everything is given, so there is no problem. Similarly, Case 16 is trivial because nothing is given.

A design procedure should apply to any of the nontrivial problems.

Purposes of Designs

The purpose of a design is to create a system to satisfy the specification; conform to applicable standards; use materials and labor economically; and sometimes, be pleasing in appearance.

A design may be required for one or more of many reasons, for example, to:

1. Set up a product line to satisfy most prospective users.   The set of designs may have a family resemblance and, where possible, use the same components.

2. Study the effect on cost and performance of changing the standards or specifications of the entire product line.

3. Satisfy one rating of a standard line.   Many designs may be made before an order is received.

4. Study the economics of changing the number, kinds, or ordering of "building-block" components.

5. Study the effect of using new materials, processes, or manufacturing tools.

6. Estimate physical characteristics and cost to permit a competitive bid.   An exacting specification may require a fairly detailed design.

7. Plan a system to perform some quite new operation.   The specification may be rather sketchy and any numbers only approximate.

What System Design Involves

A particular system design involves:

1. A choice of suitable objects or subassemblies with appropriate (mechanical, electrical, etc.) properties.

2. A choice of suitable stresses for materials used in objects and subassemblies.

3. Consideration of the operation under normal and anticipated abnormal conditions.

4. In some designs, a choice or derivation of formulas for computations of stresses and characteristics.

5. In some design problems, calculations of such things as numbers of components required, dimensions of components, performance in the usual environment and under abnormal conditions, reliability, and cost.

6. Comparing alternate designs (if such exist)

7. Deciding by a rule or rules to accept or reject any tentative solution.

In its broadest sense, design involves translating a specification into a form which describes the wanted system and its performance in sufficient detail for intended purposes of the design.

The complete solution of a system design problem may be divided into synthesis, analysis, and selection—in other words, into obtaining a tentative solution or solutions, checking, and selecting the best alternative.

Synthesis involves finding a way or ways to provide all the wanted operations. The really significant problem in the synthesis of a new system is to find a suitable collection of functional blocks. This problem may be subdivided into two problems:

1. Finding *any* collection that can perform all the functions and meets the specified requirements. To find such a collection, the available information must be found, organized, and classified. Any tentative collection must be analyzed and checked to make sure that it meets all of the requirements.

2. Reducing the results of (1) to the collection to be used for the final phase of the design process. The problem here is to achieve an optimum design. This fundamental principle is involved in almost every design selection among alternatives.

Optimizing a part of a system (sometimes called *suboptimization*) does not necessarily improve overall system performance. Suboptimizing may increase the total cost of the system or degrade some desired system property. Nor does optimizing all the parts individually always result in an overall optimum. Good system design seeks an overall optimum. Hence, suboptimization should be avoided.

Some quantity (or quantities) can be used to compare alternative solutions by either maximizing or minimizing some quantity, e.g., time, dollar cost, weight, or reliability. Instead of a single maximum or minimum there may be a range of acceptable values.

The selection of the best of several alternatives can be based on a comparison of the values of the quantities chosen for the purpose.

System Inputs

The system inputs may be (1) always of the same kind or of many kinds, (2) periodic (or infrequent) or randomly distributed in time, (3) intended to destory the system or not so intended.

Single and Multiple Kinds of Inputs

If the input is always the same, the system always responds in the same way. The designer determines the response. For example, the input to a punch press may always be the same type of raw material. The time between inputs is under design control. It can be made equal to or longer than the operation time.

For two or more kinds of inputs, a decision-making device must determine the proper output. The system complexity tends to increase with the number of kinds of inputs.

Input Time Distribution

If the system operation time is less than the shortest time between inputs, inputs can be handled as they arrive.

If the inputs are statistically distributed in time, the operation time may be longer than the shortest possible time between inputs. Then a queue, or waiting line, must form. The queue length later shortens when the input spacing lengthens. The possible design choices are: (1) a waiting place, (2) more systems, or (3) faster response.

At a turnpike toll gate, the inputs are always the same: passenger automobiles. The input arrival times are distributed statistically. Queues may form.

If the average time interval between inputs is less than the operation time, either faster operation or more systems must be provided to handle the inputs; otherwise the queue continues to lengthen for an indefinite time.

Competitive Inputs

Competitive systems may operate in different ways for identical inputs. In an air-defense system, the attacking force (inputs) is not always the same. The enemy may use missiles of several kinds as well as decoys. The input times are statistically distributed and may be intended to overload the defense system. And the enemy intent is destruction of the system.

Competitive systems must resolve conflicts in decision-making and operation time areas. The commander may be forced to make a decision based on his available resources rather than on what he would like to be able to do. Business decisions in a competitive economy are similarly affected. It follows that the response to a particular input may not always be predictable. In a well-designed and determined system, unpredictable response occurs only in response to competitive inputs.

Inputs with Low Probability

Some systems may have certain kinds of relatively infrequent inputs. Provision for their possible occurrences may lead to high costs. Analysis can often indicate the best trade-off. Too great a weight should not be given to improbable occurrences. It may be possible to arrange a system so that an improbable input sets off a signal for a human being to take over.

In a military situation, an input cannot be assigned a negligibly small probability, unless the enemy cannot control the probablility.

Steps in Analysis of Input Conditions

It is important to understand the effects of any possible set of inputs or sequence of inputs on the operation of a system. Recognition of this fact, has led Goode and Machol to describe three steps in the analysis of a tentative design:

1. Single-thread analysis. Operation with a single input of each possible kind so the designer understands exactly what the system will do to every possible kind of input.

2. High-traffic analysis. Operation with simultaneous inputs or many responses to inputs.

3. Competitive analysis. Methods of combating an agent trying to destroy system effectiveness. Reliability problems can come under this class. The pertinent mathematical tool is game theory.

Some system analyses involve all three steps.

Some Principles of Design

The principles of design are those technical, practical, and sometimes appearance factors that guide the setting up of design practices and the making of design decisions. Some principles may apply only to a particular product; others may be quite general.

Many design principles and procedures are independent of the size or complexity of a system. Newton's ideas on gravitation apply to a marble dropping to the ground or to the planets in the solar system. A very small system may have as few as ten components; an extremely large system, perhaps a million. Thus, the range is about five orders of magnitude. But in the system with a million components, not all of the components will be different, so the actual range may be nearer two or three orders of magnitude. Viewed in this way, complexity may not be intractible—if basic principles are used in design.

System design has often been treated as an art. The successful practitioners have been "old hands" in experience, and often in years. Part of the reason lies in the fact that it is sometimes as difficult to specify what is to be designed as to do the design. Further, it is necessary to include in the specification (and consider during the design) enough detail about the system environment so no undue stress or incompatibility arises. But it is always necessary to keep overall requirements in mind. Few designers have the necessary insight and experience until they have been out of the university for some years.

For an established product, the principles and design rules may be put in a "standard-practice" book. Such a book may list such things as formulas and structures to be used, standards to be met, and available manufacturing tools. Standard practices may change as a result of new developments, standards, ideas, and market requirements.

One important concept in design may be called *The Principle of Minimum Commitment*. This general principle may be stated: At each stage in synthesizing the design of a system, make no commitment beyond that necessary to solve the problem at hand. Care to observe the principle leaves all possible ways open for attacking other problems as they arise.

Extent of Novelty Involved in a Design

Some system design problems call for the design of a "completely new" system. But the design of even a completely new system can only use existing information. Any lack of existing or available information must be remedied before the design can be completed. The amount of pertinent information about a completely new system may be nearly zero and, further, may be unavailable, as, for example, information about a suitable transportation system for the possible inhabitants of Venus.

A "new" system may closely resemble a "well-known" system. For example, a special motor may bear a family resemblance to a standard motor. In an extreme case, a "new" design may differ only trivially from an existing one (for example, in the color). Therefore, there are many different degrees of "newness."

Steps in System Design

A satisfactory theory of system design should furnish a procedure (which might be loosely called an algorithm) for solving a design problem. Stated formally, the system problem is: given a set of data contained in a source document (specification), produce a second document describing the wanted system. In preparing the set of output data, relevant information is an important factor.

It will become evident that system design divides into three quite different kinds of tasks: (1) finding a set or sets of suitable devices which can jointly perform the wanted system functions, (2) making calculations of various kinds, and (3) deciding between alternatives.

When stated in this way it becomes obvious that system design is an information-handling problem. It changes an input "list" into an output "list."

The design of a system to perform a new set of functions can be divided into two quite distinct steps. In the first step, the feasibility of constructing the wanted system is carefully examined, and the most promising organization of subsystems is selected. In this book, this step is called "system design." Some other authors who have written about it have called it "system planning" or "preliminary design." In the second step, further and much more detailed design work results in drawings and other information for the construction and assembly of one or more copies of an engineering prototype of the system. In this book, such design work is considered to be part of the engineering prototype development. Elsewhere, it has been called part of the "systems development" or the "final design phase."

Definition of a Design Flow Chart

The flow chart of Fig. 14-1 shows a procedure for solving a system design problem. This flow chart is a graphic representation of the steps by which information from a source document (specification)

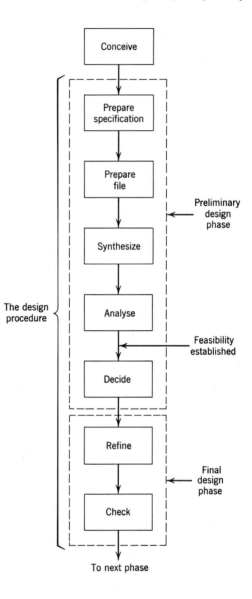

Figure 14-1

is converted into output documents (description of a system design). The procedure is put into the form of the "flow chart" with the expectation that many steps can be programmed for a computer.

The flow chart divides the steps of the design algorithm or procedure into well-defined tasks and specifies their order. It shows what tasks must be done at each step rather than how to perform them. In other words, it is a program for designing a new system or part of a system.

This new flow chart is made up of a few kinds of simple blocks—one for each kind of step in the procedure. It is possible to specify the type of information needed to perform the function called for by each kind of block, as will be shown in later chapters. There are only a few fundamental kinds of functions. Thus, a reasonable-sized tabulation of the best available methods for performing each function is possible.

For quite good reasons this flow chart differs in intent from the type of flow chart familiar to computer programmers. A computer-type flow chart places more emphasis on the documents involved than on the work steps through which they pass. In other words, such a computer-type flow chart shows what job is to be done. The flow chart to be presented emphasizes the work steps in solving a design problem rather than the documents involved. We shall later discuss the requirement to "mechanize" the steps called for by the flow chart.

Present-day computers can solve preformulated problems and process data by using predetermined procedures. Further, the exact program can depend on results obtained during a computation. However, because a computer is a very stupid machine, all possible alternatives must be foreseen.

The tasks in the design of a new system can be divided into three categories: (1) those that a computer can perform, (2) those that require human intervention, and (3) those that either may do.

No claim is made that a human being would necessarily solve a systems problem in accord with the flow chart. But the mechanization shows that certain information must be made available to a computer before it can do so.

Generality of the Procedure

No part of the procedure depends on the complexity of the system being designed. Therefore, the procedure is equally applicable at all levels of complexity. It can be applied in the design of a complex system, or of a subassembly. Also, the procedure is applicable whether the problem is in the research, development, or some other design area.

Value of the Procedure in System Design

The procedure states the system design problem in abstract terms, so all problems can be attacked by the same procedure. It also

1. Orders the design steps.
2. Indicates the kinds of information needed to solve a design problem, and the questions the designer must ask and answer.
3. Shows that solution can be made to depend on a successful file search, logical operations, and computations rather than on inspiration. However, sufficient information must exist and be discoverable by the search method used. Otherwise, a design is impossible.

In principle, a computer can make the file search, perform logical operations and do computing. Difficulties exist—but they are not insurmountable. The computer point of view can be useful, even though no machine is used. Thus, the flow chart can be a procedure for a designer to follow. On the other hand, it can be the first step toward a computer program. For certain types of product, a computer can do most of the design job. Thus, computers have been used to design power transformers both in the U.S. and abroad.

Usefulness in General Problem Solving

As one possible by-product of a design algorithm, a procedure useful in solving system design problems may also be an approach to general problem solving. Despite the temptation, we have not yet applied it to more general problems.

Another possible by-product may be in teaching system design and system engineering. At present, teaching the "art" of designing complex systems and subsystems (as opposed to individual circuits, components, etc.) is very difficult. If a procedure can be worked out that will shorten the apprenticeship of system designers, it will be an important step.

Requirements for "Solvability" of System Design Problems

Introduction

A usual system design situation can be summarized in the words: "I have a problem. The problem is not yet completely formulated. What characteristics must the formulation have for the problem to be solvable?"

A *solution* to a problem should have the following properties:

1. An action taken as a result of the solution must compare favorably with other possible actions.
2. The action must be clearly defined with no ambiguities.
3. The solution must not contain problems as complex as (or more complex than) the original problem.

In practice, it may be necessary to settle for solutions that are less than ideal.

Feasibility of Solving a System Problem

To be solvable, the problem must be capable of being completely described in a set of terms (for example, words or numbers) and a set of relations between the terms. The relations may be arithmetic or logical.

In particular, a problem is solvable if the following are available:

1. A set of variables expressed in words or numbers or letters or some combination of these.
2. A set of relations among the variables.
3. An algorithm for arriving at a well-defined and satisfactory solution.

Thus, if a system problem is in the form of a set of equations and if the equations are solvable, then the problem is solvable.

Actually, these requirements merely say that the problem is solvable if the system is feasible and enough information is available.

What Is Not Solvable

In general, what sort of problem, if any, is not solvable? As one example, Gödel's theorem states than any axiom system within which an arithmetic can be developed is incomplete. In other words, given any consistent set of arithmetical axioms, some true arithmetical state-

ments cannot be derived from the axioms. In other words, for su
problems, a proper algorithm cannot be provided.

Such a situation is unlikely in system design. A system specificatio
starts with accepted realities. The design of a complex system ca
be difficult. However, a proposed solution can usually be checke
against physical facts. If either the specification or the availab
information is inadequate, or if an algorithm produces wrong or r
results, the failure becomes apparent. With some abstract problem
—for example, a problem in esthetics—a failure might be difficult o
impossible to demonstrate.

Steps in the Design Procedure

Conceiving and Stating the Problem

A human being must recognize and need the new or improved sy
tem. Here, as well as later, the word human or human being
used to mean one or more persons. A design problem then aris
because of such unanswered questions as: Is something beyond prese
techniques? inconvenient? incomplete? too expensive? too unr
liable? too inaccurate? too time-consuming? too ugly? Such d
ficiencies point out the need for or a way to a new or improved syste
that meets some real need.

After a need has been found, it is necessary to state it clearl
This statement, the definition of the problem, is actually a specifica
tion which the design must meet.

In defining the problem two common difficulties are (1) the inabilit
to isolate the problem and (2) narrowing the problem too muc
In the first case the problem is too broad; in the second, not broa
enough.

Before going very far, it is always necessary for a human bein
to determine whether the need warrants action and whether a suitab
design seems possible. Some systems are just not worth designin
A human being must decide to start the design effort and alloca
the necessary resources.

Synthesis

The first step in deciding a course of action about a proposal
to see whether it is sound. To permit a decision on this point, feas
bility must be determined. An examination or technical estimatio
is made to see whether the system is physically realizable.

A search can be made for an existing system that meets the specification. Presumably such a system will not be found if a new set of functions is to be performed.

If a suitable system is not found, then it is necessary to synthesize one or more tentative sets of subsystems to form the complete system. Each subsystem in a set is intended to perform particular functions and is assigned a part of the overall system's tolerances. An acceptable set of subsystems must perform all of the required functions of the overall system. Moreover, each subsystem must be necessary for the overall system operation.

A search can be made for ways to realize each subsystem in a tentative set of subsystems. For each subsystem not found by the search, one or more tentative sets of subsubsystems must be synthesized, and a search made again. Subdivision and search are continued until some acceptable subassembly is found for each subdivided function. Otherwise, each realizable subfunction can be synthesized from a combination of the blocks described in Chapter 7.

A particular organization may not be feasible because suitable materials or devices are not known or not available. Under these circumstances, tentative requirements can be prepared for what is necessary. To make it available may require research, invention, or modification or extension of existing art. If it can not be made available, then the system requirements must be changed or the proposed system must be abandoned.

In the synthesis, the design questions that may arise concern possible alternate divisions of the system functions, alternate locations of functions in various subsystems, and possibly alternate ordering of the performance of functions.

Once a suitable set of subsystems has been determined, the control information requirements can be determined.

The result of synthesis is one or more alternative organizations of subsystems which seem to meet the requirements. An organization is often represented graphically by a block diagram of the subsystems. Design requirements are implied for each system making up an overall organization.

Design synthesis entails searching for information, comparing and integrating data, and logical decisions. Searching, comparing, and deciding involve little use of advanced mathematics. However, much time and considerable ingenuity may be required to figure out suitable functional arrangements. The procedure involves several mental processes, intuition, and judgment.

During the synthesis, the designer seldom has to solve complex mathematical equations, such as to analyze fields, invert matrices etc. He may perform simple but lengthy calculations (possibly with a slide rule).

Analysis

Analysis may involve an examination or estimate of each alternative synthesis to see whether theoretical limitations would make a tentative synthesis unrealizable.

For example, no system can violate the laws for the conservation of energy or the bandwidth-time relationships required for information transmission. Calculation may help to determine physical realizability. Chemical theory can help determine any chemical aspects.

Possible interactions of two or more subsystems (i.e., lack of independence of functions) must be examined.

The required number of each type of block should be determined—at least approximately.

Other studies estimate the approximate size, weight, and other physical factors to see whether they are likely to be acceptable. For some systems the effect of infrequent inputs or overload conditions must be checked. Performance under competitive conditions may require investigation.

Unless the analysis shows no alternative is feasible, the likelihood of a feasible system is established.

If the new system appears to be technically feasible, there may be one or more than one way to accomplish it.

When the required information about important criteria becomes available, the most promising alternative can be selected.

Management can then decide *whether further work and expense is economically justifiable* in comparison with possible financial and other returns. It can also decide *when* to proceed. The design and construction of a development prototype system requires far more time and effort than the system design. Hence, it is not done unless considered very likely to be worthwhile or necessary.

The analysis of a proposed design differs from the synthesis because: (1) most calculations are essentially mathematical with few logical decisions and (2) many rules and formulas for calculation are available from such sources as textbooks and manuals of standard practices.

If there is only one way, then management must decide to adopt the one way or drop the project.

If there is more than one way, then the best alternative must be selected. Almost always, there are alternative ways to achieve the wanted performance.

A rational choice between various alternatives requires information about some suitable criterion such as cost (initial cost or annual charges), performance, reliability in service, or some other factor—perhaps appearance.

To gain the necessary information, computations may be made so that the estimated performance can be compared with the specification. Preliminary cost estimates can be made. For the first cost, the estimated number of each type of component multiplied by the price of each can be summed to obtain the grand total. If annual charges are important, then first costs can be converted to annual charges by appropriate tables.

In the analysis of a proposed design, any details not believed likely to affect the choice may be given only casual consideration. The major attention is concentrated on the significant criteria. Further, at this stage extremely accurate estimates are seldom possible or necessary.

Moreover, in a product business, some designs are made for systems that may never be built. For example, a customer's inquiry may require preliminary estimates of cost or performance.

Engineering Prototype Synthesis

When the design work for the engineering prototype is authorized, presumably the feasibility of the system is established. Also, the overall system has been broken down into a set of subsystems that are believed to be realizable. Tentative specifications have been set up for each subsystem.

In the design work for the engineering prototype, the functional blocks on the system diagram must be realized by actual hardware that meets the specifications. Such components as amplifiers, motors, and gear boxes must be purchased or constructed.

To locate suitable subassemblies and components, another search is necessary. Hopefully, all of the necessary hardware is found to be available. For many items, alternatives are found.

Any missing items must be invented or developed. Otherwise, a different set of subsystems may be synthesized. The information about missing hardware may be incorporated in the overall system specification as another constraint. However, the system may not be feasible because all the necessary items are not known or are not available. Without them, a working prototype can not be constructed. For really new systems, material and device properties determine whether the system can be built.

If a system can not be built, then it is best forgotten until advances in the state of the art justify another try. Alternatively, the concepts may be used for a good science-fiction yarn.

Engineering Prototype Analysis

Subassemblies and devices for further investigation may be selected from alternative possibilities on an appropriate basis such as cost, reliability, or delivery date.

In actual practice, a "new" design may be a variation or modest extrapolation of a standard design already in production. Much so-called engineering design is of this type, as, for example, the design of a new transformer.

Standard-sized laminations are used for the core and standard sizes of copper wire for the windings. A modest number of kinds of insulation can be considered and a few styles of cases and terminals. The factory is already equipped with winding machines, and assembly methods are standardized. Despite these constraints, a very large number of combinations of such factors as core material, number of laminations, wire sizes, primary and secondary turns, and case sizes are possible. Long and tedious computations may be necessary to work out even a dozen tentative designs that can be built economically.

After information is available about promising alternative designs, a choice can be made using the criteria contained in the specification.

The final output is the record of the design effort and the drafting and manufacturing information for the prototype. The information is sufficiently detailed so that one or more prototypes can be built. Of course, changes in the information may be found essential or desirable by the builders. Except for action on such proposed changes, the design is complete when all the information has been released.

The Specification

Desired Performance

For any design problem, a specification of what is wanted is necessary. It should list the functions that the new system should perform. The specification may be vague (e.g., increase company profits over the next 20 years) or quite detailed (e.g., exact performance characteristics for an object to be manufactured). Frequently, it is initially rather vague and is made more precise as the design work proceeds. Essential requirements missing in the initial specification must sooner or later be obtained by the designer.

The specification must be consistent and detailed enough to yield some headings for a search of a file of available resources.

Tolerances

Practical system components show variations in performance. In a particular practical system, variations may or may not be important, but the consequences of variations must always be understood. For this reason, the specification must state the limits on the acceptable performance. For example, a particular performance characteristic should be within $\pm 1\%$ of a value; another characteristic, always less than some value.

As a further example, the performance of a particular mechanical system may be degraded by:

Class A errors due to fabrication tolerances, such as bearing play, misalignment, friction, improper calibration, or other mechanical shortcomings.

Class B errors arising from assumptions or approximations in the mathematical analysis or improper statement of the physical problem.

Class C human errors caused by improper system operation.

Limits for total error should be specified, as well as for each class of error and the relative importance of a given amount of each class of error.

Inputs and Outputs

Information about inputs and outputs should include the number of kinds (including both wanted and unwanted), the number of each kind, and time and space distributions.

If the range of values over which each input and output is expected to vary is not contained in the specification, such information must be supplied during the design. Of course, one kind of input is the energy from information sources.

System Transfer Function

If possible, the mathematical relation between inputs and outputs should be given, perhaps in the form of an equation. If an explicit mathematical relationship cannot be given, experimental data may be

substituted. If the wanted imput-output relation is not in the specification, it may be supplied in the course of the design.

Other Requirements

A specification may include requirements such as acceptable dimensions, weight, cost, and reliability. Some requirements may be
only a minimum or maximum value as, for example, volume less
than 1 cubic foot, weight less than 100 pounds, cost less than $500,
and average life minimum 1 year.

There are many kinds of costs, or charges, and prices associated
with systems. For example:

1. The manufacturer must consider the raw materials or costs of
system components, labor for its production, and research, design, and
development costs.

2. A buyer must consider the price he must pay.

3. An operator must consider repair part costs, labor costs for operators, maintenance costs, and depreciation.

Some or even all of these kinds may enter into the specification.

For particular systems, other requirements (such as appearance)
may have to be considered.

Some specifications may omit some or all such criteria. For example, some consumer goods may have no reliability criteria. In
other cases, performance may be so important that cost is no
limitation.

Constraints

Some requirements constrain the design. Thus, the classification
of system problems into sixteen categories shows that components
or functional building blocks may sometimes be specified, and sometimes are to be worked out by the designer. As another example,
an electrical or mechanical system may be specified. For subsystems
that are part of a complex system, compatibility with other subsystems
may be of great importance. For an addition to an existing system,
any constraints necessary for compatibility of the new functions with
the old must be specified.

For systems that must furnish extremely reliable performance, the
choice of devices may be severely restricted. No new and untried
devices can even be considered unless there is no other alternative.
For example, well-understood devices and conservative design are used
in deep-sea telephone cables because any failure both interrupts service
and requires expensive repairs.

Environment

All pertinent aspects of the environment in which the system is to operate should be stated in the specification. If not already known, they must be ascertained.

File of Information about Available Resources

A file of information about available resources plays a major role in system design.

The specification and the file must be expressed in a compatible vocabulary so they can be compared for matches. Making the vocabularies compatible is a task for a human being.

The necessary amount of information about available resources varies. The design of a simple system might require very little; of a complex system, thousands of items.

Today, designer's "files" are not too well organized for efficient searching. The available "files" may include his memory of past jobs, a personal file of memoranda, technical books and magazines, or, indeed, the Library of Congress. For well-established product lines, designers can draw heavily on a "standard-practice" book. Such a book may contain results of earlier designs. If such pertinent information is not available, then the "experts" are consulted. These are the more experienced designers, development engineers, and specialists in particular areas.

The file should contain the table of functional blocks given in Chapter 7. The blocks are a useful tool in synthesizing a subsystem.

In addition, the file contents should include lists of effectors, raw materials,* sensors, power controls, and power sources.

The list of effectors might be arranged alphabetically by name. Pertinent information about each effector might include: physical changes produced; requirements on inputs and outputs; size, weight, cost, and so on; advantages and disadvantages; special comments relevant to use; and references to other information.

It should be possible to retrieve information from the file when given either an effector name or a wanted physical change.

The other lists might be similarly organized.

---

* Raw materials and effectors are closely related. The two lists may contain some of the same material differently arranged.

Search for Available Resources

Unless a random search of the "file" of information about available resources is permissible, an order of search is necessary. For several obvious reasons, a truly random search is seldom permissible. Hence, rules for efficient searching are highly desirable. For example, it is very desirable that requirements be ordered from essential to less important.

A search based on a few essential requirements permits putting aside the less favorable alternatives without further ado. For example, if costs are very important, many alternatives can be ruled out because they cost too much. Similarly, if reliability is very important, many alternatives can be ruled out because the reliability is inadequate.

Further search on the basis of less important requirements is needed only for the alternatives that meet the essential requirements.

Decision Rules

The available information must include rules for accepting or rejecting any item located in the file search. Some rules may be quantitative, such as tolerances expressed in numbers. Rules must also be available for ordering the items tentatively accepted during the file search.

Then, to choose between alternatives, decision rules must be available. Such rules may be stated in the specification as "objectives"—for example, light weight or low cost. Other and sometimes subconscious rules are often called "designer's judgment." For example, in a particular system certain mechanical components may be rated by proneness to cause error. The ratings might even depend on the exact application. Experienced designers can and do make such ratings.

Suppose, for instance, that a system must minimize the sum of "properly weighted" Class A, B, and C errors. These classes were explained earlier. The "weights" reflect the difficulty of predicting the likelihood of the different kinds of errors.

For a particular application, it may be advantageous to reduce the possibility of Class C errors even if Class A and B errors are increased somewhat. The overall accuracy might be improved because Class C errors are harder to predict and control.

Sometimes, a compromise between Class A and Class B errors may be necessary. By adding components, Class B errors may be made small, but the added components may increase Class *A* errors. It may be better to accept some known Class *B* error to reduce Class *A* errors which may be difficult to predict.

Computation Rules

Information must be available giving the algorithms for making any necessary design computations, as must rules for altering design values to achieve an optimum design.

Synthesis

The Initial Search

As shown in Fig. 14-2, the first step in synthesis is to make an ordered hunt through the file of available resources for an existing system that meets all the important requirements.

For the hunt, two lists are assumed to be available. One is a list of requirements ordered as essential and less important but desirable. The other is a list of available resources. For each resource, the functions performed and other pertinent information are listed.

Comparison of the important wanted requirements and available performances is made to find matches. A particular resource in the file may meet all, some, or none of the important requirements. If a resource in the file meets all of the requirements, then the match

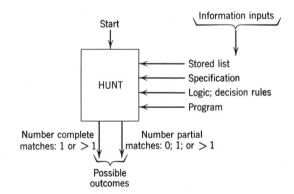

Figure 14-2

Information, Computers, and System Design

can be called *complete;* if only some requirements, then it can be called *partial.*

Figure 14-2 shows the possible outcomes of the initial hunt: (1) one, or more than one complete match, or (2) none, one, or more than one partial match. A procedure is necessary for each possible outcome.

A table can show (1) the number of complete and partial matches, and (2) the way in which each partial match differs from the specification.

The hunt through the file and comparison with the system specification is an information retrieval operation. A successful hunt sooner or later finds one or more organizations for the projected system functions and devices to perform them.

Investigation of Complete Matches

As shown in Fig. 14-3, when the first complete match is found, a decision can accept it and stop the hunt. If the first match is acceptable, no further action is necessary: the design problem is solved. Alternatively, the hunt can continue for other matches.

In some practical cases any solution—and hence the first match found—is acceptable. But in other cases all alternatives must be investigated. The initial hunt is continued until all are found.

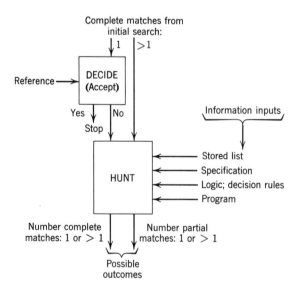

Figure 14-3

If only one is found, and if that one is acceptable, the problem is solved. Otherwise, further investigation is necessary.

If several matches are found, then one must be selected as the best. A further hunt is made for a match between less essential requirements and the performances of the tentatively acceptable matches.

Figure 14-3 shows the possible outcomes: one or more complete matches or one or more partial matches. Because there was at least one complete match at the beginning of the new hunt, there must be at least one partial match. Except for this difference, the possible outcomes are the same as for the initial hunt.

Again a table can show (1) the number of complete and partial matches (2) the way in which the partial matches differ from the specification.

It seems obvious that a designer would not like to have to investigate too many alternatives. Too many make a choice difficult—if not impossible. Six or fewer alternatives might be reasonable. For this reason, if there are too many complete matches, additional (and less important) requirements can be used in another hunt to reduce the number.

The less desirable alternatives can be temporarily put aside for reasons that seem good at the time. But it must always be possible to retrieve such an alternative. Thus, ordering the alternatives is preferable to simply rejecting the less promising.

Procedure for Partial Matches

Figure 14-4 represents the procedure to be used if at least one partial match is found. Two or more partial matches can be considered one at a time. The results of the hunt show how a particular partial match differs from the specification.

As shown in Fig. 14-4, a decision can be made to stop and accept the best partial match. Such a decision is really a change in the specification. Otherwise, further work is necessary to eliminate the differences.

Differences may be of many kinds. For example, no resource in the file may perform all the wanted functions, or none may provide adequate performance, or all may cost too much.

To find out whether an elimination is possible, a further file hunt is made by using the difference to specify what is wanted. For example, the hunt may be for a subsystem to perform a missing function. Of course, any subsystem found by the hunt must be checked for compatibility. As a second example, a hunt may be

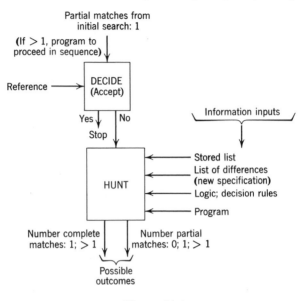

Partial matches from
initial search: 1

(If > 1, program to
proceed in sequence)

Reference ———→ DECIDE
(Accept)

Yes   No

Stop

Information inputs

HUNT

Stored list
List of differences
(new specification)
Logic; decision rules

Program

Number complete
matches: 1; > 1

Number partial
matches: 0; 1; > 1

Possible
outcomes

Figure 14-4

made for a better subsystem to replace one with deficient performance.
As yet another example, a hunt may be made for a less expensive
subsystem, or devices to reduce the cost.

The possible results are the same as for the initial hunt. Again,
these results can be tabulated. If one or more complete matches
are found, then another hunt can be made by using less essential
requirements to help order them so the best can be selected.

If there are one or more partial matches, then the hunt can be
repeated, by using the new difference for a new specification. The
iteration may continue until all differences are removed. But such
iterations may merely result in fruitless repetition. Thus, precautions
must be taken to avoid going around in circles.

Procedure When No Matches Are Found

As Fig. 14-5 shows, if there are no partial matches, a decision
must be made to (1) stop because the problem is too difficult, or
(2) get around the unwanted difference, or (3) simplify to a problem
(or set of problems) which is soluble or has been solved.

The decision necessitates assigning probable odds for success, times
for completion, and costs of obtaining any missing devices.

One possibility may be to change the specification and make another initial hunt. The possible results are the same as after Step 1, the first initial hunt. Any further work depends on whether any complete or partial matches are found.

In trying to simplify the design problem, a complex system frequently is broken down (i.e., factored or structured) into subsystems. Thus, the problem "build a system to transport people to the moon" must be broken up into many, many smaller problems. Hopefully, available resources can be found for each subsystem. Factoring involves a hunt for a set of subsystems each of which is a complete match for a part of the function of the wanted system. Together they meet the system specification.

For example, in Figs. 1-1 and 1-2, the set of functional requirements for a system was divided among a small number of subsystems. The combination of the subsystems performed all the wanted functions of the complex system. Furthermore, the subsystems were further resolved and a hierarchy of subsystems constructed. This procedure can be used on each subsystem in the hierarchy. Thus the overall design problem is factored into a large set of simpler subproblems. The solution of the set of subproblems must give an acceptable system design. In some cases it may actually provide desirable functions not called for in the specification. Thus, a complex system is synthesized from arrangements of devices into functional groups

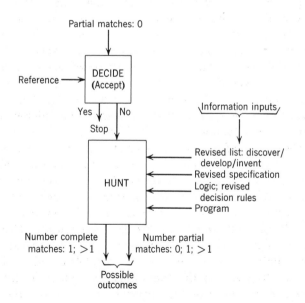

Figure 14-5

of subassemblies. These subassemblies are put together to form assemblies, and so on.

It is possible to imagine a problem that cannot be factored. In such a case, the problem must either be abandoned or else invention must solve it. However most, and probably all, complex systems can be factored into subsystems. This statement is true because any wanted function can be synthesized from the functions in the table of Chapter 7. All the basic functions are listed in the table. Hence, it should be possible to synthesize any complex system by using only the tabulated functions.

The problem should be factored in all possible ways. The phrase "all possible ways" deserves comment. In many cases alternate factorings are possible. In other words, some functions might be performed in alternative subsystems. In such cases, choosing the best location is part of the design problem.

It is possible to imagine a system that could be factored in a hundred different ways. It seems obvious that no designer would want to work out a hundred different designs. During the early design, three or four alternatives are enough to carry along.

Finding the best way to factor a system may challenge the ingenuity of the system designers and mathematicians (and programmers if a computer is used). For a new system, it is often one of the most difficult problems. A good solution may take a great deal of time.

To a considerable extent, factoring involves heuristics, the theory of step-by-step discovery. Recent applications of the theory have resulted in computer programs for solving geometrical problems and balancing the tasks performed at various stations of a production line. Some changes in these programs are necessary for the system factorization problem. These are discussed in a later chapter.

The very different answers that can result from different factorings of overall system functions is well illustrated by various telephone central offices. All of these offices set up wanted connections on request and take them down when the call is over. In some offices, the customer tells an operator the number he wants and she makes the connection. After he is through, he rings her back and she takes down the connection. The most widely used dial system is the step-by-step. As the customer dials his call, the central office switches follow each digit. When the last digit is dialed, the called line is rung immediately. When the call is completed and he hangs up, the switches that set up the connection are automatically released. Machines perform some of the operator functions, but the customer also performs some. More versatile machine switching offices such as panel, Number 1 crossbar, and Number 5 crossbar also perform the same essential functions. However they use quite different functional factorings. The still more versatile new electronic central offices differ in many important ways from all their predecessors. Yet all of these kinds of offices must be compatible so that any two customers can call and talk to each other!

A block diagram showing the subsystem functions can be prepared for each alternative system plan. A check ensures that each plan performs all the functions. If not, the plan must be modified so that it does, or else it must be discarded.

For any set of functional blocks, a hunt can be made for subsystems and devices to implement the functions.

The file may contain suitable resources for at least one factorization. If there is only one that factoring is accepted, unless there are strong reasons to the contrary. If there is more than one factorization, analysis of each alternative can provide information for a selection of the best one.

If the system is not feasible, the reason must be that some function cannot be realized by known devices. As Fig. 14-5 shows, the possible courses of action are to (1) abandon the design or (2) prepare requirements for the missing devices. Research, development, or invention may be necessary to supply them.

We can imagine a machine "inventing" by trying all possible combinations of everything in its file, but this is not done in the procedure. The invent-discover-develop state is reached only after other possibilities have been exhausted.

Analysis: Design Evaluation

General Aspects of Computations

After a set of subsystems is chosen to meet the specification, it is necessary to analyze the design. During the analysis, the performance characteristics, costs, and reliability are usually estimated or computed. For most system designs, all three aspects require evaluation.

Sometimes one order of making the evaluations may be better than another. For example, if the new system must compete with an existing system, it may be prudent to compute cost first. The cost computation may be rather simple. If the new system does not promise to be competitive, then the design has no point.

A complex system described by many performance equations with dozens of requirements is often analyzed as a set of relatively simpler subsystems. In analyzing these subsystems, only a few variables are allowed to vary at one time; the rest are held fixed. A computation is made and the results are carried over to the next subsystem. There may be many interrelated iterative loops. The order in which the subsystems are processed may depend on the relationships between variables.

Normally, some design variables are continuous functions; others are discrete—perhaps with predetermined limits. As industry becomes more standardized and automated, discreteness becomes more important. For example, nuts and bolts and their threads are available in standardized series.

Consider (1) a completely custom-built product and (2) a product completely assembled from available standard components. In the first case, the restrictions on the variables are essentially fundamental laws and the limits are set by available manufacturing processes. The task is to determine appropriate values of the variables which minimize the "value criterion" (e.g., weight, cost, or overall dimensions).

If the design equations are simple and linear, the solution is conceptually straightforward, although the computations may be long and involved. If the equations are complicated and possibly nonlinear the problem is much more difficult.

Procedures or rules must be available for making any required computation. Hundreds of rules may be necessary for computing all aspects of performance, cost, and reliability of a complex system design.

The designer may make the computations with the help of a large computer, a desk calculator, a slide rule, or just pencil and paper.

For a few variables, it may be possible to construct a chart or nomogram which relates all the variables. Then, for any desired performance, appropriate values can be determined. For larger problems, the computations may be divided into a number of subroutines. The subroutines are ordered by the computation program.

To start the computations, the designer estimates or assumes some values of the variables. Great accuracy is usually unnecessary. The difference in computing time between a very good and a rather poor set of initial values may be small.

Using the initial values, a first computation is made. The result is a set of computed characteristics. In most cases the results do not agree with the specification, so the initial values are modified and the computations repeated. The result of each computation is compared with the specification. If one or more values are unacceptable, the design is not satisfactory and at least one more iteration is necessary. Thus the design is put together step-by-step—perhaps changing only one or two variables at a time. The iterations are continued as often as necessary to meet the specification. As the design "homes in," the values are continually improved or "converge" until they cease to change.

To effect convergence the most sensitive variables are dealt with first, then the next most sensitive, etc.

When convergence is attained for one aspect of the design, the next set of computations is begun.

Figure 14-6 shows the "iteration procedure." The designer (or a computer) calculates, compares, alters values, recalculates, compares, etc.

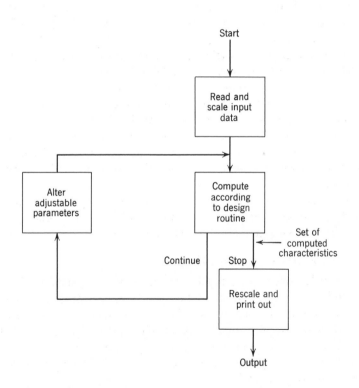

Figure 14-6

Knowledge of the relationships between variables is an important factor in deciding how to alter the values to effect convergence. Usually, the most recently computed values should be used as a guide.

Sometimes a design does not converge. There is no guarantee that the computed results will always approach the wanted values. Oscillations may occur between the values used to start a new computation and the values after the computation. Repeated jumps from too high a value to too low and then back can be very frustrating to a designer. If convergence is not attained, the computations must be stopped to save fruitless effort.

Several kinds of calculations may be necessary. For example, in designing a new transformer, it is necessary to choose the core size, and determine the wire sizes and numbers of turns for the windings.

In other systems, several identical processes may be performed simultaneously. A shop may have a number of machines making the same part. A simple, but approximate formula can help estimate how many machines are necessary to handle a particular operation. If greater precision is necessary, then more precise formulas of queuing theory may be used.

Sometimes it is impossible to compute the performance adequately. Although algorithms may be available to perform the computations, the existing information on the numbers to be put into the equations may be incomplete. In some cases, there is room for doubt even after the performance has been computed.

The time required for an analysis may depend on the designer's experience and ability. The number of steps needed depends on the system complexity and the allowable tolerances for satisfactory performance.

For good results, the designer must be familiar with the system and the design problems. He must also be creative, since precedents for the necessary steps in the evaluation may not exist.

Information Computations

A production process reduces the amount of uncertainty in the raw material. The uncertainty remaining after the process depends only on the allowable tolerances. Thus, one aspect of the process may be thought of as a means by which information is added to raw materials to shape and assemble them into a product.

Hence, the question arises: How much information is necessary to control the process?

Certainly, the narrower the final tolerances, the less the final uncertainty, and the more the added information. Also, when more processes or more complex processes are performed, then more information is added.

Hence, it may be more practical to measure the "information" added in terms of the processes applied to the raw material than of the states of uncertainty of the raw material.

The design of production methods for wanted objects to specified tolerances involves choices of suitable raw materials, of efficient production processes, and also of information generation and transmission.

The amount of information to be added in production is determined during the design step. Less information is necessary to install a purchased subassembly than to produce it from raw material. However, the supplier of the purchased part had to supply the information to produce it. The total amount of information is always increased by such a division of design. Since information generation and transmission always costs money, it is a factor in the total cost of a system. In practical cases (e.g., in making a few complexly shaped parts) it may be a very important factor.

Today, production and assembly information almost universally takes the form of drawings and instructions. The amount of information they contain is seldom or never known accurately in terms of bits. The total number of sheets of drawings and pages of typed and printed matter may be a rough measure, but only very rough.

In the future the situation may change. To automate machines, information is required to direct the tool to make a wanted part to the required tolerances. A particular machine might be evaluated in terms of the amount of information required to change the raw material into the part. The amount might depend on the possible operating ranges of the effector or tool.

An automatic machine may be directed by information stored on a tape. The directions or program for the process may be expressed in letters and numbers. These signs can be coded and stored on the tape in an appropriate form so that they can be sensed and used to control the process. The number of digits or number of feet of tape can give only a rough measure of the amount of information. However, this measure is far better than any available previously. The costs of tapes and tape preparation are strong incentives for efficient information generation and handling. These are new problems for the designer. They will become more and more important as time goes on.

The measure of information should be that required to specify the process without regard to a particular machine. Some machines require inefficient coding. Thus the important criterion is the amount necessary to specify the operation—not the amount necessary to instruct a particular machine.

To avoid needless translation, the information coding should be compatible with the machine that is to use it. Similarly, the mechanic at a lathe must be able to read the drawings describing the part he is to make. In other words, the information source and receiver must be compatible.

Information transmission occurs whether a lathe mechanic is given instructions verbally or by blueprints. The same problems are present if the lathe is controlled automatically—but may be more apparent.

By careful checking, blueprints supplied to the mechanic can be error-free. The blueprints can be handed to him. Thus there is no mutilation or loss of information in transmission. Furthermore, his reading of the information can be quite free of errors. Information punched on a tape can be so expressed that the tape reader can detect or correct many—or even all—errors.

Cost and Reliability Computations

Once the number of components, the cost per component, and the cost of assembly are known, computing the total cost—at least roughly—is straightforward. The resulting cost can be compared with the specification. If it is acceptable, then other necessary kinds of computations can be started or a decision can be made about the fate of the design. If costs are not satisfactory, a way must be found to reduce the number of components or else less expensive components must be chosen and the computations repeated. If the cost can not be sufficiently reduced, a decision about future work must be made by management.

Another aspect of some system designs is estimating the likelihood of failure in operation or, conversely, the expected reliability. Such estimates can be made when the number of parts are known, the expected stress on each part, and the expected failure rate under the stress. It is possible to evaluate the reliability of alternative arrangements of available components or the vulnerability to enemy actions.

The expected reliability is compared with the specification. If it is inadequate, sometimes it may be improved. Shannon and others have discussed the use of unreliable parts to create more reliable ensembles. These methods all require additional subassemblies or devices and thus increase the cost. A revised cost estimate is necessary.

Possible Outcomes

If one possible design is satisfactory, then a decision must be made to (1) accept it or (2) reject it and search for other possibilities.

With more than one satisfactory design, one may be chosen by invoking some new factor to permit a choice. In either case, acceptance means the problem is solved. However, all may be rejected.

If no satisfactory design is found, then the alternative to stopping work is a radical change.

Radical Change

Before stopping work, or even before making a final choice between alternative designs, sometimes it pays to consider whether some radical change could lead to an important advantage. It might be possible to: (1) change the specification, (2) alter some decision rule, or (3) search a file not previously covered.

15

An Example of System Design

The choice of a new automobile can serve as an excellent example of system design. To most families, a car is a large enough expenditure so that the purchase is given time and thought. This example is chosen because it involves many of the steps of any system design. Further, the steps can be recognized when they are pointed out.

An automobile is a system, by definition, because it is a set of components that together perform many wanted functions. It is certainly a complex system, because an automobile is an assembly of many thousands of components of which more than 2500 move.

A missile is usually regarded as a very complex system. It may be made up of 50,000 or so components—only a few times as many as a modern car.

A car can be broken down into a hierarchy of subsystems, and the subsystems can be broken down in turn. The breakdown can be made in many different ways, as, for example, into the power plant, power transmission and power assists, chassis, and body. Other accessory systems, such as the radio and heater might also each be considered to be subsystems. The power plant might be further broken down into the gasoline input and tank, carburetor, air input, ignition, and cooling and exhaust system. The other subsystems can be similarly broken down.

The United States has four major manufacturers of cars. A few other U.S. makers and many foreign producers offer cars for sale here.

General Motors alone has total sales of about $5\frac{1}{4}$ million cars a year. They offer enough choices and options so that conceivably no two cars in an entire year's production would be exactly alike! For example, in 1963 131 different models were offered; 207 designs of interior trim were available. Engines, transmissions, axle ratios, colors, power assists such as steering, windows and seats, air-conditioning, steering wheels that tilt, radios, heaters, defrosters—the list of choices and options is long and gets longer every year.

222

Other companies make many more millions of cars and offer different choices and options.

Despite the large number of choices and options, the new owner usually feels his new car is not the complex system he really wants. So he adds other objects from other suppliers—perhaps a trash bag, a compass, even a hula dancer. The result becomes a truly personally designed system—"his car." He delegates a selected maker to produce and assemble as much as possible of the systems he designed. Other suppliers provide the remaining parts. Thus, he actually factors the system into a set of subsystems.

The example is deliberately simplified. Only a few of the possible variations are mentioned. Nevertheless, enough are given to illustrate the fact that a particular car is the result of a synthesis of subsystems.

As in any system design, the first step is to conceive the need—in this case, the need for a new car. Modern advertising of new models tends to make this step fairly easy.

After some discussion about the sorry state of the present car, the next step is taken. Resources in the form of time to shop and money for the down payment are allotted, and the design project is under way.

Fifty years ago, some people had doubts about the feasibility of an automobile as a reliable method of family transportation. Today, feasibility is taken for granted. Sound mechanical design is more or less assumed.

As a result of family consultations, a tentative specification is agreed upon. The requirements are divided into essential and less essential as shown in very abbreviated form in the left hand column of Table 15-1.

The station wagon requirement eliminates all other models from consideration. The maximum price rules out all possibilities above the medium-price field.

The next step is to gain information about available cars that might meet the specification. Manufacturers' catalogs, demonstration rides, and conferences with the neighbors and co-workers in the office are often-used methods. These sources are supplemented by personal knowledge. Stock ownership may influence the choice of make. A bad experience with the old car may eliminate that make.

The available cars are determined by the manufacturers—not by the designer-purchaser. Further, particular models may be obtained with a few sizes of engines, and with certain other options. Power assists and air-conditioning may only be added with engines with enough power to operate them. These are constraints on possible designs.

Table 15-1

Specification		Information File		

Essential Requirements	Car	A	B	C
1. Station wagon		Yes	Yes	Yes
2. Automatic transmission		Yes	Yes	Yes
3. Maximum price: $X		X + 50	X	X − 50
			(list prices)	
4. Delivery date: 1 month or less		1 month	2 months	1 week
Less Essential Requirements				
5. Color: red		Available	Available	Not available
6. Upholstery: gray		Not available	Available	Available

The available information about three possible designs can be put in the form of the right-hand portion of Table 15-1.

Note that the prices are list prices. More information is necessary because the actual purchaser's cost is:

$$\text{Basic cost} + \text{options} - \text{allowance on the old car}$$

Talks with salesmen and some simple arithmetical computations give a new set of costs:

Car A	B	C
X − 50	X	X − 50

For this simplified example, possible differences in time payments are neglected.

The information about cars A, B, and C can now be compared with the specification. A and C meet the essential requirements. B is a bit more expensive and the delivery time is excessive.

The wanted color is available in car A, but not the wanted upholstery; the reverse is true for car C. So no alternative meets all the requirements.

If either car A or C is to be chosen, then either the color or upholstery requirement must be changed. Assuming the color is the more important, then car A is selected.

The example brings out another point. Two alternatives met all the essential requirements, so the choice was based on less essential requirements. In everyday living, less essential requirements dictate many choices.

16

Human and Computer Roles in System Design

The Flow Chart Verbs

The basic verbs used in the flow charts are:

1. Hunt (i.e., search the file)
2. Compare
3. Compute
4. Decide
5. Alter
6. Invent-Discover-Develop

Except for 6, these functions can be performed by appropriate functional blocks from the table of Chapter 7.

This approach to mechanizing the functions immediately shows the different kinds of information required to perform the flow-chart functions. It is possible to see what information a man must furnish.

Hunt

As used here, the word "hunt" is used to mean a particular kind of search. A *hunt* seeks any suitable available object from a group of objects. To choose an object from the group, it must first be selected and then compared with some reference to see if it is suitable.

In the mechanization of the flow chart, the hunt is conducted over the data locations in a file of available information. The data may be in the form of numbers or alphanumerics (or both). The data may or may not be coded. In a more general case, the file may contain objects or representations of objects by graphic or other means.

Random-access arrangements for selecting locations in any sequence were discussed in Chapter 6 (see also Figs. 6-21 and 6-22). A program determines the order of examination of the locations. The program may be "cut-and-try" with no real plan, or it may follow some logical procedure. The time to locate a suitable object may depend on the method of search. Effective search methods are still the subject of fundamental research.

Sequential-access arrangements were also discussed in Chapter 6 (see Fig. 6-23). In sequential selection, the order of examination is fixed. Information giving each new address is furnished sequentially in time. The sequential information may examine a new data location for each bit of address information (such as an input pulse).

A combination of the two arrangements is possible. For example, in looking up a word in the dictionary, the approximate location is first selected by opening the book to the section corresponding to the first letter. Any letter can be chosen at random. When the approximate location is found, words may be scanned one at a time in sequence.

Selection merely steers an object to one of the objects over which the hunt is made. The hunted object is merely located; in itself, the selection causes no other effect on the object. Further steps are necessary.

A comparison arrangement must compare the data at a particular location with the wanted information. At each location, a match indicator (a logic arrangement) shows a complete match, a partial match, or no match. Proper criteria for determining a match are necessary. Otherwise a suitable object may be rejected. The complete list of essential factors for a hunting function includes:

1. Addresses of the objects over which the hunt is to be conducted.
2. An order of examining the objects.
3. Information about each object when it is examined.
4. A way to recognize a suitable object when one is reached.
5. A start signal to start the operation.

In any hunting arrangement, a human being must:

1. Fill the file. Obviously, only objects in the file can be selected.
2. Set the match criteria.

A computer can then:

1. Conduct the hunt.
2. Make known the results.

Either a human being or a computer may initiate a hunt. Either may determine the search program. Figure 16-1 shows a block diagram of the functional blocks of a simple sequential-access hunting arrangement.

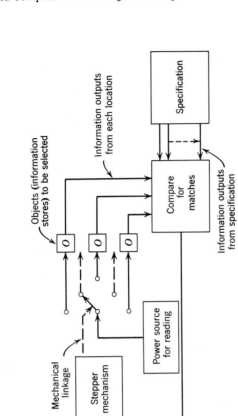

Figure 16-1

Compare and Compute

In Chapter 6, the function of *comparing* two items of information was discussed. The output information (match or no match) indicates that the inputs are or are not equal (Fig. 16-2*A*).

In *computation*, two or more sets of input data are combined according to some rule. The data can be expressed in numbers or alphanumerics (see Fig. 16-2*B*).

In comparison, the rule is logical; in computation, mathematical.

The input data and the rules for the comparison or computation operation together yield the numerical or alphanumerical output.

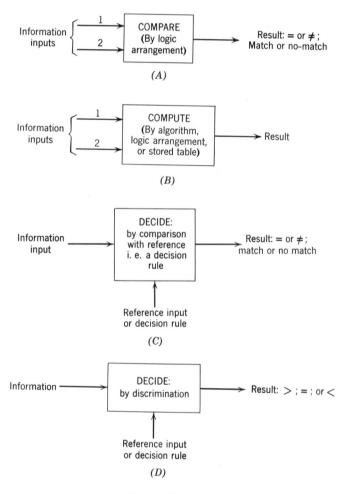

(A)

(B)

(C)

(D)

Figure 16-2

The input data can come from a store or from a human being. A man must supply the rules. If a sequence of steps is involved, a man must program them. A start signal is always necessary. A man may furnish it or a computer can be directed to do so at any appropriate point in a program.

Decide

The *decide* operation is used to accept or reject some items of information. One input for the function is the input information. The other input is a fixed reference. The two are combined by an appropriate logical rule.

An appropriate *compare* function can give an output indication of whether the two inputs are or are not equal. An appropriate "discriminate" function can show whether the input is greater than, equal to, or less than the reference (see Figs. 16-2C and D).

The input information can come from a store or from a human being. A man must supply the reference and the logical rule. A start signal is always necessary. A man may furnish it, or a computer can be programmed to do so.

These functions were discussed in Chapter 6.

Alter

The *alter* operation is used to insert or delete certain information. Destruction or complete erasure may be considered as a special case of deletion. Other possibilities are sorting or merging, translation (including changes in language, code, or efficiency), reordering in space or time, or changes of rate.

All of these kinds of information processing were covered in Chapter 6. Figures 6-50 and 6-51 are particularly pertinent block diagrams.

The input information to be altered can come from a store or from a human being. A man must supply the rules for alteration. A start signal is always necessary.

Invent-Discover-Develop

The invent-discover-develop function allows for the possibility that a human may be able to contribute knowledge not in the file. His acts may involve auxiliary use of a computer.

We can imagine a machine "inventing" by trying all possible combinations of everything in its file, but in the flow chart, the invent-discover-develop block is reached only after all other possibilities are exhausted.

Computer Capabilities

A desirable objective would be to program a computer to design a feasible system or perhaps even an optimized system. To assess the possibilities, it is necessary to know something about computers. Hence, for those who are not computer experts, some elementary facts about computers are given.

Digital Computers

A digital computer can do seven things:

1. Take in information in a form acceptable to itself (e.g., punched cards or magnetic tape). The information may be coded in binary form, or binary-coded-decimal form, or other forms. Today, it is always in numerical or alphanumerical form. In the future, character-recognition machines may be able to read handwriting or shorthand and put the information in a form acceptable to the computer. Some day, other machines may be able to understand and process spoken information.

2. Store information. The store limits the maximum problem size. Maximum store size is limited by cost and time factors.

3. Do arithmetic (e.g., add two or more numbers).

4. Do logical operations (e.g., AND and OR operations) and compare two quantities to decide whether one is less than, equal to, or greater than the other.

5. Alter input information (edit, delete, translate, reorder).

6. Put out information.

7. Perform a programmed sequence of such operations. The program may be wired in the form of cross-connections or stored in the memory. Some computers can generate a machine-coded program that can later be used by the machine itself.

The computer operation is almost always serial in the sense that there is only one central processing unit. In some problems, the time required can be shortened by adding more computer components. Accuracy is limited by the number of digits carried; computing time, by the cycle time for each kind of operation, the number of cycles per operation instruction, and the number of instructions.

Analog Computers

An analog computer can do the same things as a digital computer but the methods may differ greatly. For example, information is handled in continuous form (e.g., as continuously varying voltages or shaft rotations). If necessary, inputs must be translated into available computer variables, and outputs back into terms of the original problem. In analog computers, operations are performed in parallel; that is, each arithematical or logical operation usually has its own processing unit.

Analog computers as a class are less limited in form than digital computers. As a matter of fact, when used in a simulation, a computer can be thought of as an "analog" of a system. The variety of special-purpose analog computers is limited only by designers' ingenuity. Given any system, it is possible to construct an analog to it. In theory, in the limiting case the analog would be a duplicate system. In practice, the analog is a simplified version. Otherwise, it would be pointless.

For some kinds of problems, an analog computer may offer advantages over a digital computer. Thus, for moderate accuracy in the results, say 1%, an analog computer may be cheaper than a digital computer. It may also be faster.

The parallel operation can mean that less storage is needed.

Major Differences between Digital and Analog Computers

The major differences between the two kinds of computers are:

Analog Computers	*Digital Computers*
Data in continuous form	Data in discrete form
Operations performed simultaneously	Operations performed sequentially
Precision and accuracy limited by quality and number of components	Precision limited by maximum number of digits and thus by size of installation
Relatively inexpensive for accuracies of about 1%; more expensive for higher accuracy	Basic cost relatively high regardless of accuracy

Costs

Many operating characteristics of a particular digital computer depend on cost factors. For example, a machine can be built to take in and put out information coded in many different languages—but at a price.

Storage capacity now limits the possibility of solving some problems. In fact, storage space is often of primary importance to a programmer; the time to run the program may be secondary. More storage can be had, but at a price. More storage can make the solution of a particular problem simpler by removing limitations on its formulation.

The number of significant digits that can be handled limits the precision of results. Precision can be increased by adding more digits—again at a price.

Today's digital computers perform all the arithmetic and logical operations, so problem-handling capability can only be increased by higher computing speeds—at a price.

In an analog computer, component quality limits the attainable accuracy. And the number of computer components (amplifiers, integrators, etc.) limits the maximum problem size. With more computer components, the analogy to the system under study may be closer. But beyond a certain point, adequate accuracy is difficult—even impossible—to achieve because of component limitations.

Time Factors

In programming, several time factors may enter. For example, if a computer would take more computing time than is available before the answer is needed, then the result would not be useful. If great precision or great storage capacity is required, a particular digital computer may not be able to handle a problem in an acceptable time. Possibly, the solution may be a larger or faster computer—again, at a price.

On the other hand, few system design problems are likely to require real-time operation. Of course, a problem must not require infinite time, or even an intolerable time. Certainly, a computer should be faster than a human being—even one with a desk calculator. The value of an answer can be balanced against the computer time and cost to get it. In some situations, an analog computer working in real-time may offer advantages. For simple problems, a computer solution can be much more expensive than other alternatives.

Information Requirements for Design by Computer

A computer can help in a design only if it is given a file of adequate information in an acceptable form. The necessary information can be divided into specification and file, algorithms and decision rules, and program.

Specification and File

For a computer-directed search, the specification must be in the computer language. The computer stores it so it is available for a hunt. No difficulties should arise if the information is coded in the form of letters or numbers or both.

Each requirement may be given a numerical rating according to its importance.

Some requirements, such as those for appearance, may present rating problems. In art and architecture, some sort of standards guide the choice of desirable proportions, colors, and the like. In setting up the specification for a system, experts might develop numerical scales for such properties. To an extent the ratings would be arbitrary, but an arbitrary element is almost always present in human choices. Thus, one or a few men may choose what they consider the most attractive-looking cabinet, color combination, and other properties of a new product.

The descriptions of subsystems and devices to be stored can also be coded in an acceptable form. They should certainly include information about performance, size, weight, and cost. Ideally, they should be so complete that the specification requirements of any new system can be checked against the file.

To assist management in its problems, the file may also contain information needed to make decisions on whether to start particular projects, and the importance of alternative projects. Such information might include estimates of the probabilities of success of research and development tasks, and probable costs and time required.

The specification and descriptions must be compatible so they may be compared for matches.

Algorithms and Decision Rules

The computer must be furnished detailed information about all necessary computations. A certain number of orders are built in the computer hardware. The program must contain instructions for the wanted sequence of orders.

Among the instructions is one: "Compare A and B." The decision rules thus allow the computer to choose among alternatives.

For example, if two or more suitable designs are found that meet all the requirements, a computer can be directed to choose between them. An example of a simple decision rule is "Take the lowest cost design." More complex decision rules can easily be devised.

To permit a choice, each subassembly and component could be given a numerical rating for each important quality. For a particular design, weight might be assigned to each quality according to its importance. Each weight might be multiplied by the corresponding rating of its importance, and the products summed to give an overall rating. Then for a particular application, alternatives could be ordered.

To "pin down" qualitative decision rules for a computer program is not a trivial job. To select the qualities to be rated and to assign ratings may not be easy, but a human designer must (or should have) such information before he makes a choice. The flow chart merely emphasizes this fact.

For a particular problem, the decision rules may all be compatible. However, if two rules give contradictory answers, one must override. Human intervention might resolve such contradictions.

Some of the problems can be shown by an example. For a particular design, suppose the decision rules for weighting the various kinds of errors described earlier are (other things being equal) :

1. Avoid Class C errors if possible
2. Prefer a known and acceptable Class B error to an unpredictable Class A error
3. Avoid Class B errors if it can be done without conflict with rules 1 and 2

Moreover,

4. Prefer minimum number of operations
5. Prefer minimum number of components
6. Prefer a component elsewhere used in the design to introducing a new one

Rules 1, 2, and 3 require that components be rated on their proneness to the three types of error. Experienced designers could set up suitable ratings. Then the computer can compare alternatives.

Rules 4 and 5 require a count of operations, and a choice of the method with the smallest total.

Rule 6 requires a count of the number of kinds of components and a choice of the design with the smallest total.

Program

The computer program must contain minutely detailed instructions for the sequence of operations to be performed. It must include all possible outcomes of the called-for logical operations and computations. It must also cover the modifications of values of the variables as the design converges.

A usual computer programming situation can be summarized in the words: "I have a problem. What can the computer do about solving it?" In contrast, the systems design situation is "The problem is not yet completely formulated. What characteristics must the formulation have for the problem to be programmable?"

First, the problem must be capable of being completely described:

1. As a set of terms that can be converted by the programmer or the computer into numbers (or possibly letters, or both)
2. A set of arithmetical or logical relations between the terms

The requirement says merely that the problem is programmable if the system is feasible and enough information about it is made available to the computer. Thus, in general, a problem will be programmable if the following are available:

1. A set of values of the input variables
2. A set of relations among the input, system, and output variables
3. An algorithm for arriving at a well-defined and satisfactory solution

If a design involves only the solution of a set of algebraic or differential equations, then the problem is programmable if the equations are solvable. Logical operations can be performed if adequate input information as well as an appropriate decision rule is furnished.

Program Override

If only the specification and "standard practices" are furnished to the computer, it produces a routine design which embodies the "best" alternative. For this reason, the "standard practices" should reflect the best judgment and experience of the design groups.

In a design, the designer should be able to override the program and furnish additional input information, thus obtaining other designs to be compared with the "best" (but routine) design. This flexibility can be valuable in studying new ideas, proposed new developments, or special requirements.

Digital Computers in Design

Characteristics which make the digital computer useful in system design are:

1. Large storage capacity
2. High input and output speeds
3. Flexibility, high speed, and low cost per computation or logical operation
4. High reliability and accuracy
5. Possibility of many iterations by using stored-program and address-modification techniques
6. Continued hardware and programming improvements

The benefits of applying computers to system design lie in lower costs, improved quality, faster and better answers, as well as more interesting jobs, increased productivity, and more creative effort by the designers.

Digital computers have already been used to design electrical apparatus, such as power transformers. This application has achieved important results, both technically and economically.

A computer is well fitted to take a complicated matrix of continuous and discrete variables and find a satisfactory design. Because of its speed, a computer can sometimes cover an entire range of design possibilities. In such cases, it is unnecessary for a human to try to guess where the best alternatives lie.

Future results appear even more important, particularly in design optimization and standardization.

Indispensable Human Acts

In mechanizing the flow chart, certain human acts are indispensable. Thus, a human must conceive the need for the new system. He must decide whether to start doing something about it. Estimating the odds for success, costs, and times required for complex design tasks is to some extent an art. But such estimates can be improved by experience and common sense. Thus the calculation of odds for success of complex tasks made up out of simple ones with known probabilities of success is a science, as is the calculation of probable costs of complex tasks made up of simple ones with known costs. The same is true of calculations of the times required to perform complex tasks.

A human must choose or decide on the system requirements. He may derive them either from the needs the system is to satisfy or by computations from more primitive information about what is wanted. He must order the requirements as essential and less important.

With computer design, a human must stock the file and program the computer. It is impossible to overemphasize the fact that for design by computer to be successful, the talents of the best designers must be used in stocking the file and setting up the program.

From one point of view, the man who programs the computer really designs the system. But it does not follow that he can always choose the best design from many possibilities. Perhaps the choice can be better made by a computer.

Possibly computers could design "completely new" systems, but it is difficult to think about the programs in specific terms. Exploratory searches using heuristic programs might prove useful.

He must set up the decision rules and algorithms for logical operations and computations.

He must supply certain initial data so the computer can start to work.

Finally, he must start the entire design process.

If it turns out that the computer has been given insufficient information, he must supply it—or the computer stops.

It seems highly desirable, if not absolutely necessary, to allow him to interrupt the program at any point. Stops to prevent useless "looping" can be built into the computer program, but to make them really effective, the programmer may need more hindsight than can be expected from the designer of a new system.

Only the designer can perform the function called "invent-discover-develop." On the flow chart, this function is only necessary if some obstacle prevents a direct solution. Because the direct solution is blocked, indirect efforts are necessary.

Computer Contribution

What is left for the computer to do? Information storage and retrieval (including searching and comparing), performing logical operations and computations, and putting out results in a form usable by a man or another machine are among the computer's functions. Possibly a computer might follow a heuristic program for factoring a complex system.

When a "new" system is a variation of an older one, the entire design process can be programmed, and the human need only start the process and be able to interrupt it, as in the design of new electrical transformers or electrical wave filters.

Areas Where Either May Operate

The area where either men and machines (or both) may operate is best explained by an example. Thus, if axioms and procedures are known or can be set up for factoring a system into subsystems, then the prospects of using a heuristic program seem bright. On the other hand, if the axioms are not available, the designer may not be able to get much help from the computer.

The Doubtful Area

The extent of the doubtful area depends somewhat on the background of the problem. If very little information is available, a computer search would be wasteful. Even if a few men (or a few books or memoranda or papers) have all the available pertinent information, a computer could not help much. Again, a simple problem that must be completed within a few days would not justify writing a new computer program. In such cases, a man is superior to today's computers. But the trend is in the other direction. Except for the essential human functions, the tendency is for the computer to take over more and more of the design work.

The fact that a flow chart can be drawn for the design of a new system by a computer naturally raises many tantalizing questions such as: How does a man solve problems? In the same way as the flow chart? If not, what are the differences? In brief, how does a man *think?*

It is reasonable to speculate on possible similarities to and differences from the organization of the human brain and the procedures it may or does use in solving systems problems.

There are other interesting possibilities. The procedure should be applicable to man-machine systems in which human beings perform important functions. Also, adaptive systems can change their structure in response to their inputs and environment to perform in a "better" manner. Such system behavior simulates some aspects of "learning" by humans.

Besides such problems of individual behavior, social systems involving groups of people offer an exciting challenge. For example, we need to understand better such problems as communications in a large business organization and how decisions are made. Economic systems and the dynamic responses of large groups of people to appeals and exhortations involve even larger groups.

Human operators can be trained to perform very complex tasks. However, automation is possible only when the necessary information for a sequence of operations can be spelled out in a detailed program. Information for each step must be such that each effector can follow it and produce the wanted changes in space and time.

Much progress has been made in the automation of some manufacturing processes, but the programming of the information is costly. On the other hand, the processing may be many times faster when conditions are favorable. So far, automation has had far more limited application than it will in the future. Programming costs will surely come down. As they fall, more and more processes will be automated. But human beings will always be indispensable because human beings do the designing, the planning, and the programming.

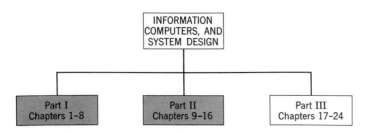

PART III

This part amplifies and justifies much of the contents of Parts I and II.

A mathematical model of a general system is set up.

A mathematical description is given for each kind of building block described in Part I. These descriptions make clear the need for certain extensions of information theory.

Heuristics (i.e., the things that aid discovery) could be more helpful in system design if they were better understood and better adapted to system design problems. For certain steps, they are the only available tool, so the need is urgent. Chapter 23 discusses heuristics and system design.

Some cost and reliability formulas and concepts that have been useful in system studies are covered in the last chapter.

17

Mathematical Description
of a System

For some purposes, a mathematical model that describes the system operation is very desirable. To create such models, the mathematical variables must be found, as well as the possible relations between them. Lacking knowledge of both the variables and the relations, quantitative treatment of a system is almost impossible.

In the molecular model, one input is always time-varying energy; one output is always an object changed by the time-varying energy applied to it. These simple facts can be used as a starting point to gain considerable insight into the operation of many different kinds of systems.

Variables and Parameters

For the present purpose, a *variable* is defined as a measurable quantity which has a definite numerical value at every instant. In other words, it is assumed that any variable can be represented by a pointer on a dial. In this sense, all quantities used in such sciences as physics and chemistry are variables.

Time is always one variable, so one pointer on a dial always represents a clock.

A model (such as the model of a particular system) can be described abstractly by a set of variables. The person describing a particular model chooses the set (which need not be unique).

For any real system, the conceivable number of variables is extremely large. Thus, in practice, the system description must select only a modest number from the set of all possible variables. In other words, the possible variables are divided into those considered to be within and those considered to be outside the system description. The two kinds need not differ in their physical nature.

243

A variable not included in the system description may be called a *parameter*. A parameter is a quantity considered to be constant in the case being considered, but varying in different cases.

For a particular system, a change in the values of some parameters may greatly affect the operation. The effects of changes in such parameters can not be neglected. For a particular study, such a parameter may be assumed to be constant at a particular value. Further studies must be made assuming other values until the effect is understood.

Changes in some other parameters may be known to produce only slight effects. Finally, an infinite number of other parameters could have no detectable effect. Such parameters can be ignored in formulating the description.

Description of a System

From the definitions, it follows that the state of a particular system at a given instant is the set of numerical values which the selected set of variables have at that instant. In a particular case, the absence of a variable can be treated as a zero dial reading. Further, the operation is described by a succession of states and the time intervals between them. Thus, time is always one variable in the description of the operation.

Formal Representation of a System

Figure 17-1 shows a general block diagram of a system. This representation is of the form:

$$\text{Inputs} \rightarrow \text{system} \rightarrow \text{outputs}$$

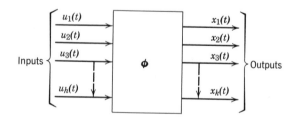

Figure 17-1

and thus may be described in terms of a model consisting of the mathematical relations between:

1. A nonempty set of input variables, $u_h(t)$, which are acted on by
2. A nonempty set of operators, ϕ, which involve the relations and restrictions between the u_h and
3. A nonempty set of output variables, $x_k(t)$,—sometimes called the objective function.

The set of variables describing the input may be thought of as the components of an input vector; the set of variables describing the output, as the components of an output vector. The set of inputs includes all inputs from the enviroment; the set of outputs, all outputs to the environment.

The operation of the system changes the values of the components of the input vector into the values of the components of the output vector. In the molecular model, the input to the system is time-varying energy, as is the output. The same set of variables can be used to describe the components of each vector.

Any equations describing the operation of the system must be dimensionally homogeneous. The operation of the system can produce no changes that violate the requirement of dimensional homogeneity of the describing equations—a fact of enormous importance.

A key step in understanding systems is to describe the set of possible input variables. This description is worked out by starting with a zero-entropy power source and then examining the additional variables necessary to describe an information-carrying energy flow.

For the system of Fig. 17-1, the output response characteristics can be formally expressed in a symbolic form:

$$X(t) = f[u_h(t), \phi] \tag{17.1}$$

$$= \sum_{t=0}^{t} [u_h(t)\phi] \, \Delta t \tag{17.2}$$

The effects can be summed only if ϕ is a linear operator so that superposition holds; in other words, only if

$$\phi(u_1 + u_2) = \phi u_1 + \phi u_2 \tag{17.3}$$

Figure 17-2 shows the operation of ϕ_1 and ϕ_2 acting in tandem. The output of the first is the input of the second. The pertinent equation is:

$$x = \phi_2(\phi_1 u) = \phi_2 \cdot \phi_1 u = \phi_u \tag{17.4}$$

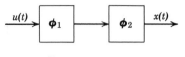

Figure 17-2

where the overall operator ϕ_u indicates the combination or multiplication of operators.

In general, the multiplication is not commutative:

$$\phi_2(\phi_1 u) \neq \phi_1(\phi_2 u) \tag{17.5}$$

An operator ϕ is linear if, and only if,

$$\phi(u_1 + u_2) = \phi u_1 + \phi u_2 \tag{17.6}$$

for all admissable inputs u_1 and u_2. A physical unit is linear only if its ϕ is linear. If the outputs are x_1 and x_2 for inputs u_1 and u_2 applied separately, then the output is x_1 and x_2 for inputs u_1 and u_2. In other words, the principle of superposition holds. Further,

$$\phi(cu) = c\phi u \tag{17.7}$$

where c is any constant.

In a time-variable system, ϕ varies with time, and $\phi(t)$ replaces ϕ in the equations.

Classification of Component Blocks of Systems

The variables describing the set of inputs and outputs and ϕ give an abstract description of the system performance.

As shown in Fig. 17-3, component blocks of systems can be classified into five categories depending on the number of inputs and outputs.

Although it is trivial, the null case is included for completeness.

Solving the System Differential Equations

The input of a molecular system is in the form of time-varying energy, as is the output. La Grange's and Hamilton's equations apply to such time-varying energy systems. But for a complex system, they present a formidable mathematical problem to the would-be designer.

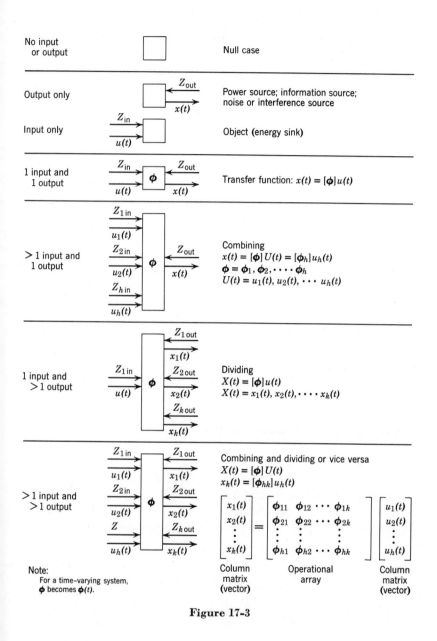

Figure 17-3

Furthermore, almost always a designer must understand how his system will perform under abnormal inputs. If he does not, overdesign is almost certain. But abnormal inputs almost certainly mean some component blocks are overstressed and operate in a nonlinear fashion. Superposition no longer holds. As everyone knows, many *linear* differential equations are insoluble in closed form. It is no great exaggeration to say that means for the solution of most *nonlinear* differential equations are pitifully weak today. Only a few special cases are tractable.

So what happens? Sometimes, a well-concealed assumption is made that the system can really be described well enough by a linear equation—perhaps over a tiny part of the operating characteristic, or that the nonlinear effects will not be too bad *in this case*. And after all, someone is going to test a prototype!

The description of a canonical model of a complex system in Chapter 8 (see Fig. 8-1) made the point that many complex systems have inputs and outputs of both time-varying energy and of objects. For such complex systems, a complete and rigorous mathematical solution of Eq. 17-1 is impossible today. A drastically simplified special case may be the subject matter for a very thick book. But the simplifications may merely result in booby traps for the unwary. Except for a few special cases, far more powerful mathematical tools must be devised to cope with the challenging design problems of complex systems. Some examples of such special cases can be cited.

Solving the Nonlinear Equations for Switching Functions

Solution of nonlinear differential equations describing a system can present a problem. The situation is quite different for the *completely nonlinear* switching system of Fig. 17-4. Here, *all of the inputs and all of the outputs are two-valued*—for example, ON or OFF. Changes from one state to the other are assumed to occur in zero time.

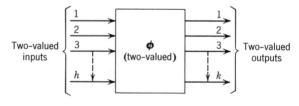

Figure 17-4

For such a switching system, every possible function of input variables can be expressed in a unique canonical form. Corresponding to any possible ϕ, a table can display the value of outputs for any set of inputs. The correspondence between the table and the canonical form can be made one-to-one. Thus the solution results from a routine procedure.

The time-varying or sequential system problem has also been solved for two-valued inputs and outputs. In a sequential system, the output due to a new input may (or may not) depend on one or more preceeding inputs. Any such system may be described by equations in a general form or by a table with appropriate headings for all possible inputs, outputs, and sequential states.

Today, the problem of the analysis of such sequential systems is completely solved. Given a system, the system equations can be written. The table can be prepared from the equations, and can show exactly how the system behaves for any initial state and input sequence.

Conversely, once a table is made up for a proposed system, the sequence of design steps may be reversed to make it possible to draw a system diagram. The only problem is to design economical arrangements. There are routine procedures to do so.

A queer state of affairs indeed! Some nearly linear equations offer enormous difficulty; some completely nonlinear equations are quite tractable.

Use of Analogs

The concept of operations on time-varying energy is applicable to systems designed for quite different purposes. By using energy, length, and time as basic variables, analogs for such fundamental concepts as force and power can be set up for many kinds of systems (e.g., mechanical, electrical, etc.). Then a solution for one kind of system can be used for quite a different system.

Analogs between mechanical and electrical systems have been exploited for a number of years, particularly in the design of acoustical devices such as loudspeakers. This idea can be extended to take in more forms of energy. Also, time variations can be introduced. For example, Schelkunoff has shown the relation between Maxwell's electromagnetic field theory and transmission line theory.

Naturally, analogs must be used with caution because they can sometimes lead to error. Yet, the literature has many articles in which such solutions of equations describing phenomena in one kind of system are used for a quite different kind of system. For example, an analogy between electromagnetism and gravitation allows calculation of various gravitational forces by considering the equivalent electromagnetic problem. Thus anyone who has competence in electromagnetic theory can study a situation of experimental interest in gravitational theory and calculate expected effects with enough accuracy to see whether they warrant further study. Again, problems in optics and photography are attacked by the methods employed in transmission theory in designing passive filters and active amplifiers.

Further, Schelkunoff has pointed out that for many (if not all) systems, a basic relation applies:

$$\frac{\text{Force or pressure}}{\text{Flow}} = \text{Impedance}$$

This relation can be used to define a generalized impedance. For an electrical system, the three possible kinds of components of impedances are resistances, inductances and capacitances; for other sysand electrical system, the three possible kinds of components of important contribution.

18

Important Concepts and Ideas of Information Theory

Introduction

An essential part of a mathematical model of a system is an appropriate mathematical description of information as a time-varying energy flow. Unfortunately, no completely satisfactory "systems information theory" is available in the literature. For these reasons, it is not only desirable but very important to have a suitable system-oriented information theory.

A well-developed "information theory" for investigating certain communication problems exists today. The literature pertaining to this "classical" information theory is quite extensive. In almost all of the work, the model assumed explicitly or implicitly describes a communication channel. The theory has led to understanding many important aspects of information handling over noisy channels. Some of this classical theory has very important implications for system designers. In particular, certain existence theorems set fundamental bounds on what is possible in information handling. Such fundamental bounds can help us to avoid trying to do the impossible.

In this chapter, some important and pertinent concepts, assumptions, and formulas of existing information theory are summarized. Findings due to many workers are included. To achieve brevity, many details less pertinent to systems design are only mentioned, or even omitted. Furthermore, no proofs of theorems are given.

Shannon's Model of a Communication System

As shown in Fig. 18-1, in Shannon's model* a communication system may be divided into five parts.

*C. E. Shannon, "A Mathematical Theory of Communication," *BSTJ*, Vol. 37, July, October, 1948.

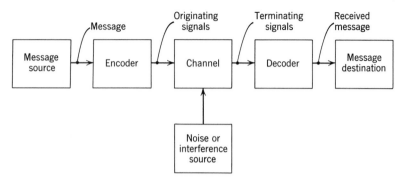

Figure 18-1

1. The "information source" produces a message or series of messages.

2. The "transmitter" or "encoder" operates on the message and produces signals suitable for transmission over the channel.

3. The "transmission channel" (frequently shortened to just "the channel") carries the signals from the transmitter to the receiver (e.g., a pair of wires, the band of radio frequencies assigned to a particular station).

4. The "receiver" or "decoder" operates inversely to the transmitter to reconstruct the message from the signal.

5. The "destination" is the person (or thing) for whom the message is intended.

This model (sometimes with minor variations) has almost always been assumed by writers on information theory ever since Shannon's results appeared.

In many practical situations (e.g., in telephony) one such five-element communication system is the input for the next.

In the 1920s, two fundamental concepts were developed: Nyquist's Sampling Theorem, and Hartley's Bandwidth-Time Relation. These famous theorems were derived for telegraph and telephone channels, in other words, for communication systems represented by the model of Fig. 18-1.

The Sampling Theorem

Nyquist's famous "sampling" theorem states that a function of time, $f(t)$, limited to a band 0 to W cycles per second can be completely specified for a time, T seconds, by $2TW$ numbers. Stated differently, the numbers are the ordinates of the function at discrete points $\frac{1}{2}W$ seconds apart. This statement is a restricted (but widely used) form of the sampling theorem.

A similar statement can be made of any function for which Fourier analysis is applicable. This fact will be used later in deriving a mathematical description of a zero-entropy energy source.

The $2TW$ numbers can be obtained by sampling the function twice per cycle of the highest frequency contained in the function for an interval of T seconds. Thus functions limited to a band W cycles per second wide and T seconds long correspond to points in a space of $2TW$ dimensions.

Hartley's Bandwidth-Time Relation

Hartley implied that the "quantity of information" which can be transmitted over a channel in a bandwidth W in time T is proportional to

$$2WT \log S$$

where S is the number of distinguishable values in the signal (e.g., values of amplitude, frequency, or power). Thus to transmit a given amount of information, a definite minimum product of bandwidth and time is required.

Further

$$I = \log \text{ (number of possible choices)} \qquad (18.1)$$

where I equals the amount of information.

If the number of possible choices is two, a unit amount of information is often called a "bit."

Nyquist's Theorem on Telegraph Signaling Speed

In signal-on–signal-off telegraphy, the speed of signaling is usually specified in dots per second, i.e., the number of signal elements per second divided by two.

Nyquist showed that (subject to a few idealizing assumptions) it is possible to transmit two bits per second of digital information for each cycle of bandwidth while maintaining at least one position in each bit that is not influenced by adjacent bits. Then, neglecting

noise interference, a sample taken at the undisturbed point can determine whether the signal is on or off.

The Uncertainty Principle

Gabor has stated an "uncertainty principle" based on the inverse
relationship between signal duration and the effective spectrum bandwidth. For time-varying signals with a limited bandwidth ΔW, the
shortest signal which may be measured is ΔT, where

$$\Delta W \cdot \Delta T \simeq \text{a constant near 1} \tag{18.2}$$

The exact constant depends on an arbitrary definition of ΔT and
ΔW.

Gabor compares the situation to Heisenberg's Uncertainty Principle.
He also shows that some of the mathematical ideas of quantum theory
may be applied to signal analysis. Of course, quantum theory is
not applied—only some of the mathematical tools.

The Communication Theory Problem

In information theory a fundamental communication problem is
to reproduce at some point or points either exactly or approximately
a message selected at another point. The important word is "selected,"
because the actual message is assumed to be selected from a set
of possible messages. Stated another way, the transmitted message
must be unexpected and hence unpredictable, because if the receiver
knew what it was beforehand, no information whatever would be
gained by receiving it. Thus the amount of information conveyed
by a message depends on the unexpectedness of that information.

Brillouin describes this central problem of the theory: Suppose
we have a set of possible events whose probabilities of occurrence
are

$$p_1, p_2, \ldots p_n$$

The communication system must operate adequately for each possible selection from the set of possible messages. This broad requirement determines the properties of the channel or channels that must
be provided and also the properties of the devices that generate and
receive the signals carrying the messages.

The operation of converting a message into physical signals suitable for transmission is called *coding;* the operation of recovering the message from the signals is called *decoding.* In general, decoding is the inverse of coding. To perform these operations, input signal energy is supplied to the coder and the output energy flows from the decoder. The coder and decoder are sometimes called *transducers.*

If the output signs of one transducer can be identified with the input signs of a second, they can be connected in tandem and the result is also a transducer. If a second transducer operates on the output of the first and recovers the original input, the second is called the inverse of the first.

In many practical cases, the signal transmission is interfered with by noise or other disturbances. Then the receiver cannot always be certain what was transmitted. Sometimes it can not be certain whether anything at all was transmitted. For satisfactory performance, the noise and other disturbances must be kept within tolerable limits. Otherwise, acceptable delivery of the message information may be impossible. Shannon's original paper discussed the effects of noise on information transmission. Many workers have followed the trail he blazed.

Shannon's Model for Discrete Signals

Shannon generalizes Hartley's concept about the amount of information. He takes into account several effects encountered in trying to transmit information over a noisy channel. His model (Fig. 18-1) is idealized except for noise in the signal medium connecting the signal transmitter and the receiver.

The Information Source

For his analysis, Shannon assumes a discrete message source that generates information sign-by-sign. The source chooses successive signs according to certain probabilities that depend both on preceding choices and the sign in question.

The source is the input of a discrete transducer. Its input is one sequence of signs and its output is a second sequence.

Under these assumptions, the receiver can only guess what sign was sent. From the viewpoint of the receiver, such a source falls into the class of devices described by mathematicians as "conjectural" or "stochastic," and such a physical message source (or the mathematical model of such a source) is called a *stochastic process.*

Conversely, any stochastic process producing a discrete sequence of signs chosen from a finite set of signs is a *discrete source*. This definition includes such examples as (1) English and French syllables or words, (2) continuous information sources rendered discrete by some quantizing process, and (3) mathematical models which merely define a stochastic process that generates a sequence of symbols.

Shannon analyses such discrete transducers in terms of Markoff processes.

Markoff and Ergodic Processes

Mathematicians call a stochastic process producing a discrete sequence of signs chosen from a finite set of signs a discrete Markoff process: discrete, because it deals with discrete signs rather than continuous functions; Markoff, because Markoff was the mathematician who investigated the theory of such processes.

The theory of Markoff processes or chains deals with an arrangement which can exist in several states, p_1, p_2, . . . p_n. If the arrangement is in state p_a, the probability that it will change to state p_b is given by a transition probability p_{ab}. Markoff processes are found in many fields other than information theory such as in biology and genetics, and in the blocking of calls in telephone central offices.

Among the possible discrete Markoff processes, one group, the *ergodic processes,* has special properties of significance in information theory. In this group every sequence produced by the process has the same statistical properties: roughly speaking, *an ergodic process is statistically homogeneous.* Take printed material as an example of such a process. To be statistically homogeneous, the letter frequencies, two-letter-sequence frequencies, and so on, of particular groups of letters must approach definite limits as the length of the groups increase. These limits are independent of the particular group examined. Spoken and printed English, French, and other languages are usually considered to meet the definition.

Encoding as a Markoff Process

With finite internal memory, the number of possible states of the encoder is finite. The output depends on both the present state and present input symbol. The next state is a second function of these quantities. Thus in terms of a Markoff process, the transducer can be described:

$$x_n = f(u_n, a_n) \qquad a_{n+1} = g(u_n, a_n) \qquad (18.3)$$

where u_n is the nth input symbol; a_n the transducer state when u_n is introduced; and x_n the output symbol or sequence of symbols produced when u_n is introduced and the state is a_n.

Shannon's Entropy Formula

For this encoding model, in some senses a quantity which Shannon calls H measures the amount of information produced by an ergodic process. In such a process,

$$H = -K \sum_{i=1}^{n} p_i \log p_i \qquad (18.4)$$

where p_i is the probability of state i and K is a positive constant, a scale factor.

If the logarithmic base is 2, then H is expressed in bits per sign.

H has the form of entropy as defined in certain formulations of statistical mechanics, for example, the H in Boltzmann's theorem, which states that starting with any distribution function, the entropy must increase until equilibrium is reached at the maximum possible value.

The entropy of a system is a measure of its disorder. It always tends to increase. Information is a measure of order—hence the minus sign in Eq. 18-4.

Negentropy

Brillouin has pointed out that a source of energy not in equilibrium is necessary in any information system. This source pours negative entropy into the system. From this negative entropy, information is obtained. With this information, we may operate and rebuild negative entropy and complete a cycle:

$$\text{Negentropy} \rightarrow \text{information} \rightarrow \text{negentropy} \qquad (18.5)$$

Brillouin coined the abbreviation *negentropy* to characterize entropy with the opposite sign. Entropy always increases; negentropy always decreases. Shannon's results can be put:

Information → signal → negentropy on the channel
→ signal received → information received (18.6)

Power Source Requirement for Perfect Encoding: Zero-entropy

For perfect coding, the source of energy to be encoded must be perfectly predictable—in other words, it must have zero-entropy; otherwise it would contribute some uncertainty to the transmitted signals. Moreover, the coding operation should produce only wanted signals without mistakes.

Definition of a Zero-entropy Energy Source

In information theory, H can be thought of as the uncertainty of the generating process. Thus a source that can produce only one particular information sequence—however long or complex—has zero entropy. This definition has some strange consequences. For example, take a computing machine calculating the successive digits of π. According to the theory, no channel is required to transmit this information to another point, because another machine could compute the same sequence. As a practical matter, if you do not have such a machine and need the information, a handbook can be very helpful.

Condition for Maximum Entropy

For maximum H, the transmitted signs should all be equally likely, because from the viewpoint of the receiver this is the most uncertain situation. In other words,

$$H_{max} = \log m \qquad (18.7)$$

where m is the number of signs in the alphabet.

Further, for maximum uncertainty successive signs or groups of signs should not be correlated.

If there are only two possible events, such as the signs 0 and 1,

$$H = -p \log p - (1 - p) \log (1 - p) \qquad (18.8)$$

and H is a maximum when $p = q = \frac{1}{2}$ (i.e., the signs are equally likely).

Efficiency and Redundancy

The ratio of the actual H to the maximum possible H using the same signs (see Eq. 18-7) is called the *relative entropy* or *efficiency E*.

Redundancy is a property of languages, codes, and sign systems when excess information is present that helps communication despite interference during transmission.

$$\text{Redundancy} = 1 - E \qquad (18.9)$$

Repetition is a simple form of redundancy, as is writing the amount of a check in two different ways.

Ordinary written English is about 50% redundant, if statistical structure over more than about eight letters is disregarded. In other words, about half the letters can be omitted and the original test can still be recovered.

Amount of Information in a Particular Message

For a particular class of messages, the amount of information in a particular message I is the number of bits needed to encode the message using the most efficient code for the class as a whole. For a message of M signs:

$$I = M\mathrm{H} = -\log p_m = \log 1/p_m \qquad (18.10)$$

where p_m is the probability of a particular sequence of M symbols.

As an example, a four-digit number may be expressed by 13+ bits, so this is the amount of information. If the four digits are encoded less efficiently, the redundancy is increased, but the amount of information is unchanged.

Capacity and Information Rate of a Noisy Channel

Let $\mathrm{H}(u)$ be the entropy rate of source u. If messages are received as sent, the sending and receiving rates are obviously the same. Reception removes the uncertainty as to what was sent. But noise or interference with the messages in transit causes some information to be lost. Now because entropy is a measure of uncertainty, the conditional entropy of the messages at x (i.e., of the received signal), $\mathrm{H}_x(u)$ measures the average rate of information loss. The actual information-carrying rate of the channel, R is:

$$R = \mathrm{H}(u) - \mathrm{H}_x(u) \qquad (18.11)$$

Shannon calls $\mathrm{H}_x(u)$ "equivocation." It is the average amount by which the transmitted and received messages differ.

If $\mathrm{H}(x)$ is the uncertainty of the mutilated message and $\mathrm{H}_u(x)$ the uncertainty of (or false information in) the received message, then the net rate of receiving information is $\mathrm{H}(x) - \mathrm{H}_u(x)$.

Combining the two expressions gives the total loss of information:

$$\mathrm{H}_x(u) = \mathrm{H}(u) + \mathrm{H}_u(x) - \mathrm{H}(x) \qquad (18.12)$$

The capacity of a noisy channel C is the maximum rate for all possible input sources:

$$C = \max [\mathrm{H}(u) - \mathrm{H}_x(u)] \text{ in bits per second} \qquad (18.13)$$

Equation 18.13 states that for an arbitrarily small error frequency exceeding zero, it is possible to transmit at rate C but not faster.

If $\mathrm{H}_x(u) = 0$ in Eq. 18.13, the channel is noiseless; and the entropy and therefore the capacity are maximum.

An equation similar to Equation 18.13 for a binary code is:

$$C_s = 1 + p \log_2 p + (1 - p) \log_2 (1 - p) \qquad (18.14)$$

where C_s is the channel capacity. The subscript s differentiates it from the general case. The probabilitity of error in receiving any sign is denoted by p.

Several techniques may be useful in signaling over a noisy channel. A trained radio operator can read signals—even distorted signals—in the presence of severe static. Prediction techniques, based on the self-correlation of the signals from instant to instant is useful under some circumstances, such as tracking a target. "Maximum-likelihood" detectors try to make the best guess as to which of several possible signs was actually sent.

But there are optimal ways of "encoding" the message to minimize the information loss due to noise or interference. Equation 18.13 shows the statistics of the source can be adjusted to maximize the information rate. More information can be sent when the noise is less, and vice versa. This adjustment is the statistical analog of impedance matching in transmission networks.

Also, it is possible to encode and transmit supplementary data over a correction channel with a capacity equal to $H_x(u)$ and correct all but an arbitrarily small fraction of the errors, but not with a channel having a capacity less than $H_x(u)$.

Shannon's Model for Continuously Varying Signals

Entropy Formula

Theoretically, signals or messages (or both) that are continuously variable functions of time can assume an infinite number of values and so require an infinite number of bits for exact specification.

Formally, by analogy to Eq. 18.4, the entropy of a continuous distribution with the density distribution function in a function space $p(x)$ can be defined:

$$H = - \int_{-\infty}^{\infty} p(x) \log p(x) \, dx \qquad (18.15)$$

Note that the integration extends from $-\infty$ to $+\infty$.

In practical situations, the messages or signals do not—in fact, can not—require an infinite frequency band for *adequate* transmission and interpretation.

By the sampling theorem a function of time, limited to a band
0 to W cycles per second, can be specified for a time T seconds
long by $2TW$ numbers. In physical arrangements, the bandwidth
is always limited, so the $-\infty$, $+\infty$ integration limits are replaced
by finite values.

Capacity and Information Rate of a Channel Disturbed by White Gaussian Noise

A channel input that is a nonbandwith-limited, continuous function
of time requires an infinite channel capacity for exact recovery at
the receiving point. Furthermore, a noisy channel has finite capacity,
so exact transmission is theoretically impossible in such cases.

But a definite rate for a channel carrying continuously varying
functions of time can be found if only a certain approximation to
exact recovery is required.

With the bandwidth restriction in mind, the information transmission rate R for a continuous channel is defined analogously to the
discrete channel case:

$$R = \mathrm{H}(u) - \mathrm{H}_x(u) \qquad (18.16)$$

The channel capacity is the maximum information rate for the
most-demanding input signals.

If the signal and noise are independent and the received signal
is the sum of the transmitted signal and the noise, then

$$R = \mathrm{H}(x) - \mathrm{H}(N) \qquad (18.17)$$

i.e., R is the entropy of the received signal $\mathrm{H}(x)$ less the entropy
of the noise $\mathrm{H}(N)$.

For a given average power, white Gaussian noise has the maximum
possible entropy; so it is the worst kind of noise from the standpoint
of interference.

With average transmitted power S, the capacity of a channel with
bandwidth W carrying continuously varying functions of time and
perturbed by a white Gaussian noise of average power N is:

$$C = W \log_2 \left(\frac{S + N}{N}\right) = W \log_2 (1 + S/N) \qquad (18.18)$$

Coding methods have been devised that can approach the ideal
maximum rate; but so far they have been little used.

In general, more and more delay is needed in the encoder as ideal

encoding is approached. The encoder must examine more and mor
input information before it can decide how to encode most efficiently.

Encoding against White Gaussian Noise

It follows from Eq. 18.18 that by proper encoding for the particula
channel, a maximum number of bits per second can be transmitte
with arbitrarily small error frequency; no higher rate can be trans
mitted. This conclusion from Eq. 18.18 is another important resul
of Shannon's work.

To approximate the maximum rate, the transmitted signals mus
approximate white Gaussian noise in statistical properties. With sucl
a signal source, the received signals have a flat spectrum, i.e., th
power is uniformly distributed over the used band. Hence, the sourc
and noise spectra must be complementary—more signal must be ser
where there is less noise, and vice versa.

The derivation of Eq. 18.18 does not tell how to encode, merel,
that as the maximum rate is approached the statistics of the signa
approach those of white noise.

Simple codes, such as those used in telegraphy, fall 7 or 8 d
short of the ideal. Much effort has been devoted by many peopl
to the study of codes for high-speed data transmission over nois·
communication channels.

Equation 18.18 gives the same rate as Nyquist's theorem (2 bit
per second per cycle of bandwidth) for a signal-to-noise ratio o
3. For many practical cases, this ratio exceeds 3. For these cases
Shannon's formula indicates a greater capacity than Nyquist'
formula.

Bandwidth-power Trades

Equation 18.18 also shows that bandwidth can be traded fo
signal power, or vice versa. For example, an increase in W ca
allow a decrease in S.

Successful applications of the capacity formula have been mad
to the detection of very weak signals in noise (such as in ultralong
range radar detection).

Decrease of Entropy by a Transducer

Shannon proved that a transducer must decrease (or at best main·
tain constant) the entropy of its information input. This is ye
another of the numerous important results of his work.

Information and Energy

H is expressed in bits per sign; in thermodynamics, in joules per degree. In suggesting a link between information and energy, Felker has worked out the minimum energy cost of a bit as 0.114×10^{-19} joules.

Contributions of Information Theory to System Design

Despite some built-in limitations, "classical" information theory can make definite contributions to the solution of system design problems.

Information theory literature is quite extensive. Almost all of it uses the communication model, because the theory is used to explain some important aspects of the communication of information. Much of the material is devoted to three principal topics: the communication system model itself, mathematical theory of information (actually a branch of probability theory and statistics), and various considerations of entropy and uncertainty applied to physical, biological, and other systems.

A word of caution is in order. At present, it is not a completely general theory. For example, to-and-fro speech is not completely explained. Also, if there are only a few possible signals and messages are always short, coding to approach the theoretical maximum capacity of a channel runs into some difficulties. Despite such shortcomings, the theory provides a powerful tool for choosing optimum detection methods for weak signals in the presence of Gaussian noise and in the analysis of signal statistics. However, combating the effects of noise in a communication channel is not the central problem in the design, manufacture, and operation of many other kinds of systems. For example, the objective in specifying how to make a machine is to provide unequivocal information and noise-free transmission. Expressed differently, the drawings describing the parts to be made and the assembly methods should be clear and error-free. The information carried on the drawings is handed to the appropriate shop people who make the parts. In the transportation of these drawings from the sources to the users, the "noise" due to the transmission is usually negligible.

The information theory model and the system models are similar in some respects but differ in others. For this reason, it is interesting

Table 18-1   *Some Contributions of Information Theory to System Design*

    Important:
        Sampling theorem
        Hartley's bandwidth-time equation
        Concept of a zero-entropy generator
        Measures of amount of information
        Input and output entropy of any machine
        Information is carried by time-varying energy
    Less Important:
        Coding to combat noise
        Bandwidth-power trades

to classify some of the major concepts of classical information theory into those of lesser importance for most system design and those of major importance. Of course, any such classification must be somewhat arbitrary since it can only represent one opinion. Table 18-1 shows such a classification.

Take the concepts considered to be of lesser importance first. Much of the content of information theory actually is a theory of coding of messages to combat the effects of noise in a communication channel. Efficient use of the transmission channel is a major objective. White Gaussian noise is usually assumed. In a telemetry channel to a space satellite, cosmic noise from the sky and thermal noise in the early stages of the receiver are very important sources of interference. If the satellite is far away, sophisticated coding and optimum (but expensive) detection circuits are justified—because otherwise the information is not received. But all communication channels are not thus noise-limited. Today's telephone channels are engineered so that you are seldom conscious of any noise at all—much less of noise loud enough to interfere with information exchange.

In America, exchange of data between computers takes place over telephone channels. Rather unsophisticated codes that permit detection of an error are frequently used. The portion of the information containing the error is then repeated upon request from the receiving equipment. The background noise is so low that the noise interference that does cause errors is not Gaussian, but short, intense pulses (impulse noise). European telephone and telegraph administrations have had the same experience.

Armstrong's bandwidth-power trade gives us the pleasures of high fidelity, static-free FM radio.

Thus, these concepts of information theory have practical applications—even important applications. The point is that the applications are to rather specialized kinds of systems.

On the other hand, the Sampling Theorem, the Bandwidth-Time Concept, and the Zero-entropy Generator Concept lead to a classification of all possible types of system building blocks. New applications and necessary extensions of existing information theory are presented in the next few chapters.

Measures of amount of information are essential in the design of any measuring system, of any information-handling system, or of any automated process.

It seems that Shannon's proof that a transducer can at best maintain equal input and output entropy has far-reaching implications. Certainly, his proof is valid for *any machine*. Is it valid for a human being? If so, then what? If not, why not? These are important philosophical questions.

Finally, the concept that information is a form of time-varying energy is important for all system designers. By using this concept, Felker has shown that information is quantized—as are other forms of energy.

Discussion

The model of a communication system represented by Fig. 18-1 is idealized except for the presence of unwanted noise in the transmission medium. For such systems, the designer cannot know the exact behavior of either the physical embodiment of his system or the environment in which it will operate. Hence he can not describe the operation with complete certainty. Shannon appreciated that uncertainty or unexpectedness is an essential concept in any information theory. Unexpectedness can be described mathematically in terms of probabilities. Shannon did so—with some surprising results.

A modest number of such ideas have served to bring many diverse thoughts about communication systems into a unified conceptual framework. On the other hand, these unified concepts have not been too much concerned with many details of the building blocks which a designer must use to synthesize a new system.

McMillan and Slepian point out that various authors define the content of information theory differently. Some use a "Strict-Sense" definition; others, a "Wide-Sense" definition; still others, principally those working in Europe, use an extremely broad definition.

According to the "Strict-Sense" definition, information theory includes the study of: (1) *entropy*, (2) *channel capacity*, and (3) *coding* of information for transmission so that the available channel capacity is used most efficiently.

Implicit in the concept of entropy or information rate is the idea of coding the information into signs suitable for transmission. Also implicit in the concept is the idea that the output of any coder transducer, or decoder can contain no more information than the input. Studies of channel capacity examine means of combating the effects of unwanted noise in the medium on the wanted signals Essentially, performance is evaluated in terms of channel time per unit of offered information. Thus far, such abstract mathematical studies have not given system designers many useful answers in term of hardware.

The "Wide-Sense" definition covers the studies included in the "Strict-Sense" definition, but goes further and includes several allied areas. Many theoretical and mathematical studies have been devoted to *signal detection and extraction* in the presence of noise. Certain aspects of such work is akin to the testing of hypotheses. A decision must be made between the possibilities that a weak signal is or is not present in a mixture of noise and possible signal. Mathematical studies of *filtering* and *prediction theory* show the best *linear* operator to separate a signal from unwanted noise. They have been useful for some special systems and have advanced statistical communication theory.

Some parts of *modulation theory* are considered to be part of Information Theory in the Wide Sense. These parts help in a choice of the best modulation method to combat the kind of noise expected to be encountered. For example, frequency modulation systems offer considerable protection against many forms of static that can plague radio communication.

Information-processing studies complete the list of topics. Such studies have been very helpful in understanding how to design certain radar systems and other systems where the signal-to-noise ratios are very small.

The broadest definition also includes many other areas to which the word "information" might be applied. The meaning of the word is interpreted very broadly indeed under this definition. We give some subject matter already included in published studies:

Parts of physics
Parts of psychology
Linguistics; semantics; language translation by machine
Cryptography

Cybernetics
Pattern recognition
Data storage and retrieval

The list is long. And it grows longer year by year.

Despite the impressive technical achievements of existing Information Theory, it has had only modest success in helping to design new systems. Even if the broadest definition is used, outstanding practical applications have been few.

The point of view adopted in this book is that the findings of the theory do have wide application. Some of the formulas show how to divide the possible from the impossible. They define fruitless pursuits equivalent to trying to build a perpetual motion machine.

Furthermore, a corollary of the theory is that only a few kinds of operations are possible on information-carrying energy or on information itself. Recognition of this corollary can give further insight into the system design problem. It may have many other important applications—for example, in biological systems.

For the design, production, operation, and maintenance of systems, error-free generation, coding, transmission, detection, and use of information are all essential. To meet these requirements, we have several people check proposed information for errors. Editors check for meaning, grammar, and syntax. Proofreaders check the coding for spelling and typographical errors. Printed sheets are examined for noise in the form of streaks and smudges. Ophthalmologists check for defects in the vision of the human beings who receive and use the information.

Systems involving information in graphic form have been used and improved for centuries. Life today would be vastly different if they did not exist. Recent advances have been made by the introduction of rapid, relatively cheap processes for copying, microfilming, and storing all sorts of graphic material.

Graphic systems are examples of systems in which the signal is deliberately maintained far above the noise level. High-fidelity radio systems are another example. By the design, noise interference with the wanted information is made very small. Information Theory, even Information Theory under the broadest definition, has devoted only meager time to the almost-perfect systems. Most of the published studies consider the small signal-to-noise ratio end of the spectrum of possible systems. The present approach tries to take a broader view. By so doing, system design can learn what Information Theory has to teach.

Description of a Predictable
Power Source

A zero-entropy (i.e., completely predictable) power source and an information (i.e., unpredictable) source are each assumed to have one output and no input.

Description of a Planar Energy Flow at Any Instant

In Fig. 19-1, the output from the zero-entropy power source across a plane of observation A is to be described. A set of variables can describe the flow at any instant. These variables may be thought of as components of a multidimensional vector. One or more of the components may vary with the time in a predictable manner.

Assume a rectangle is drawn to include the maximum spatial extent of the power source plane in fhe x and y coordinate directions (Fig. 19-2).

The location of the plane in space may be described in terms of any suitable set of coordinates.

Note that the surface of observation is a plane. But certain three-dimensional surfaces (e.g., cylindrical or spherical) can be mapped onto a plane by known mathematical methods. In theory, such a

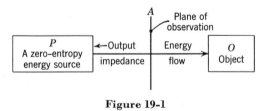

Figure 19-1

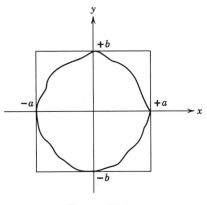

Figure 19-2

mapping of a three-dimensional surface is always possible.   In practice, the mathematical difficulties may be extremely great.

Obviously, point or line sources can be considered as special cases of a planar source.   Flow from an idealized point source is sometimes assumed in heat and optical problems.   Examples of flow from one-dimensional sources occur in electrical circuits; flows in three dimensions may occur in radiation from a line source (cylindrical waves) or an isotropic radiator (spherical waves).   The sun is an example of a three-dimensional energy source.

The division of the planar extent into elementary cells is accomplished by applying two well-known results.

First, the wave form of the energy distribution over the plane at any instant is described in terms of sines and cosines.   To do so, Mertz' and Gray's method for analyzing the scanning of a scene by a flying spot is used.   Actually, Foucault used similar mathematics to solve some optical problems about a hundred years earlier.   For the analysis of the wave forms, sine and cosine waves have at least two advantages (1) the mathematics is relatively simple and (2) analogous wave forms exist in many branches of physics (e.g., in optics, in electromagnetic waves, and in vibrations of strings).   Hence, the results have wide application.

Second, if the wave forms are described in terms of sines and cosines, the cell dimensions can be determined with the help of the Sampling Theorem.

Now, let Fig. 19-2 represent a time-invariant planar energy source of dimensions $2a$ and $2b$, with reference axes x and y.   The flow is out of and perpendicular to the paper. This source is scanned horizontally by an infinitesimal aperture.

Then along any horizontal line, Mertz and Gray show that the energy amplitude $E(x)$ may be expressed by a single Fourier series.

$$E(x, y_1) = \sum_{m=-\infty}^{+\infty} A_m \exp j\pi(mx/a) \qquad (19.1)$$

For Fourier's theorem to apply, $E(x)$ must be finite, continuous, and single-valued. In the practical cases to be discussed, these requirements are met.

In Eq. 19-1, the complex amplitude A_m represents both the absolute intensity and the phase angle of the mth component; $j = \sqrt{-1}$. The complex amplitude of the corresponding component with a negative subscript is the conjugate.

The fundamental space period is $f_1 = 1/x_1$. Each harmonic component mf_1 is an integral multiple of f_1. Its complex amplitude A_m represents both the absolute intensity and the phase angle. The dimensional units of $f(x)$ and A_m are the same.

Along each line in the x direction, a similar series holds with different coefficients, so the A's are functions of y and may be written as a Fourier series along y:

$$A_n = \sum_{n=-\infty}^{\infty} A_{mn} \exp j\pi(ny/b) \qquad (19.2)$$

Substitution in Eq. 19.1 gives the double Fourier series:

$$E(x, y) = \sum_{m=-\infty}^{+\infty} \sum_{n=-\infty}^{+\infty} A_{mn} \exp j\pi(mx/a + ny/b) \qquad (19.3)$$

For physical interpretation, the $+m$, $+n$ term can be combined with the $-m$, $-n$ term to give the single $(m, +n)$th component. Similarly, the $+m$, $-n$ term can be combined with the $-m$, $+n$ term to give the single $(m, -n)$ component. Then Eq. 19.3 can be expressed as a cosine series

$$E(x, y) = \sum_{m=0}^{+\infty} \sum_{n=0}^{+\infty} a_{mn} \cos [\pi(mx/a + ny/b) + \varphi_{mn}] \qquad (19.4)$$

Where
$$A_{mn} = \tfrac{1}{2}a_{mn}(\exp j\varphi_{mn})$$

and
$$A_{-m-n} = \tfrac{1}{2}a_{mn}(\exp -j\varphi_{mn})$$

where a_{mn} is always real. Each term represents a real, two-dimensional sinusoidal variation in amplitude across the plane.

The description is built up by superposing waves of various periods extending across the plane in various directions. Using amplitude as a third dimension, Fig. 19-3 shows examples of such components. A component (m, n) passes through m periods along a horizontal line, and n periods along a vertical line. The slope with respect to the x axis is the negative reciprocal of the slope of the line of fastest intensity variation, $-mb/na$.

For the same values of m and n, the $m, +n$ component and the $m, -n$ component have equal space wavelengths but slope in opposite

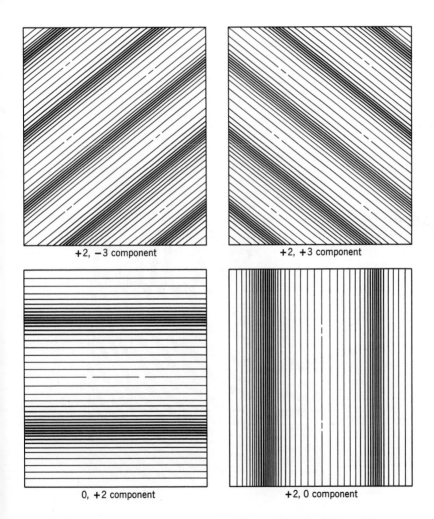

$+2, -3$ component $+2, +3$ component

$0, +2$ component $+2, 0$ component

Figure 19-3 (Courtesy of the Bell System Technical Journal.)

directions to the x axis. If m is zero, the crests are parallel to the x axis; if n is zero, parallel to the y axis. Both m and n equal to zero gives a uniform intensity distribution over the entire plane.

The wavelength of a component is

$$\lambda_{mn} = 1/\sqrt{(m/2a)^2 + (n/2b)^2} \tag{19.5}$$

Figure 19-4 shows components up to m and $n = 4$. This and Fig. 19-3 are reproduced from Mertz' and Gray's monograph.

The component wavelengths and orientations vary only with the

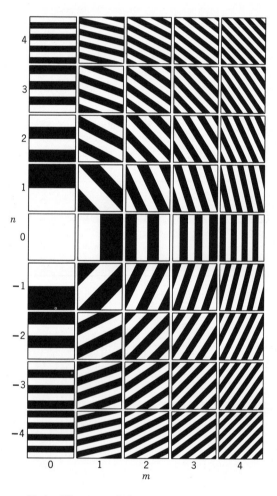

Figure 19-4   (Courtesy of the Bell system Technical Journal.)

shape and size of the rectangular plane. A change in the relative amplitudes or phases of the components (or both) changes the representation.

In a physical system, a perfect discontinuity is impossible. So "discontinuous" spatial structures (edges) are describable in terms of sines and cosines; but an accurate description requires spatial harmonics with very short space periods.

The Sampling Theorem, Cell Dimensions, and Resolution

The Sampling Theorem states that a one-dimensional wave in time can be described by a set of $2TW$ numbers. By analogy, a one-dimensional wave in space can be described by a set of $2LW_s$ numbers. L is the extent in space in meters. The number of spatial periods per meter is between 0 and W_s.

At any instant, a two-dimensional or planar wave in space can be described by two sets of such numbers—one for the x coordinate and one for the y. Similarly, a three-dimensional wave in space can be described by three sets.

For a planar wave, the period of the shortest space-period cosine term in the x and y directions determine the sides of the minimum cell, δx and δy, and hence the size of the smallest spatial detail that can be resolved.

The resolution limits the maximum possible information density per unit area that can result by modulating the zero-entropy source.

Direction of Energy Flow

Within each elementary cell of the plane, the direction of energy flow is perpendicular to the plane. An appropriate vector can represent both the energy amplitude and the direction of flow.

In mapping a three-dimensional flow onto a plane, the mapping function must describe changes in both amplitudes and directions.

Form of Energy

The form of energy is one component of the multidimensional vector describing the flow.

Different forms may conveniently be given numerical values by assigning them numbered tags—for example, 1, to electrical; 2, to mechanical; 3, to acoustical; 4, to thermal; and so on.

Each form of energy uses a system of units, for example, volts, amperes, and ohms for electrical energy. Analogous units exist for mechanical, acoustical, and other forms of energy.

Variations with Time

For an unvarying zero-entropy source or a "snapshot" of the instantanous value of a changing but predictable source, the mapping d the space variables are constants. The form of energy does not vary with time.

For a changing planar source, the flow of energy from the elementary cells describing the spatial energy distribution varies with time. Further, the mapping function may vary with time.

In describing the operation of a power source, time is assigned a separate coordinate, t. T stands for an extent in time; and δt for the maximum possible resolution in time.

Now, for a particular elementary cell, any periodic wave variation in time can be described in terms of a Fourier series:

$$f(t) = \sum_{n=-\infty}^{\infty} A_{nt} \exp\left(j2\pi nf_{1t}t\right) \tag{19.6}$$

The restrictions stated previously apply here also.

The fundamental frequency is $f_{1t} = 1/t_1$. The frequency of each harmonic component is an integral multiple of f_{1t}.

Because $f(t)$ is real, the imaginary parts of each component in the summation must cancel. This cancellation occurs between the amplitudes A_{nt} of the components of equal positive and negative values of n. The dc component ($n = 0$) always has a real amplitude $A_o \geq 0$.

The complex amplitude A_{nt} of a component of frequency nf_{1t} is:

$$A_{nt} = \int_{-t_1/2}^{t_1/2} f(t) \exp\left(-j2\pi nf_{1t}t\right) dt \tag{19.7}$$

The highest frequency in $f(t)$, f_{nt}/t_1, determines the bandwidth W.

The sinusoidal nature of each component can be seen from the several equivalent expressions for a unit vector rotating at frequency nf_1,

$$\exp\left(j2\pi nf_{1t}t\right) = \cos\left(2\pi nf_{1t}t\right) + j\sin\left(2\pi nf_{1t}t\right) = \operatorname{cis}\left(2\pi nf_{1t}t\right)$$

Equation 19.6 can describe any changes with time of the energy flow of any particular cell in the space pattern of a zero-entropy source. Hence, the time variations of the energy flow can be expressed in terms of sines and cosines.

Fourier Integrals

Representation of a transient or nonperiodic wave form is possible by "Fourier Integrals." A photographic flash bulb is an example of such a zero-entropy energy source. Instead of a number of distinct components, the distribution of energy over a frequency spectrum is described. Thus, the Fourier series and Fourier integral are analogous to the line spectrum and band spectrum of light waves.

In extending the series concepts to the integral, a transient is assumed to occur only once. Thus t_1 is made very large and the corresponding f_{1t} very small. Also A_{nt} is changed to the frequency spectrum $A(f)$, representing the "amplitude-frequency density" or "amplitude per unit of frequency" in the vicinity of frequency f instead of nf_{1t}. This density has the dimensional units of $f(t)$ multiplied by time. For example, if $f(t)$ is in volts, $A_t(f)$, is in volts per cycle per second or volts-seconds.

With these steps, the Fourier integral for describing the wave form of a transient or nonperiodic wave in terms of its frequency spectrum follows:

$$f(t) = \int_{-\infty}^{\infty} A_t(f) \exp{(j2\pi f_t t)} \, df \tag{19.8}$$

Another form describes the frequency spectrum in terms of the transient or nonperiodic wave

$$A(f) = \int_{-\infty}^{\infty} f(t) \exp{(-j2\pi f_t t)} \, dt \tag{19.9}$$

A useful corollary of the Fourier integral is the "energy integral":

$$\int_{-\infty}^{\infty} |A|^2 \, df = \int_{-\infty}^{\infty} f^2 \, dt \tag{19.10}$$

Thus, the energy of the transient is proportional to the area under the energy distribution curve (plotted in terms of $|A|^2$) over the frequency range. This concept can be used to evaluate the energy of random noise. Random noise can be considered to be composed of many pulses of random amplitudes occuring at random times. The energy $|A|^2$ is independent of the phases.

The Sampling Theorem for Time Variations

By invoking the Sampling Theorem, time variations of the energy flow in any cell may be described by $2TW$ numbers. The highest period term in the description determines the minimum cell length and hence the resolution in time.

The resolution limits the maximum possible information rate per unit time that can result from modulating the source.

Potential Information Capacity

At any instant along a coordinate of space x_1, x_2, . . . x_i, the length is L_i. Thus the maximum possible number of cells along a space coordinate

$$N_i = L_i/\delta i \qquad (19.11)$$

For a planar zero-entropy source, the total number of dimensions is the sum of the number required to describe both the cells in the plane and any variations with time of the energy flow through the cells. Then, the maximum number N of possible states at any instant is:

$$N = \Pi N_i \qquad (19.12)$$

Within the boundaries drawn for the plane, some cells may not lie within the boundaries of the power source. Such cells may be called "unoccupied." An unoccupied cell cannot be controlled to generate information.

If the number of unoccupied or vacant states in the rectangle is N_0, then the potential information capacity of the zero-entropy power source at any instant is:

$$N - N_0 \qquad (19.13)$$

Further, along the time coordinate, the maximum possible number of time cells for a duration T is

$$T_i = T/\delta t \qquad (19.14)$$

If the number of unoccupied intervals during T is T_0 then the potential information capacity of the power source during the occupied intervals is:

$$(N - N_0)(T - T_0) \qquad (19.15)$$

Thevinin Equivalent Source

The concept of a Thevinin equivalent circuit for a zero-entropy power source is useful for computations involving energy flow from the source into an object such as a receiver.

For two terminal networks, Thevenin's theorem can be expressed: With respect to any pair of terminals considered as output terminals, the network can be replaced by a branch having an impedance Z_s equal to the driving point impedance at these terminals in series with an electromotive force E equal to the open-circuit voltage across these terminals.

An analogous theorem can be expressed in terms of the short-circuit current flowing through the output node of the network.

Thevenin's theorem may be generalized to describe an equivalent source for an elementary cell in the plane of observation. The generalized pressure may vary as a function of time E_{xyz}, ω_t. It is in series with a generalized impedance Z_{xyz}, ω_t.

Except in a one-dimensional case, the coordinates in space for pressure and impedance may vary with direction.

This "source" impedance (internal impedance of an appropriate generalized Thevenin generator) of an elementary area or cell is a generalized vector impedance as described by Schelkunoff.

Description of an Object

In Fig. 19.1, the energy flow is assumed to flow across a plane at A to cause some change in the object. The object is assumed to have no output. Thus, it dissipates all of the input energy. In other words, it is an energy sink. If all of the energy is not dissipated, it must appear at one or more outputs. Objects that transmit some energy are considered in a later chapter.

The energy flow into the object may be described in terms of the variables discussed previously in this chapter.

The object is assumed to contain no sources of energy. The input impedance of an elementary area or cell of the object is a generalized vector impedance. Generalized vector impedances have just been discussed in connection with a Thevenin equivalent source.

20

Description of an
Information Source

In Fig. 20-1, information-carrying energy is assumed to flow across a plane at B. A three-dimensional source can be mapped onto the plane.

To convey information, zero-entropy energy is changed or modulated so that it becomes unpredictable. The variables to describe the information-carrying flow must include:

1. The energy flow in space and time. The necessary variables are the same as those for the zero-entropy energy flow from a power source.

However, to convey the information, the flow must not be com-

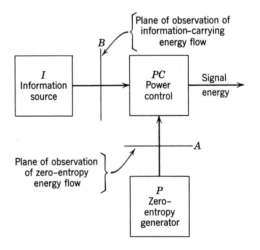

Figure 20-1

pletely predictable. Hence, additional variables are necessary to describe

2. The information structure in space or time or both and finally, variables to describe

3. An equivalent Thevenin source.

Information Structure

The information structure is made up of a set of signs distributed in some way over the cells describing the zero-entropy source. Letters or figures in printed material, telegraph signals, and television or motion pictures are examples of structural sets of signs. The signs in printed material are structured in space; the signs in telegraphy, in time. Television and motion picture signs are structured in both space and time.

Stored Information

A space structure that does not vary with time in sometimes called "stored" information. Of course, a change occurred when the information was stored. A time-varying expenditure of energy must take place to effect the storage.

Description of an Information Structure

In constructing the description of an information structure, the spatial coordinates x_i are laid out and extended to the limits L_i of the space to be described. The domain volume is clearly the product of the L_i values.

The x_i may involve dimensions other than length. For example, in quantum mechanics, phase space has six coordinates q_1, q_2, q_3, and p_1, p_2, p_3. Three are distances; three are moments.

Time is a separate coordinate with extent or duration T.

The word *resolution* is defined as "the act, operation, or process of separating the parts which compose a · · · mixed body." The maximum possible resolution along a space coordinate is represented by δx_i, along the time coordinate, by δt. Thus each x_i is divided into segments of lengths δx_i; T, into segments of δt.

The number of cells along a space coordinate is $N_i = L_i/\delta x_i$; along the time coordinate, $N_t = T/\delta t$.

The total number of cells is

$$N = \Pi N_i N_t \tag{20.1}$$

The maximum energy flow in a cell is E. The minimum possible discrimination between nearly alike energy levels is δe_s in the space domain and δe_t in the time domain. So, the maximum number of distinguishable energy levels is

$$N_{ES} = E/\delta e_s \quad \text{and} \quad N_{ET} = E/\delta e_t \tag{20.2}$$

The *gross* or *maximum possible descriptive capacity* depends on the extent of each space coordinate, the duration of the time coordinate, the maximum energy level in each cell and the maximum possible resolution in each of the coordinates.

The *actual descriptive capacity* of an information structure may be far less than the gross descriptive capacity. The actual resolutions in the spatial coordinates, Δx_i; in the time coordinate, Δt; and in the energy amplitude coordinates Δe_s and Δe_t—all of these may be far less than the corresponding δx_i, δt, δe_s, and δe_t. Even more, some possible coordinates may not be used at all.

The description of the information structure of a printed page is interesting. The plane of the page can be divided horizontally and vertically to form cells that may or may not contain a letter or number. The size of the smallest letter on the page determines the necessary cell size and thus the actual resolution. Some of the cells are empty: for example, those around the edges of the page. These empty cells form part of the structure. The signs may be the letters of the alphabet, Arabic numerals, or punctuation marks. Certain signs may take several forms—for example, upper and lower case letters or normal, bold and italic typefaces. Depending on the size of a particular sign, it may occupy one or many cells. Conceivably, one extremely large sign might almost cover the page.

Thevenin Equivalent Source

Thevenin's theorem by generalization may be used to describe an equivalent source for each elementary cell of an information source.

21

Other Functional
Building Blocks

One-input, One-output

In Fig. 21-1, the purpose of the physical unit represented by ϕ is to change a quantitative input into a quantitative output.

The input and output may be either zero-entropy or information-carrying energy. The input "forcing" function, or the output, or both may vary with time. Either the input, or the output, or both may be continuous functions, step functions or impulses, or sequences of pulses. Thus, a particular flow may be described mathematically by any one of an extremely large class of functions. They need not be continuous functions nor have prescribed bounds. For certain operations, the input may be an object. In all cases, the output depends on the input and the operator. In some cases, it may also depend on an appropriate number of input conditions.

The action of such a physical unit may be represented symbolically by the equation:

$$x = \phi u \qquad (21.1)$$

Here, ϕ is the operator representing the conversion of the input into the output. In the general case, ϕ may vary with time, or it may vary with the properties of the input, or it may vary with both time and input properties.

Variation of ϕ with time and input properties can enormously in-

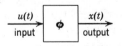

Figure 21-1

crease the difficulties of system design. Yet physical units *do* vary with time; they *do* deteriorate; and they *do* wear out sooner or later. And *excessive inputs always change them;* they may destroy them.

If ϕ is a linear operator, then powerful mathematical tools are available to study the performance. Unfortunately, in many actual cases, ϕ can not be a linear operator. Such practical considerations as size, weight, or cost force the designer to use nonlinear operators.

If ϕ is not linear, then superposition does not hold and ϕ may vary with the properties of the input.

For a nonlinear system, the input-output relations may sometimes be expressed by a set of integro-differential equations. For such a set of relations, a simple solution is usually not available.

For small changes in the variables, nonlinear relations are often assumed to be linear for small perturbations. The variations may be defined in terms of small deviations from steady-state or reference ᵛˡues. The resulting relations may be correct only for infinitesimal variations. But they are assumed to hold approximately for finite variations. Sometimes the approximation is useful; sometimes not.

Certainly, the available mathematical tools for handling nonlinear operators are less than adequate. Each case is attacked more or less *ad hoc.* All sorts of tricks and subterfuges are used to try to use a linear approximation to a nonlinear ϕ.

A medium is a particular form of operator. The input to a medium may be either zero-entropy or information-carrying energy at a location in space. Ideally, a medium delivers its input energy as an output at another location in space. Thus, the action of a medium may be described by an operator that changes only the space location of the input without affecting any other properties. Actually, transmission of energy through any medium takes a finite time. Whether the transmission time requires consideration depends on the particular ɔpplication. The operator (and hence the output location) may vary or be made to vary with time.

An analogous transport operator changes the space location of an object.

Delay or storage is another particular form of operator. Its input may be either zero-entropy or information-carrying energy at a location in space. Ideally, a delay or storage device delivers its input energy at a later time with no change of location in space. Thus, the action may be described by an operator that changes only the time location without affecting any other properties. The operator φ (and hence the output location in time) may vary or be made to vary with time.

An analogous storage operator changes only the time location of an object. Of course, there is no inverse operator for a time delay or change in location in time.

The input to an effector is information-carrying energy at one location in space. The effector applies energy to an object at another location to make some wanted change in the object. The operator φ and hence the output location in space, or time, or both may vary or be made to vary with time.

The input and output of a transducer-operator may be zero-entropy energy or information-carrying energy. It has been shown that a zero-entropy energy flow may be described in terms of a set of space and time variables. Table 21-1 gives a complete list. A suitable transducer can change any one of the variables. Thus, there are many possible kinds of such transducers. But it is possible to classify, tabulate, and study all the possible kinds.

Each kind of transducer can be described by an appropriate φ. Such a φ is sometimes called the transducer transfer function.

Tandem arrangements can change more than one of the variables. As pointed out earlier, such tandem arrangements are not necessarily commutative.

To continue, an information-carrying energy flow is merely a zero-entropy energy flow that has been changed or modulated to make it unpredictable. The information content has a structure in space and time.

Again, a suitable transducer can change any one of the variables describing the information-carrying energy flow. Because the set of variables is the same as for zero-entropy energy flow, the possible kinds are the same in the two cases. The requirements on such properties as linearity of the operator may be more severe for information-carrying transducers. Each kind of transducer in this class can also be described by an appropriate operator.

Finally, a suitable transducer can change any aspect of the information structure in space or time or both. However, the amount of output information from a transducer can never exceed the amount of input information. The operation of transducers that change information structure can be described by an appropriate φ.

Appropriate φ's composed of linear devices can shape input waves and thus perform the operations of integration or differentiation on either a continuous or discontinuous input wave. These operations

Table 21-1 *Summary of Variables to Describe a Zero-entropy Power Source*

Form of energy (e.g., mechanical or electrical)

At any instant, the energy flow across a plane of observation can be described in terms of:

A mapping function (if required)

Space variables for the:
  Location of the plane in space
  Extent of the plane

Number of terms in a double Fourier series	$m \times n$
Periods of terms	mx/a and ny/b
Amplitude coefficients of terms (some may be zero)	A_{mn}
Relative phases of terms	φ_{mn}

The highest period term determines the maximum possible resolution, δ_{xy}.

The mapping function or any of the space variables or both may be predictable functions of time.

For any elementary cell in space, the time variation of the energy amplitude within a particular interval may be described in terms of:

Time variables for the:
  Location of the interval in time
  Extent of the interval

Number of terms in a Fourier series	n_t
Periods of terms	f_{nt}
Amplitude coefficients of terms (some may be zero)	A_{nt}
Relative phases of terms	φ_{nt}

The highest period term determines the maximum possible resolution in time, δ_t.

A suitable Thevenin equivalent circuit for the source.

are frequently used in analog computers. Integration is used in pulse amplitude modulation systems to reconvert the sampled wave to analog form.

Other ϕ's composed of linear devices can shape an input wave in other ways. One example is the change of square pulses into raised-cosine shaped waves. Filters and tuned circuits are also used to shape waves by selecting or rejecting certain frequency components. They usually employ passive linear elements but may include active elements (power sources). The reference frequencies (cut-off frequencies) of filters are usually determined by the design and do not depend on nonlinear elements.

One Input, More than One Output, and Vice Versa

Dividing

In Fig. 21-2, the physical unit represented by ϕ has one input $u(t)$ and k space-separated outputs $x_1(t), x_2(t), \ldots, x_k(t)$. A compact symbolic representation is

$$X = \phi u \qquad (21.2)$$

where X is a column matrix representing the outputs produced by the operation of ϕ on the input.

Here, ϕ may vary with time; it may vary with the properties of the input; or it may vary with both.

The one input may be either a zero-entropy or an information-carrying energy flow. Thus, the input may be described by any one of an extremely wide class of functions.

The operator ϕ may divide the input energy among the several outputs in one of several ways:

1. A planar energy flow may be divided so that the energy flow in particular input areas is delivered to particular outputs.

2. The input energy may simply be divided among the several outputs, so that each receives a fraction. The fractions may or may not be equal.

3. The input energy flow may be divided among the outputs, so that a particular output receives only the input energy in a particular frequency band.

4. The input energy flow may be divided among the outputs, so that a particular output receives only the energy flowing during a particular time interval after some reference instant.

5. The input energy flow may be divided among the outputs so

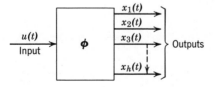

Figure 21-2

that a particular output receives only the energy flow bearing a particular phase relation to a reference phase.

Combining

Similarly, in Fig. 21-3, the physical unit represented by ϕ has h space-separated inputs $u_1(t), \ldots u_h(t)$ and one output $x(t)$. A compact symbolic representation is

$$x = \phi U \tag{21.3}$$

where U is a column matrix representing the inputs and ϕ is an operator representing the conversion of the inputs into the output.

If, the only if, $x(t)$ depends linearly on the h inputs can the input-output relations be written in the form

$$x(t) = \sum_{h=1}^{h} \phi u_h(t) \tag{21.4}$$

In the general case, ϕ may vary with time; or it may vary with the properties of one or more of the inputs; or it may vary with both time and the input(s).

All of the inputs may be zero-entropy energy flows; or all may be information-carrying energy flows; or some may be zero-entropy and some information-carrying. Not only may the vector describing each input be any one of an extremely wide class of functions, but combinations of different kinds of inputs are also possible. For this reason, various physical units with more-than-one input and one output can perform many quite different kinds of operations.

Moreover, the inputs may be objects which are combined to form a single object.

Simple Combining

Combination of zero-entropy energy flows from two or more inputs may be described by the operator. The contributions of the separate sources may or may not later be separated by another operator. For example, two single-phase 60-cycle generators may feed a bus-bar

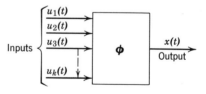

Figure 21-3

that furnishes energy to many motors. Separation of the contributions of the two sources is unnecessary in such an arrangement. For another example, take generators arranged to furnish three-phase 60-cycle power to a high-voltage transmission line. At the receiving end of the line, the three phases are separated for delivery to customers who require a single-phase power supply. For these examples, ϕ may be a linear operator that simply adds or superposes the inputs.

With a linear operator, reversing the polarity of an input causes amplitude subtraction instead of addition.

Two or more zero-entropy energy flows with extents in space may be combined to form a single energy flow. Similarly, two or more pulse trains may be combined to form a single train.

Zero-entropy and information-carrying energy flows may be combined as in the plate circuit of vacuum-tube amplifier.

Multiplexing

Two or more information-carrying energy flows may also be combined by an operation often called multiplexing. Multiplexing of energy flows may be accomplished in the space, frequency, phase, or time domains. In principle, all combinations are possible. Almost always, the intent is to recover the separate inputs by later dividing the combined energy flow among several outlets. This inverse operation is often called demultiplexing. A number of requirements must be met if such arrangements are to recover the input flows without either loss of information or unwanted interference.

Generation of Information-carrying Energy by Modulation

Figure 21-4 represents an information source varying the flow from a zero-entropy power source with time to create information-carrying energy, that is, signals. The signal output depends on the instantaneous values of both the zero-entropy power source and the infor-

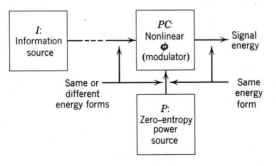

Figure 21-4

mation source energies. Obviously, the signal is conveyed by the form of energy furnished by the zero-entropy power source. This signal-generating operation is called "modulation," "encoding," or "mapping" by various authors.

The zero-entropy power source furnishes only one form of energy. Further, its output impedance may or may not be constant with time.

The energy forms of the zero-entropy and information sources may or may not be the same. For example, both may be electrical. For another example, one may be acoustical, the other mechanical.

Any one of the variables or some combination of the space or time variables used to describe the output of a zero-entropy power source may be modulated to generate the signals.

The signal energy may be one-, two-, or three-dimensional in space.

In modulation, the information-carrying the zero-entropy flows are not simply superimposed. To map the message information onto the zero-entropy flow and thus create the signals, the ϕ must be a nonlinear operator. On the other hand, the system specification may state that the information-carrying features of the message should be accurately represented in the signal. Such a requirement is implicit in any high-fidelity sound-reproduction system. The necessary conditions to meet such a requirement are discussed in a later chapter.

In Fig. 21-4, the action of the power control may change the space variables of the zero-entropy power source by:

1. Reducing the extent along one or more space coordinates. In the limit, the extent along one or more space coordinates may be reduced to zero.

2. Changing the mapping function (if a three-dimensional flow is mapped onto a plane).

3. Changing the fundamental space period along one or more coordinates.

4. Changing the relative space harmonic amplitudes. This may reduce the resolution.

5. Changing the relative space harmonic phases.

The power control may change the zero-entropy time variables by:

1. Changing the extent in time.

2. Changing the fundamental period.

3. Changing the relative harmonic amplitudes. This may reduce the resolution.

4. Changing the relative harmonic phases.

The power control is assumed to act instantaneously. For this reason, the message and signal energy flows have the same extent in time.

Types of Modulation

For one-dimensional information sources and zero-entropy power sources, Table 21-2 gives some possible types of modulation.

In a particularly important special case called "base-band modulation," the zero-entropy power source furnishes a constant amplitude of zero frequency—in other words, direct current.

With a single-frequency sinusoidal zero-entropy power wave, the amplitude, frequency, or phase may be changed by the information source. Combinations are possible: for example, both AM and FM.

A constant amplitude (dc) or a sinusoidal zero-entropy wave is often called the "carrier" or "carrier wave" by communication engineers.

Similar modulation operations are possible if the zero-entropy energy is in the form of a train of pulses.

In pulse amplitude modulation (PAM), the amplitude of a zero-

Table 21-2

Power Source Wave	Information Source Wave	Type of Modulation
Continuous	Continuous	
Constant amplitude (i.e., direct current)		Amplitude $\Delta_k = k_{ma}\,\Delta_m$
Sinusoidal		Amplitude $\Delta_k = k_{ma}\,\Delta_m$ Frequency $\Delta_f = k_{mf}\,\Delta_m$ Phase $\quad \Delta_\varphi = k_{m\varphi}\,\Delta_m$
Non-sinusoidal		A photograph is an example
Continuous—any shape	Discontinuous	On-off keying is an example
Discontinuous	Continuous	Pulse amplitude (PAM) Pulse frequency (PFM) Pulse duration or width (PDM) Pulse position (PPM) Pulse time (PTM)
Discontinuous	Discontinuous	Certain secrecy systems are examples

Δ = change in amplitude, frequency, or phase
$k_{(a,\,f,\,\text{or}\,\varphi)}$ = modulation gain or loss constant

entropy pulse source is varied to create the signal. The value of each very brief sample of the information input waves determines the amplitude of a pulse. The Sampling Theorem specifies the minimum number of pulses per second necessary to recover the input information without some loss. The information input wave is assumed to be arbitrary, except that the bandwidth is finite; and it may take on an infinite number of different values during any finite time interval. Such a wave can be reproduced exactly from a knowledge of its samples if the number of samples exceeds twice the maximum significant frequency in cycles per second.

In pulse frequency modulation (PFM), the pulse width and amplitude are held constant but the repetition frequency of the pulses is varied by the information input.

In pulse width modulation (PWM) the pulse amplitude and repetition frequency are held constant, but the width and hence the area is varied.

In pulse position modulation (PPM), the position of the leading or trailing edge (or both) of each pulse is varied.

Any continuous wave (e.g., an FM wave) or any discontinuous wave may be sampled if the zero-entropy power source pulses are narrower than the input pulses (strobing).

The zero-entropy energy flow may have a complex character such as smoke from a fire. If the zero-entropy power source furnishes a complex wave, the amplitude of the envelope of the wave may be varied, or the relative amplitudes, frequencies, or phases of the Fourier components may be varied. Combinations are possible.

The same principles apply in both the space and time domains. Thus, zero-entropy energy transmitted by fields in free space or in a wave guide can be amplitude modulated or have their extent in space varied. A light beam may be chopped by rotating blades, its color changed by filters, or its extent in space reduced.

Modulation Ratio or Index

The ratio of the information source amplitude to the zero-entropy power source amplitude is called the modulation ratio. It may vary from 0 to more than 1. Values exceeding 1 cause "over-modulation."

Similar ratios can be defined for the frequency ratio in frequency modulation and for analagous ratios in other forms of space or time modulation.

Linear and Nonlinear Modulation

Over the modulation range, the operation may be over a linear portion of the zero-entropy power source output characteristic. In this case, the modulation process may give a linear input-output relation.

If the operation is over a nonlinear portion of the characteristic, the modulation operation results in a nonlinear input-output relation (e.g., in the case in which AM compression or expansion of the input wave takes place). Similarly, in taking a picture, the photographer can produce "high key" or "low key" effects by his choice of the location on the density-exposure time curve relating the input light and film response. Such nonlinear operations may be compensated by an appropriate inverse operation if certain conditions are met.

Information-rate Carrier-frequency Ratio

For a dc or sinusoidal carrier wave, the possible modulation methods depend on the value of the ratio of the bit rate to the carrier frequency (see Table 21-3).

As the table shows, if the ratio is $\gg 1$, then only the carrier amplitude can be changed to generate the signal. Obviously, neither a change of the carrier frequency or phase is possible. The dc telegraph and the telephone transmitter use ratios $\gg 1$.

In practical situations, a ratio near 1 is almost always less desirable than other possibilities. Amplitude modulation is possible and frequency and phase modulation are theoretically possible if the bit rate is somewhat less than the carrier frequency. With the bit rate and carrier frequency equal, that is, synchronous digital data transmission, frequency modulation of the carrier information source has no meaning. However, the amplitude of a single cycle of a sine wave (dipulse) can be varied. In a binary or two-state system, the dipulse is present or absent. In a two-state system, phase modulation

Table 21-3   *Bit-rate/Carrier-frequency Ratio*

	$\gg 1$	~ 1	1	< 1
Modulation methods	Amplitude	Amplitude	Amplitude (e.g., dipulse)	Amplitude (double, single, vestigial side band)
		Frequency	—	Frequency, frequency shift
		—	Phase (e.g., dipulse same or different phases)	Phase-two or more phases

methods are also feasible. For example, 0° from a reference phase can be used for one condition and 180° for the other. Or one condition can be indicated by no phase change in two successive cycles; the other condition, by a 180° change. Both methods have been used.

For a bit rate low with respect to the carrier, either amplitude, frequency, or phase modulation of the carrier can be used.

It is likely that all possible modulation methods have been studied. Further, almost all are in use. Those that are not in use have drawbacks.

Parallel channels may be used for the simultaneous signals denoting a character. To provide parallel channels, the possible arrangements can be tabulated (see Table 21-4).

As Table 21-4 shows—and as everyday knowledge confirms—plural information channels can transmit information simultaneously. The information may, but need not be, parts of the same message. Parallel telephone wires in a single cable sheath provide a familiar example.

With a single space channel and a bit rate/carrier frequency ratio of 1 or >1, two signals can be transmitted using two kinds of modulation. At the destinations, receivers responding to only one kind of modulation can separate the signals. Such systems have been built but because they tend to be complex they have not been extensively used.

Table 21-4

Channels	Possible Modulation Methods
>1 Space-separated	Any listed in Table 21-3
1 Frequency band over 1 space-separated channel	Bit-rate/carrier frequency ratio = 1: a combination of amplitude and phase modulation can give four or more conditions
	Bit-rate/carrier frequency ratio ≫1: a combination of amplitude and frequency or amplitude and phase modulation can give four or more conditions
>1 Frequency band over 1 space-separated channel	Each frequency band can be made independent and use any of the methods listed immediately above
>1 Frequency band over some or all of >1 space-separated channels	Combinations of the methods listed above

Simultaneous radio transmission of telegraph, voice, and television signals uses more than one frequency band over a single space channel. Another example is the coaxial cable systems widely used here and abroad. Many examples of combinations of space separation and AM, FM, ϕM and pulse modulation are found in various parts of the widespread wire and cable network of the Bell System.

Recovery of Information

Figure 21-5 represents an incoming signal applied to the input of a device that recovers the message information. This operation has been called "demodulation," "decoding," "detecting," or "sensing."

The energy forms at the input and output of the device may or may not be the same. For example, both may be electrical; or the input may be electrical and the output, mechanical. If the energy forms are different, one input to the sensor must be appropriate energy flow from a zero-entropy source.

Information-carrying energy flows differ from zero-entropy energy flows only in that they are unpredictable. Hence, a sensor must measure the unpredictable variations of the input signal with time and furnish the result as an output. To be able to make such a measurement, the sensor must either compare the signal with a zero-entropy energy source exactly like that used in the modulation or some other suitable equivalent reference. Only by comparing the input signal with a reference can the sensor know whether information is present or not.

The functions of comparison and discrimination were discussed in Chapter 6. The possible changes in zero-entropy energy to create the signal have also been enumerated. A particular system uses one or more of the possible changes in the modulation operation. Obviously, the receiving sensor must be able to measure the results of the changes. In other words, the modulator and sensor operations must be inverse.

In sensing, the operator ϕ does not simply superimpose the informa-

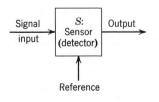

Figure 21-5

tion-carrying input and the reference. To extract the information from the signal, ϕ must be nonlinear. However, accurate recovery of the message information may be necessary for proper system operation. The sensor (usually called the discriminator or detector) in a high-fidelity FM radio receiver is a carefully designed precision device.

Computing

Computing operations may be divided into arithmetical operations and logical operations. Logical operations may be equivalent to arithmetical operations if the arithmetic is binary; otherwise not.

In arithmetical operations, the inputs may be continuous or discrete energy waves or objects which represent digits.

Two continuous input waves may be combined by a suitable operator. If they are to be superposed—that is, added or subtracted—then the ϕ must be linear. Multiplication, division, squaring, or taking the square root require an appropriate nonlinear ϕ.

The inputs may be in the form of waves conveying information in the form of discrete numbers. The output or answer is another number. Thus, the inputs and output are both numbers. In this case, the operator ϕ must also be digital.

For logic operations, some of the useful ϕ's describe the AND, OR, NAND, and INHIBIT functions. In an AND arrangement, the output appears if, and only if, all inputs are simultaneously present. In an OR arrangement, the output appears if any input is present; in a NAND (not-AND) arrangement, if no input is present. An INHIBIT input overrides all other inputs and prevents any output.

All of the possible kinds of logical operators have been tabulated and studied. Many physical realizations of such operators are in use in digital computers. In such physical realizations in computers, both the input and output waves are pulses. Clearly, superposition does not hold and ϕ is nonlinear.

Other important logical operations are compare and discriminate. These operations have been discussed in Chapter 6. Two continuous or discontinuous wave inputs may be compared with respect to such properties as extent in space, amplitude, frequency, or phase. The comparator output indicates whether they are equal or which is the greater. The output of a discriminator indicates equality of two inputs or the magnitude and sign of any difference. As a special case, one of the inputs may be a reference or standard wave, and the other input an unknown or unpredictable energy wave. Depending on the system requirement, the appropriate ϕ may be linear or nonlinear.

22

Information Conservation

Introduction

The information transfer between the input and output of any block may be conservative (total information out equal to total information in) or nonconservative (total information out less than total information in). Shannon showed that the third case (total information out more than total information in) is impossible. These fundamental concepts are as important to a system designer as the laws of thermodynamics are to a physicist dealing with heat phenomena. They separate the possible from the impossible.

Early work by Nyquist and Hartley is pertinent to the necessary conditions for information conservation in processing telegraph and telephone-type signals. Ideal telegraph signals are on-off square pulses. Telephone-type signals can be described by a Fourier series in time. Then, by the Sampling Theorem due to Nyquist, for a sequence of $2TW$ ordinates each having one of n different values n^{2WT} different wave forms are possible. This relation may be interpreted as describing $2W$ cells per unit time for a time duration T. Each cell may contain any one of n objects.

Hartley's formula states that a given amount of information can be handled with any combination of bandwidth and time, or:

$$WT = \text{a constant} \tag{22.1}$$

The bandwidth W can be provided in or by one or more devices. Also, the more information elements processed simultaneously, the shorter the time required to handle them.

Some Important Generalized Relations

By a generalization of Hartley's formula to include the spatial coordinates of energy flow, a given amount of information can be handled with combination of cells in space, bandwidth, and time. At any instant, the number of cells in space can be furnished by any combination of area and cell size. For any space cell, the variations with time may be described by Hartley's relation, Eq. 22.1:

$$WT = \text{a constant} \tag{22.1}$$

Hence, if the space cells and their W's are all the same, the total amount of information that can be handled is the product:

$$N_s WT = \text{constant} \tag{22.2}$$

Somewhat more complicated formulas are necessary if the resolution and hence the minimum cell dimension differs in different directions in space, or if W is not the same for all space cells, or both. Nevertheless, the underlying principles are simple.

The generalized relation can be used to study the information conservation requirements for a one-input, one-output block; for a one-input, more-than-one-output block; or for a more-than-one-input, one-output block.

Gabor's uncertainty formula, and Shannon's entropy and equivocation concepts can also be broadened to include all possible information-carrying energy flows. The necessary steps to make the extensions seem obvious.

Information Conservation in One-input, One-output Blocks

For equal amounts of information into and out of a transmission medium or a store, the output wave is an exact duplicate of the input wave except possibly for uniform changes in the amplitude of some or all space and time components. For such information conservation, a number of requirements must all be met:

1. Equal numbers of input and output dimensions in space and time (i.e., equal number of coordinates).

2. Space and time bandwidths adequate to reproduce exactly at the output all details of the input.

3. Equal numbers of cells in each space coordinate and in time in the output and input. The individual input and output cells may be the same size, or larger, or smaller (i.e., magnification or reduction). The energy flow in corresponding cells in the input and output may be greater or less (amplification or attenuation).

4. Because of the finite velocity of energy transfer, the output wave

is always delayed in time with respect to the input. For real-time operation, the input and output rates must be the same.

5. All space-period terms within the required bandwidth must be transmitted without (a) any change depending on the input amplitude (compression or expansion); (b) any change of relative input amplitudes as a function of space period; or (c) any shift of relative phases. Similar requirements apply in the time domain. Here, item c may be rephrased to say that the delay must be the same for all frequencies within the band. The human ear is not very sensitive to relative phase shifts in the frequency components of speech waves. Thus, the equal-delay requirement is not too important in telephone transmission systems. On the other hand, the square pulses much used for data transmission are relatively intolerant of phase distortion.

6. Equal input and output signal-to-noise ratios. Hence, for equal susceptibility to extraneous noise at input and output, if the amplitude variations are less at the output than at the input, the noise amplitude must be less at the output.

The output waves of many transducers are not intended to be exact duplicates of the input waves. For information to be conserved by such transducers, the operation must be described by Eq. 22.2.

Many different kinds of transducers are required to make all of the possible kinds of conversions. Thus, a suitable transducer can increase or decrease the number of space dimensions in the input information. For example, transducers and dividers can be arranged so that radar information about a distant airplane may be presented on three separate oscilloscope screens—one for the azimuth, one for elevation, and one for range. Information about the plane's location in three-dimensional space is split among three two-dimensional displays.

Trades are possible between the input and output bandwidths in space and time and also between the number of cells in the space and time domains. Suitable transducers can take in information in the space domain and put it out in the time, frequency, or phase domain. Other transducers can perform the inverse operations. Pairs of such transducers are frequently used. Thus, a television camera scans a scene in space, and delivers the video information as an electric wave which is carried by a coaxial-type cable. At the television receiving set, the input video wave controls the movement of a beam of electrons to present the scene on the screen.

An appropriate transducer can change the structure of the information carried by its input energy. Such transducers are inherently complex. The input information must first be sensed. At least some must be stored so that rearrangement in space or time or both is possible. Then the rearranged information must be used to generate the output signal. Some small loss of information is almost certain as each operation is performed. These losses are cumulative, as each operation causes some loss.

One-input, More-than-one-output Blocks

With one input and more than one output, the input energy is divided among the space-separated outputs. In such dividing, for equal amounts of information into the block and into each output, each output wave must be an exact duplicate of the input wave except possibly for uniform changes of some or all space and time components. To conserve the information between the input and each output, requirements 1 to 6 already stated for the one-input, one-output case must all be met.

Duplication of printed or graphic information is an important example of such an operation. Many, even tens of thousands, of copies of a newspaper page can be printed from a single plate.

In a quite different type of operation, the input information may be divided among the outputs. The input energy to a space medium may be the outputs of channels that have been combined in space, frequency, time, or phase domain—or even some combination of these. An appropriate device (such as a wave filter) can select the energy from a particular input and reject the energy from all other inputs. Imperfect rejection causes unwanted energy or noise in the selected channel and degrades the information-conservation performance. So-called guard bands are often used to help make adequate separation of the wanted and unwanted energies possible.

In dividing, information may be lost in another way. For example, input information may be carried in a frequency band not selected by any output. Clearly, the energy flow from that input band is dissipated and the information is lost. Similar considerations apply in the space, time, and phase domains.

A divider and a combiner may be used as an inverse pair. Thus a piece of paper (such as a letter) may be torn to bits (divided). Later the scraps may be patched together (combined). Or information energy from many inputs may be combined for transmission over a single medium and then divided among appropriate receivers.

More-than-one-input, One-output Blocks

With more than one space-separated input, the output information may be the sum of the amounts of information from the several sources. If all of the sources supply equal amounts, the output amount is obviously the amount from one source times the number of inputs.

If the inputs are combined to cover a greater extent in space, then for information conservation, the space areas being combined must not be overlapped. If they do overlap, then the information in the overlapping area is lost. The amount lost depends on the number of overlapping space cells.

Similarly, if information in the space-separated inputs is to be combined in the frequency domain, then for information conservation, the frequency bands must not overlap. Analogous requirements must be met for combining in the time or phase domains.

To facilitate later recovery of the information carried by each input, guard space or guard bands in the space, frequency, time, or phase domains may be provided by the design. Of course, allottment of cells to guard duty reduces the possible amount of information that can be handled to less than the amount of an ideal arrangement.

Modulation

Signal generation is a particular case of combining. Because of the importance of the modulation function, it merits special examination. The two inputs to a modulator are a source of information-carrying energy and a source of zero-entropy energy. The output is information-carrying signal energy. Figure 21-4 showed a block diagram representing the modulation process.

The maximum possible information content of the signal is determined by the properties of the zero-entropy power source. The power source limits the maximum information content of the signal output in:

1. Each space dimension
2. Duration in time
3. Maximum energy amplitude
4. Frequency range of the energy (bandwidth)
5. Resolution in each space dimension
6. Resolution in time

Only energy flow in occupied cells in the space and time dimensions of the power source may be changed by the power control. Unoccupied cells within or outside the maximum extent of any coordinate cannot be controlled to create signals.

The information source may offer more information than the zero-entropy power source can handle. Then, the power source is limiting, and potential signal information may be lost. In such cases, signal generation can not be on a real-time basis unless information is lost. To avoid a loss, input information must be stored and transmitted at a lower rate for a longer time interval. Further, the information and power sources may each have one, two, or three dimensions in space. But an ordinary camera can not take a three-dimensional picture. A still camera can take only a snapshot of a scene containing movement.

Conversely, the information source may offer less information than the power source can handle. In such cases, the information capacity of the power source is not fully utilized. The input information can be handled in real time. In fact, a suitable transducer might be added to store the slower-rate input information and, at an appropriate time, release it for handling at a higher rate in a shorter time interval.

The information source may have a smaller number of dimensions than the zero-entropy power source. For example, a one-dimensional information source can control a power source that generates a planar wave (two-dimensional) or a spherical wave (three-dimensional). Despite the increase in the number of dimensions, the signal wave can contain no more information than the input information wave.

The variables used to describe the zero-entropy power source and information source flows have been discussed in detail. For information conservation between the information input and signal output of Fig. 21-4, requirements 1 to 6 for one-input, one-output blocks must be met. The energy changes of the information source must be mapped exactly on the zero-entropy energy flow.

There are many interesting examples of the possible relationships between information and zero-entropy power sources. As an example of a spatial limitation, take a stage illuminated by a spotlight. Only the areas in the light beam (i.e., the power source area) can reflect light energy. In this case, the power source determines the visible area. The power source may limit the extent of the signal in time. Certainly, before the power source is turned on and after it is turned off, signals can not be generated. Similarly, the maximum signal energy is determined by the maximum power source output.

Photography offers examples of the effects of a limited power source bandwidth: quite different pictures of a colored object are obtained with white light and light of restricted bandwidth.

A power source may limit the actual resolution of the signal output. As an example, the resolution of an electron microscope can exceed that of an optical microscope, because the electron beam (power source) has spatial components with shorter periods than those of visible light. Of course, for greater resolution capability to be useful to a human being, a transducer (photograph) must be used. This makes the ultra-fine details visible to the human eye.

As an interesting example in which the information source is limiting, take a daily newspaper. The "news" is proclaimed in 2- or 3-inch headlines—and is read in light good enough to see things finer than a human hair.

23

Heuristics and System Synthesis

Introduction

Available knowledge can aid in solving problems. Thus, it may suggest the order of examining possible solutions, or provide a test to distinguish likely from unlikely possibilities. Such kinds of knowledge may be called "heuristics"—things that aid discovery.

A heuristic approach can be particularly useful in attacking problems in which the variables or criteria are not numerical or the available information is incomplete. For this reason, the synthesis of a new system often must be attacked heuristically.

A heuristic approach to a problem can lead to empirically valid knowledge. Often it "works," but it can seldom guarantee a solution.

At present, the use of heuristics is an art with little analytic framework. There are many unanswered questions. For example: How may kinds of heuristics are there? What heuristics do humans actually use? How can new heuristics be discovered? The ultimate intent of some workers in this new field is to program a computer to solve appropriate kinds of problems.

Formulation of the Problem

Newell, Shaw, and Simon discuss two kinds of heuristics: a means-ends analysis heuristic; and a planning heuristic. Their heuristics have been applied successfully to the solution of certain mathematical problems by a sequence of steps. The synthesis of a new system design is a somewhat different problem: in a complex system, the joint operations of all the subsystems perform all of the wanted functions. Although differences exist, the problems also have some similarities.

In discussing a General Problem Solver, Newell, Shaw, and Simon make two important observations: (1) objects can be characterized by their "features," and by the "differences" that can be observed between pairs of objects* and (2) an effector† can be applied to an object to produce a different object (as a saw applied to a log can produce boards). Effectors may be restricted to apply to only certain kinds of objects. Some effectors can produce more than one object as an output.

Many problems can be formulated in terms of objects and effectors. Two examples are (1) transforming one object into another and (2) modifying the object so that a given effector may be applied to it.

In proving a theorem in a formal mathematical system, the objects are theorems, and the effectors are the admissible rules of inference. To prove a theorem is to transfer some initial objects, the axioms, into a specified object, the desired theorem.

Means-Ends Analysis

Two very general kinds of heuristics are (1) means-ends analysis (2) planning. Means-ends analysis proceeds step-by-step and does not look far ahead. Planning constructs a proposed solution in general terms before working out the details. The two kinds are discussed in order.

Means-ends analysis assumes:

1. Detectable differences exist between the given and desired object.
2. Effectors alter some but not all features of their operands. Hence, effectors can be characterized by the changes they produce and can be used to try to eliminate differences between given and desired objects.
3. Some detectable differences are more difficult to effect than others. So it is better to try to eliminate "difficult" differences, even if new differences of lesser difficulty are introduced. This process can be repeated as long as progress is made toward eliminating the more difficult differences.

The first step should be to get a useful set of differences. Lacking a good set of differences between the wanted object and the object

---

*In some problems, the initial object is not specified. Then the first step is to find a suitable object satisfying any given rudimentary specification.

† The word "effector" is used here in preference to "operator", the word used by Newell, Shaw, and Simon.

at hand, different sequences of effectors can be tried at random. Progress is hard to measure, because the best clue to progress is elimination of the existing differences.

After obtaining a useful set of differences, the next question is: What effector will remove a particular difference? The list of effectors can be searched randomly or systematically until one is found that affects the difference in question. A more efficient procedure is to make, once and for all, a table to indicate which effectors remove which differences. Then, only those effectors that can remove a difference in question need be considered.

Problems and subproblems amenable to means-ends analysis can be divided into a few types:

Type 1: To transform object a into object b.

Type 2: To apply effector E to object a (or to an object obtained from a by admissible transformations).

Type 3: To reduce a difference Δ between object a and object b by modifying a.

Means-ends analysis uses one method for attacking each type of problem.

The method for Type 1 consists in:

1. Finding a difference Δ between objects a and b. Tests for the more important differences are made first.

2. Setting up a Type 3 problem to reduce Δ. If this is successful, a new transformed object c is produced.

3. Setting up the Type 1 subproblem for transforming c into b. If this is successful, the original problem is solved.

The method for Type 2 consists in:

1. Determining if the effector E can be applied by setting up a Type 1 problem for transforming a into q', the input form of q.

2. If successful, the output object is produced from q'', the output form of q. This method is useful where an effector is described in terms of the input and the output objects.

The method for Type 3 consists in:

1. Searching for an effector that can reduce the difference Δ.

2. If one is found, setting up a Type 2 subproblem to apply the effector. If successful, this produces the modified object c.

Planning Method

The Planning Method consists of:

1. Omitting certain details of the objects a and b and effectors.
2. Forming an abstract problem corresponding to the simplified one.
3. Solving the simplified abstract problem.
4. Using the solution to provide a plan for solving the original problem.
5. Translating the plan into the terms of the given problem and executing it.

Skillful use of lemmas in the proof of a difficult theorem may be an example of Planning.

The Planning Method is claimed to offer two advantages. First, all available skills can be used to solve the abstract problem. The omission of detail gives a simpler problem with fewer steps than the original. Second, the subproblems in the plan are collectively simpler (each has fewer steps) than the original problem. The exploration required to solve a problem generally increases with the number of steps in the solution. Replacing a large problem by several smaller ones may greatly reduce the difficulty.

Like the other heuristics, Planning does not always work. It may generate no plan, a single plan, or several plans. More serious, a plan may prove impossible to carry out; for example, proof of a crucial lemma may be impossible.

Appraisal for System Design

Newell, Shaw, and Simon originally worked out their heuristics for the solution of mathematical problems by a sequence of steps. Their Means-End heuristic seems to be applicable to finding a sequence of manufacturing processes to convert raw material into a finished object. Essentially, this is their Type 1 plus Type 3 problem. Their Type 2 problem also has application where possible changes by an effector are described. For example, a particular lathe can make cuts on material within definite dimensions set by its maximum swing and bed length. One manufacturing problem may be to prepare an object so the available effector (the lathe) can be used.

Some Known Methods of System Synthesis

A system is made up of a set of components. By acting together, the set performs all of the wanted functions. Thus, system synthesis is concerned with joint actions—not with a sequence of steps. The difference is important.

The synthesis of some systems has been put on a routine basis by the discovery of appropriate algorithms. Brief mention of a few of these synthesis problems that have been solved may be helpful.

Figure 23-1 represents a multiple-input, multiple-output switching circuit. Each input and each output is two-valued—for example, either ON or OFF. For the outputs to be limited to the two values with two-valued inputs, ϕ must not introduce gradations in the output changes. Hence, ϕ itself must be two-valued.

Given the combination of output values for every possible combination of input values for a particular design, it is always possible to synthesize a logical system (i.e., a ϕ) to provide the wanted input-output relations. Straightforward methods for finding a logical system for any possible input-output combination are known. After such a ϕ is synthesized, the next step is to reduce the number of components, or the cost, or both. Methods of doing so are also known for many important practical cases. Heuristics are almost unnecessary where such powerful methods are available.

Methods for the synthesis of the electrical networks used in communication systems have also been extensively studied. Wave filters and equalizers are examples of such networks. Synthesis of a network for any arbitrary characteristic is not always possible. To separate the possible from the impossible, mathematical "realization" criteria have been discovered and developed.

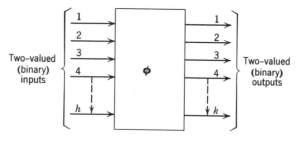

Figure 23-1

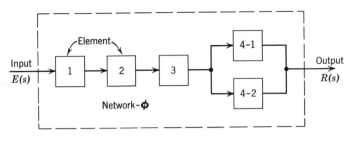

Figure 23-2

Most such network problems specify an amplitude or phase characteristic or an impulse response characteristic. The first step in a solution is to obtain a realizable transfer operator from the wanted characteristic. For a low-pass filter, the cut-off frequency, the maximum deviation from a prescribed amplitude in the pass band, the rate of "cut-off," and the minimum attenuation in the stop band might be specified. The required operator is constructed from these amplitude specifications. A body of "approximation" theory is available to help in the construction.

In Fig. 23-2 the input is $E(s)$ and the output $R(s)$. The starting point for synthesis is the operator function:

$$\phi = \frac{R(s)}{E(s)}$$

The ratio $R(s)/E(s)$ is decomposed into a product of simpler ratios. These are then connected in tandem.

The first step in network synthesis is to see whether ϕ can be realized as a physical, linear, passive network. To be realizable, it must meet two important considerations: causality and stability. Causality requires that a voltage cannot appear at any input or output before a current flows, or vice versa. In other words, the impulse response must be zero prior to zero time. These conditions result in specific mathematical requirements on realizable shapes of transfer characteristics. If a network is to be stable, then for a bounded input, the response must also be bounded. This condition results in further mathematical restrictions on realizable shapes.

For a realizable curve, the possible structures of networks having the required transmission properties for ϕ must be examined and a suitable structure chosen. After a suitable structure is found, the whole synthesis process can be performed by a "continued-fraction" expansion following a known algorithm. The quotients obtained in

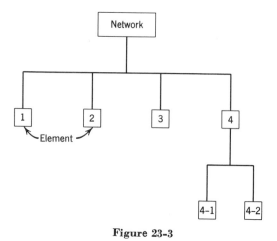

Figure 23-3

the expansion represent the elements of the network. Thus, a ladder network design is worked out element-by-element.

A network design can also be looked at as a system design problem. In Fig. 23-3, the elements 1, 2, 3, and 4-1 and 4-2 that jointly compose the network (system) are represented as a hierarchy. A suitable structure of the elements and their ordering in tandem is recognized and chosen by the designer. Then an algorithm first determines the value of element 1. At this stage, the remaining elements are unknown. The values of the remaining elements are determined step-by-step. The procedure results in a network that is known to meet the requirements.

Similarities and Differences

Heuristic synthesis of a system and the network design procedure are similar in some respects and different in others. In network synthesis, a suitable structure must be chosen. Then the values of the elements of the structure are found one-by-one. When all are found, the synthesis is complete.

In system synthesis, the problem can be described in terms of functional model in the form of a hierarchy. The wanted functions are all allocated to the functional blocks, together with any limiting constraints. The functional model does not indicate components or means. For a complex system, the allocation of functions may be difficult, because a general algorithm appears impossible. Yet experience shows that one or more allocations can be made. A major hazard is that some important or even essential requirement or constraint may be overlooked. Vigilance and checks for errors of omission are essential. The network designer is faced with the same possibility of working from incomplete requirements. But given the requirements and knowing a suitable structure, he can proceed with confidence. The system designer is not nearly so well off. He must find a set of realizable blocks that together can perform all the wanted functions.

Heuristic Procedures for System Design

The network design proceeds step-by-step. A system designer must also proceed step-by-step. Instead of a Means-End Analysis, he can follow a procedure, such as:

1. Match the set of functional requirements and properties of available objects to find complete or partial matches between them. Tests for more important requirements are made first.

2. If a complete match is found the problem is solved. A network designer may find a suitable filter already exists. A mathematician may find the solution to his integral in a table.

3. If no object is found that meets all requirements, enter the objects that meet some requirements in a preliminary representation of a hierarchy containing signs for the objects. Include all the inputs, outputs, and pertinent information such as, size, weight, and cost. Some functional requirements can now be realized by a known object or objects.

4. Match unfilled requirements with available objects to find a complete or partial match between them. Step 2 or 3 and then 4 can be repeated until all requirements are met or those that cannot be met are found.

The Planning Method is often applicable. However, deliberate or inadvertent omission of an important functional requirement can result in an unpleasant surprise.

Cost and Reliability Computations

Introduction

Four questions must be answered in many system design studies:

1. Number of each kind of component block
2. Estimated cost
3. Operation under overload
4. Estimated system reliability

Almost always, some or all of the answers are needed to compare alternative versions of a proposed system. Great accuracy is seldom essential. For many studies, 10% is quite good enough.

Competent management knows that early estimates are quite likely to be in error because of optimism or pessimism. Difficulties may be underestimated or even overlooked completely. Less often they may be overestimated. For such reasons, good management often will not authorize resources unless the chances of good returns appear to be excellent. Occasionally, a "policy" decision may say "go" even though the chances do not look too good. In neither case are extremely accurate estimates necessary.

The rest of this chapter presents some approaches that have proved useful under actual design conditions.

Number of Each Kind of Component Block or Machine

In the design and engineering of systems, the question often arises "How many component blocks or machines are needed to handle the offered inputs?"

A simple formula helps to point out the fundamental variables and to understand some useful principles. The formula is not new.

It is really a definition of the machine occupancy. The notation is:

N—the number of items to be processed. Sometimes only one or more subprocesses are involved.

M—the number of machines.

τ—the machine cycle time, or holding time.

N_c—the number of items processed during one "machine cycle," i.e., one complete operation which repeats as long as the machine is working.

In many processes, a machine handles one item at a time, so $N_c = 1$. In other processes, a machine handles several items simultaneously, so N_c equals the number of such items.

T—the time interval available for processing N items, measured in any convenient unit; for example, an hour, or 3600 seconds. For some problems, it is convenient to measure T in units of τ.

ϵ—the occupancy or efficiency: the time a machine (or group of machines) is in use divided by the total available machine time.

In symbols, the formula is

$$N = M \frac{T}{\tau} N_c \epsilon \tag{24.1}$$

where $\dfrac{T}{\tau}$ is the number of cycles which can be complete during T.

Solving for M

$$M = \left(\frac{N}{T}\right) \frac{\tau}{\epsilon N_c} \tag{24.2}$$

where M is the number of machines needed. Spares may be added to take care of breakdowns and maintenance.

For some systems (such as dial-telephone central offices), expected occupancies can be obtained from tables. Otherwise they may have to be estimated.

N/T may vary during T. The variation may be expressed by a probability distribution with an average, a dispersion and a shape. To determine the distribution parameters precisely, extensive statistical studies may be necessary. They may be only indirectly affected by the system design.

Further, τ may be a constant or it may have to be described by a distribution function—perhaps determined experimentally.

The "efficiency factor" ϵ must be chosen to provide acceptable performance under peak loads. Depending on the system, queing of inputs may or may not be allowable.

The formula emphasizes the basic variables involved: the number of items to be handled per unit time, the efficiency or occupancy, and the machine cycle time.

Operation under Overloads

Over a "long" interval

$$N\tau \leq MT \tag{24.3}$$

Otherwise, the excess input items simply continue to pile up indefinitely. For few systems does such a pile-up result in acceptable operation. Thus, equality in the relation of Eq. 24.3 sets the upper limit on processing capacity.

Over a "short" interval, for no delays in processing offered items

$$M \geq \text{maximum number of simultaneous input}$$
$$\text{items at every instant} \tag{24.4}$$

If some delays are acceptable

$$M \geq \text{number required so delays in processing}$$
$$\text{offered items are } \leq \text{ some tolerable value} \tag{24.5}$$

The required number of M can be computed using queing theory. With delay operation, any costs due to storing the delayed items must be balanced against the costs of providing more machines and eliminating the delays. Such a balance can show how to obtain the minimum cost for the operation.

Estimation of Costs

When the number of machines M_1, M_2, . . . M_n required to implement a particular version of a system is found, then the total cost is simply

$$\Sigma(\$_1 M_1 + \$_2 M_2, \cdots + \$_n M_n)$$
$$+ \Sigma(\$_1' M_1 + \$_2' M_2 \cdots + \$_n' M_n) \tag{24.6}$$

where $\$_1$ is the cost of the machine M_1, and so on, and
$\$_1'$ is the cost of input information to M_1, and so on.

Thus, the cost of a system is the sum of the costs of the information and effector portions. Sometimes cost estimates omit the information costs. Such an omission can lead to unhappy results for the designer.

For identical systems in parallel, such as two production lines, the total cost is the cost of the separate systems. Correction terms can be added to take care of second-order effects or constraints caused by the increased capacity. For example, existing floor space might not be adequate for the additional capacity so that construction would be required. As another example, some information costs might be less because the same shop drawings could be used and new training manuals need not be provided.

Some system studies involve costs that may be deferred for a number of years. The present worth of such costs (today's value) can be found by consulting annuity tables. Long-range cost studies of public utility systems such as electric power and telephone systems are often made on a present worth basis.

Another formula is useful in estimating the cost of producing objects from raw material:

$$\sum_{ijk} N_{ijk} U_{ij} \tau_{jk} \$_{jk} \tag{24.7}$$

N_{ijk} is the number of units of the ith object assigned to kth machine to receive the jth change of property.

U_{ij} is the number of units of the jth change of property in the ith object.

τ_{jk} is the cycle time of the kth machine to produce the jth change of property.

$\$_{jk}$ is the total cost of using the kth system to make the jth change of property.

In words, the cost of producing objects is the sum of all the terms of the form "number of kinds of objects to be produced times the number of units of each kind of change per object times the cycle time to produce each kind of change using a specified machine times the total cost of the machine per cycle."

Estimation of System Reliability

A useful method for predicting trouble frequencies can be applied to a part of a system, or, with additional assumptions, to an entire system.

Predictions are based on component counts and stress-adjusted component failure rates. They can be made for paper designs long before tests are possible on completed equipment. They can indicate where studies should be concentrated to improve performance. Such studies must include any necessary analysis work. Also, alternative approaches to obtaining improved reliability can be compared, for example, paralleling, duplication, information coding, and better environment.

The accuracy of predictions depends on that of the base failure rate data and stress factors that degrade component reliability. As knowledge of these factors increases, the predictions improve.

Each component block or subsystem can be appraised separately. In a system, if some failures are more serious than others, they can be treated accordingly.

The Procedure

1. Preferably, redraw the system block diagram according to the principles explained later in this chapter.
   Divide the system into sections according to effects of failure. A weight determined by the importance of failure can be assigned to each section. For example, a system might be divided into sections where:
   a. Failure does not hamper operation—at least over a short interval, for example, certain lights and alarms.
   b. Failure reduces system capacity, for example, one of a group of machines. The importance of such failures may vary with time of day, inputs, etc.
   c. Failure prevents performance of some essential system functions, for example, some but not all operations can be performed.
   d. Failure closes down the system.
2. Count components of each type for the section under consideration.
3. For each type of component, find the base failure rate as discussed under "Component Failure Rates."
4. For each component, determine and make the stress correction to obtain the expected failure rate for continuous use under the specified conditions for an entire year.
5. If the stresses are not always present, multiply the result of Step 4 by the fraction of the year the stress is expected to be present.
6. To find the expected failure rate for the section, multiply each component failure rate by the number of components to which it applies and add the products. All failures are assumed to be independent and any failure causes section failure.
7. To predict the failure rate for an entire system, add the section failure rates (multiplied by any appropriate weighting factors).
8. If a section or system failure rate is too large, use redundancy to improve the expected performance. Redundancy is discussed later.

Assumptions

Experience indicates that the number of troubles is high at first, drops off rapidly, and becomes relatively constant until component wearout effects become important. During the period of relatively constant failure rate, failures are assumed to be randomly distributed in time. These failures are frequently called "catastrophic" in the literature. Under these conditions, the exponential failure law holds:

$$P = e^{-\lambda T} \tag{24.8}$$

where P is the probability of survival for time T and λ is the (constant) failure rate during the period.

The exponential law can also be written:

$$P = e^{-TL} \tag{24.9}$$

where L, the predicted mean life, is the reciprocal of the failure rate. Equation 24.9 says that if failures are not repaired, the number of equipments diminishes exponentially during a given period. Mean life has been reached when 37% of the initial number remain.

With random failures, the times between failures vary greatly and have no central tendency toward the mean life value. Thus, mean life is *not* a guaranteed period of failure-free service, but it does indicate the uninterrupted potential.

The following additional assumptions are made:

1. The component failures to be counted are independent and each one causes section failure.

2. The system has been debugged: initially defective components have been removed.

3. Wearout either does not occur or can be forestalled by preventive maintenance (e.g., tests for and removal of components approaching the end of their useful life).

4. When a failure rate is valid for both component tests and application in a section of a system, the section failure rate is the sum of the component failure rates.

Component Failure Rates

Failure rate data are available for many frequently used electronic components. Failure rate is given as a function of ambient temperature and electric stress.

Ambient temperature normally varies from point to point in an assembly depending upon cooling conditions and the location of thermally active components. A resolution of about 5°C. is adequate.

The measure of electrical stress used depends on the component, for example, for a silicon diode the ratio of operating to rated wattage.

For missile or other military applications, pressure, vibration, shock, and maintainability can affect component failure rates.

Experience indicates a method of appraising individual high-population components in their application in a complex system need not be exact since the large number of components tends to "smooth" the results.

Possible Methods for Improving Reliability

Redundancy is a method of increasing reliability. In some cases, it may be the only one. The consequences of two kinds of redundancy are discussed later in this chapter.

Component improvement is always at least theoretically possible. A small improvement in a high-population high-failure rate component can greatly increase reliability.

Derating and conservative design are "musts."

Reliability Diagrams

Given a block diagram of a system, a reliability diagram can indicate how failures of particular sections affect the system reliability. Tandem or parallel grouping, effects of packaging, power supplies, etc., and the consequences of interdependence are evident.

Figure 24-1 shows the block diagram of a simple telemetering system used in explaining a sample reliability diagram. In this example, if either transmitter fails, the other also fails.

The considerations in constructing and using a reliability diagram:

1. A line represents a one-way path of information flow. For electrical systems, information flow may be interpreted as signal flow.

2. A block in the diagram represents a part or group of parts that must function satisfactorily for information to pass from input to output. The information need not pass through all the parts.

3. Preferably, the parts in a block should be describable by a probability of successful performance independent of the performance of any other part. Dependence between parts in different blocks is admissible if the dependence is between a particular part of one block and an entire second block.

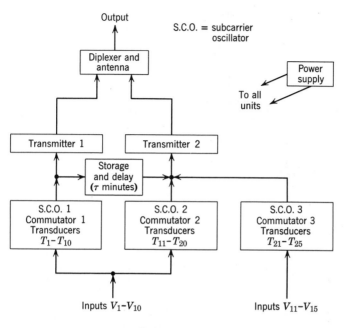

Figure 24-1

4. A path of information transfer consists of a single tandem connection of successive lines and blocks from system input to output. Successful transmission along a particular path occurs if each of the blocks operates successfully. Redundant parts omitted from one path are included in other paths. A particular part may be included in several paths.

Figure 24-2 is the reliability diagram corresponding to Fig. 24-1. It shows the blocks connected by lines of signal flow. The blocks in the signal flow lines must operate properly for transmission to be satisfactory. Blocks added as tandem elements indicate effects of transmitter dependence, power supply, and packaging. Each block is located on the basis of the way its reliability influences system reliability. A set of transducers, the related commutator and SCO are put into a single block because these parts perform a particular task, independently of others.

A block with some portions associated with individual input signals and others common to all signals would be represented by several blocks in the reliability diagram.

Cables and connectors may introduce additional blocks, or, the reli-

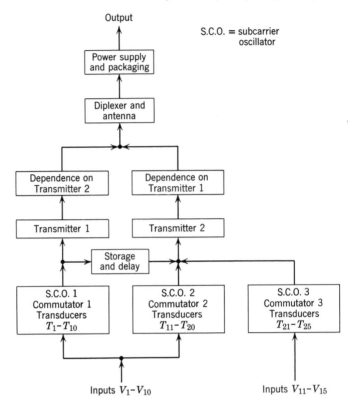

Figure 24-2

ability of a block may include that of the cables and connectors leading to and from the block. When cables interconnect parts of different blocks, half may be assigned to each block.

Weighting factors determined by the relative importance of failure of the various blocks may range from 0 to 1. If failure of a block is of primary importance, the weight is 1; if less so, less than 1 and proportional to the importance of failure.

Paralleling

System Reliability

Let p_1 be the reliability of block 1, p_2 the reliability of block 2, and so on. Here, a block is defined as a subassembly of components with specified inputs and outputs and functioning within a system. Assuming block failure means system failure, the basic system reliability is

$$P = p_1 p_2 \cdots p_{N_T} = \prod_{i=1}^{N_T} p_i \qquad (24.10)$$

If the block reliabilities are identical, then

$$P = p^{N_T} \qquad (24\text{-}11)$$

This model is oversimplified. Nevertheless, it permits some general statements. For high reliability, the block reliabilities must be high and the number small. The reliability is less than or equal to the reliability of the *least reliable* element. But block reliabilities are limited by the state of the art, and the number of elements depends on the required functions.

Reliability of Blocks in Parallel

Assume m blocks of reliabilities, p_1, $p_2 \ldots p_{N_P}$ are connected so only one block is actually used. If it fails, another takes its place: a parallel reliability connection. There is a tandem analog. Consider a silicon diode, high-voltage rectifier. Suppose that the number of diodes connected in tandem is more than is needed for the peak inverse voltage. If the extra diodes fail by shorting, the rectifier will not fail. This situation can be called a tandem reliability connection.

If the probability of system failure, or the unreliability is Q, then

$$Q = \prod_{i=1}^{N_P} (1 - p_i) \qquad (24.12)$$

But $P = 1 - Q$, so

$$P = 1 - \prod_{i=1}^{N_P} (1 - p_i) \qquad (24.13)$$

For the special case of equal reliabilities,

$$P = 1 - (1 - p)^{N_P} \qquad (24.14)$$

The reliability of an aggregate of parallel blocks is greater than or equal to the reliability of the *most reliable* block.

Complete Standby Systems

One or more complete standby systems may be provided.

Then $\qquad P_A = 1 - (1 - P_0)^{N_P} = 1 - Q_0^{N_P} \qquad (24.15)$

where P_A is the reliability achieved with system standby, P_0 and Q_0 are the reliability and unreliability of a basic system, and N_P is the number of parallel systems. But if

$$P_0 = p^{N_T} \qquad (24.11)$$

then

$$P_A(N_T, N_P) = 1 - (1 - p^{N_T})^{N_P} \qquad (24.16)$$

If p is constant, the reliability approaches 0 with an infinite number of tandem elements, even if the number of parallel systems increases without limit. So this approach may be expensive.

Block Standby

With n blocks in tandem and each block paralleled $N_P - 1$ times, the reliability of each group is $1 - (1-p)^{N_P}$, and the system reliability is

$$P_B(N_T, N_P) = [1 - (1 - p)^{N_P}]^{N_T} \qquad (24.17)$$

where P_B is the reliability of the whole system employing block standby. The reliability of block standby tends toward 1 as N_P increases, even if the number of tandem blocks approaches infinity. The reliability tends toward 0, only if N_P remains finite and N_T approaches infinity.

Effect of Switch Reliability

Assume each block used for paralleling has an associated "sensing and switching" equipment of reliability p_s, to determine when the operating block fails and to switch in a standby. Then the reliability is:

$$P_B = [1 - (1 - p)(1 - p_s p)^{N_P-1}]^{N_T} \qquad (24.18)$$

Assuming perfect switching, system standby reliability is:

$$P_A = 1 - Q_0^{N_P} \qquad (24.15)$$

For P_B to be larger than P_A

$$p_s \geq \frac{1}{(1 - Q_0)^{1/N_T}}\left[1 - \left[\frac{1 - (1 - Q_0^{N_P})^{1/N_T}}{1 - (1 - Q_0)^{1/N_T}}\right]\right]^{1/N_P-1} \qquad (24.19)$$

Or for one standby block per operating block:

$$p_s \geq \frac{(1 + Q_0)^{1/N_T} - 1}{1 - (1 - Q_0)^{1/N_T}} \qquad (24.20)$$

Debugging

Reliability prediction assumes initially defective parts are removed during "debugging."

The debugging period may be defined to end when the *next* failure is as likely to be a random failure as a debugging failure.

Assuming reduction of defectives is an exponential function, and failed defectives are replaced, the defective population is:

$$n_d = N_d e^{-t/G} \tag{24.21}$$

where n_d is the defective population at any time t, N_d the number of initial defectives, and G a constant of proportionality dimensionally equal to time. Differentiating:

$$\frac{dn_d}{dt} = \lambda_d = -\frac{N_d}{G} e^{-t/G} \tag{24.22}$$

where λ_d is the failure rate during the debugging. Assuming $\lambda_d = \lambda$ when $t = t_d$, then

$$t_d = G \ln \frac{G\lambda}{N_d} \tag{24.23}$$

where λ is the ultimate failure rate.

If, as an approximation, λ is considered proportional to total components, since N_d is proportional to the total component count, N_c, then

$$\lambda = \alpha N_c \text{ and } N_d = \beta N_c$$

where α is the average failure rate per part and β the percent of initial defectives.

Either 0 ultimate failure rate or 100% defectives implies infinite debugging time; zero total defectives, 0 debugging time. The boundary conditions agree with the equation.

Wearout and Its Possible Relation to Catastrophic Failures

After debugging is complete, dividing the physical phenomena into random and wearout failures simplifies analysis and permits engineering decisions for each region more or less independently.

As a first approximation, the failure rate in a wearout region can be represented by a normal distribution:

$$\lambda_w = \frac{N_w}{\sigma \sqrt{2\pi}} e^{-(t-t_0)^2 / 2\sigma^2} \tag{24.24}$$

where λ_w is the failure rate; N_w is the total number of wearout failures, and σ is the standard deviation.

For wearout, a time t_0 has a unique significance. With random failures, no particular time is characteristic of the phenomenon.

Knowing t_0, σ, and the total failures allowed for wearout, the contribution of wearout to the total failure rate can be anticipated and steps taken before t_0 to avoid trouble. This is not true for random failures.

An "accelerated life" test is an attractive concept. Going one step further leads to "test-to-failure." A potential difficulty is that laboratory observations may find t_0, a characteristic of wearout, while in practice random phenomena are the important factors.

For components that fail because of a combined time-energy stress, there may be a definite relation between the time of wearout failure and the "pure" or random failure rate prior to wearout.

Consider two special cases: (1) a thermal dissipator and (2) a dielectric medium. In each instance, the operation involves a composite of electrical and thermal (environmental) stress.

For components of a thermally dissipative or dielectric nature, there seems to be a *linear* relation between the random failure rate λ and the time of wearout t_w under practical conditions.

Within the random-failure phase, only some random weak elements succumb to the normally low time-stress condition. Only when a large number of samples fail from the same cause is group wearout observed. Thus, during its useful life, a component survives according to the usual exponential relation.

Bibliography

CHAPTER 1. Massachusetts Institute of Technology has an experimental program in the application of system concepts to the management of enterprises and to social and economic systems. *Industrial Dynamics*, Jay W. Forrester, The M.I.T. Press, Cambridge, Mass., 1961.

CHAPTER 3. Shannon's now classical paper is cited in a footnote.

On Human Communication, Colin Cherry, John Wiley and Sons, Inc., New York, 1957, contains much pertinent material.

CHAPTER 4. A less complete list of the properties of messages and signals is given in *A Methodology for Systems Engineering*, A. D. Hall, Van Nostrand, Princeton, N.J., 1962.

An excellent book on various aspects of modulation is *Modulation Theory*, H. S. Black, Van Nostrand, Princeton, N.J., 1953. Modulation in the space domain is not discussed.

Information signals, codes, and structures in space and time are discussed in Colin Cherry's book referred to in Chapter 3.

Measures of information and units are discussed in the papers "Transmission of Information", R. V. L. Hartley, Bell Sytem Technical Journal, VII, July, 1928; "Theory of Communication," D. Gabor, Proceedings IEE, London, England, 93, November, 1946; and D. M. MacKay, "The Nomenclature of Information Theory", Transactions of the IRE Professional Group on Information Theory, PGIT-1, February, 1953.

Some compatibility problems in telephone systems are covered in a paper "Compatibility in Communications," F. J. Singer, Electrical Engineering, 81, February, 1962.

CHAPTER 5. Two excellent books on feedback-type time-varying systems are: *Network Analysis and Feedback Amplifier Design*, H. W. Bode, Van Nostrand, Princeton, N.J., 1945 and *Servomechanisms and Regulating System Design*, Harold Chestnut and R. W. Mayer, John Wiley and Sons, Inc., New York, 1959.

CHAPTER 7. *Wave Forms* by Britton Chance, et al., Volume 19, Radiation Laboratory Series, McGraw-Hill Book Company, Inc., New York, 1949, discusses many of the basic building blocks for handling electrical waves and their use in microwave and radar systems.

The Design of Switching Circuits by W. Kiester, A. E. Ritchie, and S. H. Washburn, Van Nostrand, Princeton, N.J., 1951, and *Switching Circuits and Logical Design*, S. H. Caldwell, John Wiley and Sons, Inc., New York, 1958, present many arrangements used in dial-telephone switching systems employing relays and other mechanical devices.

"Translators and Identifiers" by H. H. Schneckloth, Bell System Technical Journal, 30, July 1951 describes many such devices that have been used in dial switching systems in America and abroad.

"Some Basic Relay Circuits" by W. Kiester, S. H. Washburn, et al., Transactions of AIEE, 67 and 68, 1948 and 1949 was reprinted as Bell System Monograph B-1688. "Relay Preference Lockout Circuits in Telephone Switching," A. E. Joel. Transactions of AIEE, 67, 1948 was reprinted as Bell System Monograph B-1641. "Magnetic Devices for Memory and Logic," D. H. Looney, R. H. Meinken et al., Electronics Components Conference, Washington, D.C., May 1960 (Bell System Monograph B-3650), describes a different way to implement some of the functional building blocks.

Selected Semiconductor Circuits Handbook, Seymour Schwartz, ed., John Wiley and Sons, Inc., New York, 1960, has a self-explanatory title.

Many ways to implement the storage function are the subject of Chapter 19 of the *Handbook of Automation, Computation and Control,* E. M. Grabbe et al., Volume 2, John Wiley and Sons, Inc., New York, 1959.

Two interesting books dealing with information storage and retrieval are: *Textbook on Mechanized Information Retrieval* by Allen Kent, Interscience Publishers, New York, 1962, and *Electronic Information-Logic Machines* by L. I. Gutenmakher, translated from the Russian by Rosalind Kent, Interscience Publishers, New York, 1963.

A block diagram of a Russian-English translator is shown on page 47 of *Machine Translation of Languages* edited by W. N. Locke and A. D. Booth, The M.I.T. Press, Cambridge, Mass., 1955. This book and *Mechanical Resolution of Linguistic Problems* by A. D. Booth, J. P. Cleave and L. Brandwood, Academic Press, New York, 1958, take up many of the difficult information-processing problems encountered in translating from one language to another.

CHAPTERS 9 AND 10. *The Design of Engineering Systems,* W. Gosling, John Wiley and Sons, Inc., New York, 1962; *A Methodology for Systems Engineering,* A. D. Hall, Van Nostrand, Princeton, N.J., 1962; *Introduction to Design,* Morris Asimow, Prentice Hall, Englewood, N.J., 1962; and *System Engineering,* H. H. Goode and R. E. Machol, McGraw-Hill, 1957; and Chapter 14 of *Systems: Research and Design,* D. P. Eckman, ed., John Wiley and Sons, Inc., New York, 1961, all contain material pertinent to the subject matter of these two chapters.

Introduction to Metamathematics, S. C. Kleene, Van Nostrand, Princeton, 1952 and *Logic for Mathematicians,* J. B. Rosser, McGraw-Hill Book Company, Inc., New York, 1953, are advanced treatments of symbolic logic and set theory. A delightful book, *Faster than Thought,* B. V. Bowden, ed., Sir Isaac Pitman and Sons, London, 1953, in Chapter 15 discusses "Machines for the Solution of Logical Problems." Chapters 1 and 11 of *The Handbook of Automation, Computation and Control* Volume 1, E. M. Grabbe et al., John Wiley and Sons, Inc., New York, 1958, discuss "Sets and Relations" and "Boolean Algebra and Logic" in summary form. "Symbolic Logic: The Propositional Calculus, D. P. Ling, Bell Laboratories Record, June 1962, and July–August 1962.

A classic book on probability and queing theory is *An Introduction to Probability Theory and its Applications.* Volume 1, 2nd ed., W. Feller, John Wiley and Sons, Inc., New York, 1957. Many articles dealing with particular high-traffic problems can be found in the Bell System Technical Journal.

Network theory: *Synthesis of Passive Networks*, E. A. Guillemin, John Wiley and Sons, Inc., New York, 1957; *Network Analysis and Synthesis*, F. F. Kuo, John Wiley and Sons, Inc., New York, 1962; *Circuits, Matrices and Linear Vector Spaces*, L. P. Huelsman, McGraw-Hill Book Company Inc., New York, 1963; *Theory of Linear Physical Systems*, E. A. Guillemin, John Wiley and Sons, Inc., New York, 1963.

Feedback, Cybernetics, Servomechanism Theory: *Network Analysis and Feedback Amplifier Design*, H. W. Bode, Van Nostrand, Princeton, N.J., 1945; *Cybernetics*, N. Wiener, John Wiley and Sons, Inc., New York, 1948; *Servomechanisms and Regulating Systems Design*, H. Chestnut and R. W. Mayer, John Wiley and Sons, Inc., New York, 1951; "Regeneration Theory," H. Nyquist, Bell System Technical Journal, 11, 1932.

Optimization: A recent translation from the original Russian *The Mathematical Theory of Optimal Processes*, L. S. Pontryagin et al., translated by K. N. Trirogoff, Interscience Publishers, New York, 1962.

Game Theory: *Introduction to the Theory of Games*, J. C. C. McKinsey, McGraw-Hill Book Company, Inc., New York, 1952; *The Compleat Strategyst*, J. D. Williams, McGraw-Hill Book Company, Inc., New York, 1954.

Decision Theory: *Design for Decision*, I. D. J. Bross, The Macmillan Company, New York, 1953.

PERT: *Schedule, Cost and Profit Control with PERT*, Robert W. Miller, McGraw-Hill Book Company, Inc., New York, 1963; "PERT in Research Management," J. Sterling Livingston, Industrial Research, June 1963.

CHAPTER 11. The references for Chapters 9 and 10 are pertinent. The problems of information and mechanical design encountered in automatic control of machine tools are well described in a series of papers in English publications: "Digital Control and Programming," Peter J. Farmer, Aircraft Production, July and August 1956; "Computer Control of Machine Tools," D. T. N. Williamson, Control, July, August, September 1958; "Automatic Control of Machine Tools," Conference on Technology of Engineering Manufacture, Institution of Mechanical Engineers, London, March 1958; "Developments in Machine Tool Design to Keep Pace with Electronics and Numerical Control," H. Ogden, Machine Shop Magazine, April 1960.

CHAPTER 12. *Introduction to Operations Research*, C. W. Churchman, R. L. Ackoff, E. L. Arnoff, John Wiley and Sons, Inc., New York, 1957; *Operational Research in Management*, R. T. Eddison, K. Pennycuick, B. H. P. Rivett, John Wiley and Sons, Inc., New York, 1962; *Operations Research in Research and Development*, Burton V. Dean, ed. John Wiley and Sons Inc., New York, 1963; *Systems: Research and Design*, Donald P. Eckman, ed., John Wiley and Sons, Inc., New York, 1961.

CHAPTER 14. *System Engineering*, H. H. Goode and L. E. Machol, McGraw-Hill Book Company, Inc., New York, 1957, discusses the several kinds of system inputs and the analysis of a tentative design in some detail.

Despite the title, "A Method for Synthesizing Sequential Circuits," George H. Mealy, Bell System Technical Journal, 34, September 1955 discusses both the synthesis and analysis aspects. Some of his assertions are reworded and generalized in this chapter.

Mechanization of Motion, Lee Harrisberger, John Wiley and Sons, Inc., New York, 1961, has the appropriate subtitle: Kinematics-Synthesis-Analysis.

"The Automatic Handbook," Nathaniel Rochester, Proceedings of the IRE, 50, May 1962.

CHAPTER 16. *The Computer and the Brain,* John von Neuman, Yale University Press, New Haven, Conn. 1958.

"Communications between Man and Machine," J. E. Karlin and S. N. Alexander, Proceedings of the IRE, 50, May, 1962.

Some examples of the diverse kinds of design problems for which computers have been found useful are described in these papers: "The Computer as an Aid to the Design and Manufacture of Systems," T. H. Crowley, also "Automated Logical Design," H. F. DeFrancesco and T. R. LaCrosse, IEEE International Convention Record, Part IV, 1963; "Digital Computers in Power System Analysis," P. P. Gupta and M. W. Humphrey Davis, IEE London, Paper No 3484, January 1961, and also The Proceedings Vol. 108 Part A; "The Digital Computer Applied to the Design of Large Power Transformers," W. A. Sharpley and J. V. Oldfield, Proceedings of IEE London, Vol. 105 Part A, No. 20, April 1958; "Computing Machine Aids to a Development Project," C. W. Rosenthal, IRE Transactions on Electronic Computers, Vol. EC-10, September 1961; "Computer Program for Preparing Wiring Diagrams," D. B. Kirby and C. W. Rosenthal, AIEE Transactions Part 1- Communications and Electronics, 57, November 1961; Engineering Outside Plant with Computers," R. W. Amory, Bell Laboratories Record, July–August 1963; "A Computer-Aided Parts Data Processing System," T. J. O'Connor, Bell Laboratories Record, September 1963; "Machine-Aided Preparation of Electrical Diagrams," H. M. Kalish, Bell Laboratories Record, October 1963; "New Concepts in Library Service," W. K. Lowry, Bell Laboratories Record, January 1964; "A New Calculation Method for the Design of Filters by Digital Computer with Special Consideration of the Accuracy Problem," T. Iedokoro et al., IEEE International Convention Record, Part 2, 1963.

CHAPTER 17. *The Mathematical Theory of Linear Systems,* B. M. Brown, Chapman and Hall, Ltd., London, 1961, on page 173 has a block diagram representing systems with multiple inputs and outputs and expresses their input-output relations in matrix form.

"From Circuit Theory to System Theory," L. A. Zadeh, Proceedings of the IRE, May 1962, surveys the evolution of a mathematical system theory, with an exposition of some of its concepts, techniques and problems.

The "Summary of the History of Circuit Theory," V. Belevitch, Proceedings of the IRE, May 1962, among other topics discusses the progress in the development of the theory of nonlinear and linear variable circuits. Pertinent books are: *Analysis of Non-Linear Control Systems,* D. Graham and D. McRuer, John Wiley and Sons, Inc., New York, 1961; *Introduction to Non-Linear Analysis,* W. J. Cunningham, McGraw-Hill Book Company, Inc., 1958; and *Non-Linear Electrical Networks,* W. L. Hughes, Ronald Press, 1960. Also, "Non-Linear Systems Analysis and Synthesis," Ming-Lei Liou, Paper 17.1 Wescon Show of IEEE, San Francisco, 1963, and Technical Report No. 6554-6 Stanford Electronics Laboratories, October 1963, SEL-63-095.

For references to switching circuit design see bibliography for Chapter 7.

Analogs in system design: *Dimensional Analysis and Theory of Models,* H. L. Langhaar, John Wiley and Sons, Inc., New York, 1951; *Dynamical Analogies,* H. F. Olson, Van Nostrand, Princeton, N.J., 2nd ed., 1958; *Heat Transfer Phenomena,* R. C. L. Bosworth, Associated General Publications

Pty, Ltd, Sydney Australia and John Wiley and Sons Inc., New York, 1952; "The Impedance Concept," S. A. Schelkunoff, Bell System Technical Journal, 17, January 1938.

CHAPTER 18. Many important references were named in the list for Chapter 3.

"Maxwell's Demon Cannot Operate: Information and Entropy I" and "Physical Entropy and Information II," L. Brillouin, Journal of Applied Physics, 22, March 1951.

"Information Theory," B. McMillan and D. Slepian, Proceedings of the IRE, 50, May 1962.

CHAPTER 19. "Theory of Scanning," Pierre Mertz and Frank Gray, Bell System Technical Journal, 13, July 1934.

"The Impedance Concept," S. A. Schelkunoff, Bell System Technical Journal, 17, January 1938.

CHAPTER 21. Modulation and Demodulation: *Modulation Theory*, H. S. Black, Van Nostrand, Princeton, N.J., 1953.

Computers and Logic Operations: *Logical Design of Digital Computers*, M. Phister Jr., John Wiley and Sons, Inc., New York, 1958; *Digital Computer Technology and Design*, 2 vol., W. H. Ware, John Wiley and Sons, Inc., New York, 1963; *Handbook of Automation, Computation and Control*, E. M. Grabbe et al., 3 vol., John Wiley and Sons, Inc., New York, 1958, 1959, and 1961.

CHAPTER 22. "Transmission of Information", R. V. L. Hartley, Bell System Technical Journal, VII, July 1928.

CHAPTER 23. "Programming the Logic Theory Machine" and also "Empirical Explorations of the Logic Theory Machine," A. Newell, J. C. Shaw, and H. A. Simon, Proceedings of the 1957 Western Joint Computer Conference, IRE, February 1957. "The Processes of Creative Thinking," A. Newell, J. C. Shaw and H. A. Simon, The RAND Corporation Paper, P-1320, August 1958. "The Use of Heuristic Programming in Management Science," Fred M. Tonge, Management Science, 7, April 1961, is a partial survey of the present and potential applications of heuristic programming.

CHAPTER 24. "The Reliability and Quality Control Field from Its Inception to the Present," C. M. Ryerson, Proceedings of the IRE, 50, May 1962 is not only an interesting historical survey, but also a source of references to many of the most important military and other publications.

Glossary

ALGORITHM. An *effective* computational procedure.

ALLOTTING. The act of selection in which the object to be selected is specified before the selecting action is initiated.

ALPHABET. The letters or signs of a language.

ALTERING. An operation to insert change, or delete information.

BIT. A unit for expressing a quantity of information when using the unexpectedness concept.

CODE. A set of rules on any subject; a system of military or navigational signals.

CODING. A transformation or mapping according to a set of rules.

COMBINER. A functional block that merges two or more space-separated inputs to form one output. The inputs may be energies or objects.

COMPARE. To set or bring energies or objects together (in fact or contemplation) and to examine the relations they bear to each other and especially to ascertain their agreement or disagreement or the prints of resemblance or difference. A compare function can give an output indication of whether the two inputs are or are not equal.

COMPONENT. A widely used unit of equipment with a definite name and performance standard.

COMPUTER. A machine that changes its input information in some way to form output information.

CONNECTING. The operation of establishing a path from an energy source to a selected object, so that energy may be supplied to the object. A selection operation must furnish information about when a suitable object has been selected and also the location of the object.

An analogous operation involving two or more objects in space occurs in assembling.

CONTROL. To exercise such an influence over (something) as to guide, correct, manage, or restrain it; to check.

CONTROL. To exercise such an influence over (something) as to guide,

DECIDING. An operation used to accept or reject some items of information. One input is the information; another is a fixed reference. The two inputs are combined by an appropriate logical rule to give the output.

DELAY. The time required to traverse a distance in space; the transmissions time through a component.

DESIGN. To map out in the mind; to plan mentally; to conceive of as a whole (e.g., a system); to invent.

DISCRIMINATION. The act of distinguishing; the act of making or observing a difference.

DISTORTION. A definite difference between a particular input signal and the corresponding output signal; an unwanted change in the relation of the output wave to the input wave caused by some component of a system.

DIVIDER. A functional block that divides its one input among two or more space-separated outputs. The input may be energy or an object.

EFFECTOR. Something that causes the wanted change in an object in response to its input energy.

ENTROPY. A message of disorder or the improbability of the next state. It always tends to increase and is a maximum where the sequence of events is completely unpredictable.

ENVIRONMENT. Everything outside a system that either affects the operation of the system or is affected by the system.

EQUIVOCATION. The average amount by which transmitted and received messages over a channel differ.

FINDING. The operation of identifying and then selecting. One object among a group starts the operation with a request to be found. The selection is ended when the requesting object is found.

GRAMMAR. The order of words in a communication or portion of a communication such as a phrase, clause, or sentence.

HEURISTICS. An aid or guide to discovery; the theory of step-by-step discovery.

HUNTING. The act of selection according to a particular set of rules; a particular kind of search that seeks any suitable available object from a group of objects.

IDENTIFYING. The operation that gives the source of a particular information mark and hence of an object or a location. The operation involves both selection and translation.

INFORMATION, AMOUNT OF. Three possible measures are unexpectedness, complexity of structure, or the precision of measurement.

INFORMATION, AMOUNT IN A MESSAGE. The number of bits in the message.

INFORMATION, COMMUNICATION OF. The reproduction of generated information at some other location or locations either exactly or approximately.

INFORMATION EFFICIENCY. The ratio of the actual negative entropy to the maximum possible entropy using the same set of signs.

INFORMATION-IN-GENERAL. That which can add to a representation of what is known, believed, or alleged to be so. Information is the *capacity* for increasing knowledge. Actually, it may or may not do so.

INFORMATION THEORY, "STRICT SENSE." The study of (1) entropy; (2) channel capacity; and (3) coding of information for transmission so that the available channel capacity is used most efficiently.

INFORMATION THEORY, "WIDE SENSE." The studies included under the "Strict-Sense" definition, and also signal detection and extraction in the presence of noise, filtering and prediction theory, some parts of modulation theory, and information processing studies.

INFORMATION TRANSFER, CONSERVATIVE. Total information out of a channel or component equal to the total information in.

INFORMATION TRANSFER. NONCONSERVATIVE. Total information out of a channel or component less than the total information in.

LANGUAGE. A vocabulary and a way of using it; any mode of conveying ideas.

LOGON. The unit for expressing a quantity of structural information.

MACHINE. Any combination of mechanisms for utilizing, modifying, applying or transmitting energy, whether simple or complex.

MECHANICS. The branch of physics that treats of phenomena caused by action of forces on material bodies.

MECHANISM. A system that constitutes a working agency.

MEDIUM. A transmission path for energy.

MESSAGE. An ordered selection from an agreed set of signs intended to convey information; the original modulating wave in a communication system.

METRON. The unit for expressing a quantity of metrical information.

MODEL. An approximate or simplified representation of the actual system being studied.

MODEL, ICONOGRAPHIC. A pictorial representation used to describe the system and its functional relationships.

MODEL, MATHEMATICAL. An equation or set of equations that express the relations between the inputs and outputs of a system.

MODEL, UNDERSTANDING A. Understanding how the system outputs vary with the inputs.

MODULATION. A change of some property or properties of a zero-entropy energy flow to create an information-carrying signal.

NOISE. Any unwanted signal may be called "noise."

NOISE, GAUSSIAN. Noise with a particular voltage distribution specified in terms of probabilities.

NOISE, IMPULSE. Noise highly localized in time and covering a broad frequency spectrum.

NOISE, SINGLE-FREQUENCY. Noise highly localized in frequency but lasting a significant time.

NOISE, WHITE. Noise with equal energy at all frequencies. Band-limited white noise has equal energies within a specified band and zero energy elsewhere.

OBJECT. An information or energy sink in a system.

OPERATION. The bringing about of an effect.

OPERATOR, MATHEMATICAL. A symbol that briefly indicates a mathematical process describing the relations and restrictions between the input variables and output variables of a system.

PARAMETER. A variable not included in the description of a system, a quantity to be considered constant in a case being considered, but varying in different cases.

PART. A portion, piece, or fragment of a component.

SCANNING. The operation of looking over a group of objects to find any that may be generating a particular information mark.

PROBLEM. A situation in which someone desires a certain state of affairs and does not immediately know how to attain it.

PROBLEM, SYSTEM DESIGN. A problem of the following form: given a specification which lists the desired properties of the system, produce a document which describes an optimum (or close to optimum) realization of these properties. System design is almost entirely an information-handling process.

REDUNDANCY. A property of languages, codes, and sign systems when excess information is present that helps communication despite interference during the transmission.

RESOLUTION. The act, operation or process of separating the parts which compose a mixed body.

RETRIEVAL. The operation of recovery of energy or an object previously stored. Retrieval involves (1) selection of one or more space locations at which there are usable objects; (2) applying energy to the object or objects to determine their state; and (3) sensing the read-out energy or object.

SELECTION. The act of choosing and taking from a number of alternatives; a taking from another by preference. Selection alone causes no effect on the selected energy or object.

SENSE, COMMON. Sound or ordinary sense; specifically good judgment or prudence in estimating affairs, especially as free from emotional bias or intellectual subtlety.

SENSOR. A functional block that receives input signal energy, measures it, and delivers the resulting information at its output.

SIGN. A written mark conventionally used for a word or a phrase; thing used as a representation of something; a natural or conventional motion or gesture used instead of words to convey information.

SIGNAL. The only physical embodiment of the information contained in a message. Any operations on information can only involve operations on the physical phenomena carrying the message.

SOURCE. That from which an effect or energy proceeds; an origin.

SOURCE, INFORMATION OR MESSAGE. A generator of information. The output is assumed to be error-free.

SOURCE, NOISE. A source of any unwanted signal.

SOURCE, ZERO-ENTROPY. A source of completely predictable energy that furnishes no information whatsoever.

SPELLING. The order of signs within written or printed words.

STORING (or STORAGE). An operation that changes the time location of an amount of energy or of an object. Storing always occurs at a location in space. Storing always involves selection of a space location at which an object is to be changed and application of energy to make the change.

STRUCTURE. The arrangement of organic units or parts in a whole; the arrangement of constituent parts of a structure or body; the manner of organization.

SYMBOL. A thing regarded by general consent as naturally typifying or representing or recalling something by possession of analogous qualities or by association in fact or thought.

SYNTHESIS. The operation of finding one or more ways to provide all the wanted operations specified for a new system.

SYSTEM. A regular or orderly arrangement of components or parts in a connected and interrelated series or whole; a series or group of components necessary to some operation.

SYSTEM, INFORMATION TRANSMISSION. A system that takes in input information and delivers it at the output without change.

SYSTEM, INFORMATION PROCESSING. A system that takes in information, changes it, and delivers the resulting information at the output.

TRANSDUCER, ACTIVE. One whose output waves depend on one or more sources of power apart from those supplied by any of the activating waves, which power is controlled by one or more of the input waves.

TRANSDUCER, PASSIVE. One whose input waves are independent of any sources of power controlled by the actuating waves.

TRANSLATE. To interpret; to render into another language; to express in words of a different language.

VARIABLE. A measurable quantity which has a definite numerical value at every instant.

WORD. A group of signs; a single articulated sound or a group of articulate sounds or syllables uttered by a human voice and by custom expressing an idea or ideas.

SUBSYSTEM. A series or group of components that perform one or more operations of a more complex system.

ZERO-ENTROPY ENERGY. Completely predictable energy that furnishes no information whatsoever.

Index

335